# TREATING THE ADOLESCENT IN FAMILY THERAPY

## A Developmental and Narrative Approach

*by*
ANNE K. FISHEL, Ph.D.

JASON ARONSON INC.
*Northvale, New Jersey*
*London*

This book was set in 11 pt. Century Schoolbook and printed and bound by Book-mart Press, Inc. of North Bergen, NJ.

**Library of Congress Cataloging-in-Publication Data**

Fishel, Anne K.
    Treating the adolescent in family therapy : a developmental and narrative approach / by Anne K. Fishel.
        p.  cm.
    Includes bibliographical references and index.
    ISBN 0-7657-0192-8
    1. Adolescent psychotherapy. 2. Family psychotherapy. I. Title.
RJ503.F56 1999
616.89'00835—dc21                                             98-51012

Printed in the United States of America on acid-free paper. For information and catalog write to Jason Aronson Inc., 230 Livingston Street, Northvale, NJ 07647-1726, or visit our website: www.aronson.com

To my mother and father,
Edith and James Fishel

# Contents

## Part III: Developmental Variations

## Part IV: Stories That Professionals Live By

# Preface: How I Came to Write This Book

I confess that I am a great fan of adolescence. There is a little adolescent in all of us, if by adolescent we mean *in the process of becoming someone*. The energy and sense of possibility that are part of becoming an adult have been compelling to me at every stage of life I have experienced so far. As a mother, wife, therapist, and teacher, I try to reclaim the exuberance that my adolescent self possessed—the exuberance that made it possible in a single day to plan a political action, rehearse a play, volunteer at a storefront day care center, and by nightfall still want to play in a jugband in a basement coffeehouse. What I appreciate now, more than when I was an adolescent, is the energy and potential of families to promote the development of each member of the family.

In my twenties I became a clinical psychologist so that I could work intensively with adolescents. Like many therapists drawn to adolescents, my interest began early on. Before going to graduate school, while I was still an adolescent myself, I worked on an adolescent inpatient unit at McLean Hospital in Belmont, MA, where I was intrigued and terrified by the young people I encountered who were so like me but were also mute, or talking to invisible people, or unable to control their tempers. When I arrived at graduate school in North Carolina, my first practicum was at a state mental hospital, again working with hospitalized adolescents. I was assigned to conduct therapy twice a week with a 17-year-old girl who didn't speak to me for a month. Through events not related to my clinical work I appeared on a national talk show that was broadcast on the inpatient unit. Only then did she find any words for me. Her first statement to me was, "Your dress was cold," meaning that I had dressed in a way that she liked. I knew that appearing on national TV to break through an adolescent's silence was not an intervention I could easily count on in the years to come. So, I continued learning about psychotherapy with adolescents during the next two years of graduate school, first consulting at a public junior high school and later working at a college counseling service. In my third year, my training director pulled me aside and told me that I seemed to be avoiding working with any one older than me and that it was time to work with some adults. I cooperated but the younger age group still remained my favorite.

I continued to hone my skills as an individual therapist throughout graduate school and as an intern at Massachusetts General Hospital, where I resumed my work with adolescents. Then came a sea change. I decided to do two years of postdoctoral training in family therapy at Judge Baker Guidance Clinic. This training precipitated many clinical revelations that were grounded in what I already knew personally: that when one member in a family changes, everyone is affected; that children are transformed by their parents and are also active agents in transforming their parents; and that no therapist, no matter how superb, can ever replace a parent. Once I encountered the family systems perpective, I never turned back. After my postdoctoral training I began teaching family therapy and went on to start a couples therapy training program at Massachusetts General Hospital. But first I took one very difficult job.

My first job out of training was working at a private psychiatric hospital, Westwood Lodge, on the children's and the adolescent units, where I hoped to apply what I knew about family therapy to inpatient work. I had been hired, however, to be the individual therapist for children and adolescents. Family therapy was really the domain of the social work staff. Much of my time was spent hearing from my adolescent patients about their families' failures and abuses and then finding an alternative family for each of them after discharge—foster homes, Department of Youth Services placements, and residential schools. Many mornings I awoke at dawn to worry and wonder: Could some of these kids have been kept out of the hospital if I had worked with their families as intensively as I had worked with them individually? Was I doing a disservice by helping many of these kids extricate themselves from their families?

After a year, I left the hospital and began working in the psychiatric emergency room at Massachusetts General Hospital. My job was to be on hand to do family consultations and to teach the psychiatry residents how to do family crisis intervention. I found this work tremendously exciting. Families in crisis were far more fluid and willing to let in an outsider like me than were the families of hospitalized adolescents. Many times, during the crisis, the family's own resources were mobilized and hospitalization was not only prevented, but the family emerged from the crisis stronger and more resilient. Within a few years of teaching and supervising in the emergency room, I decided to start an adolescent crisis team to see whether hospitalization could be prevented if more were done on an outpatient basis.

Many of the clinical cases in this book come from my years of seeing adolescents with their families during a crisis—a suicide attempt, a disclosure of sexual abuse, a first psychotic break, a sudden onset of mutism, an adolescent's violent outburst, a discovery of substance abuse, a teenager's running away, an unplanned pregnancy. Of course, I have not always been able to prevent hospitalization or keep a family intact, nor should these always be the goals in every case. But I begin with the premise that adolescents still need their families and that my job is to help maintain their connection whenever possible.

In the years since my family therapy training, I have worked in a variety of settings besides the emergency room. I have worked with adolescents struggling with eating disorders. I have taught pediatric interns a course in normal family development, a course that always seems to focus on families with adolescents. I have supervised dozens of psychology interns and psychiatry residents in their work with adolescents. In my private practice, I have seen many adolescents and their families. Even during individual therapy with an adolescent, I have usually ended up scheduling some family meetings, a move that has run counter to the traditional training I received that stressed keeping individual therapy confidential.

Was it merely my idiosyncrasies that always led me to meet with the entire family even when doing individual work with adolescents? Was it just me who found my work changing as I became a parent and became closer in age to the parents of adolescent patients than to the adolescents themselves? To satisfy my curiosity, I interviewed more than a dozen experienced family therapists who work primarily with adolescents. There were several commonalities to our experiences. One was a sheepish admission that when it comes to working with adolescents, we bend a lot of rules: we use humor, tell stories about ourselves and our families, and meet with the adolescent, the parents, and the family rather than refer the various subsystems out to different therapeutic specialists. Most of the therapists I interviewed reported being drawn to work with adolescents very early on in their careers because the work felt more "real" and emotionally present.

By the time of our middle age and parenthood, these therapists and I experienced an eagerness to empathize with parents as well as with their adolescents. Maturity as a family
therapist seems to come with the willingness to see both generational perspectives simultaneously. (See Chapter 8 for a
fuller discussion of the study of family therapists.) Much of
my maturity has come from becoming a parent, although I
must admit that both my sons are preteens, so the clinical
ideas presented here have not been tested at home.

In contrast to my evolving view of the adolescent as a viable, vital part of the family, I have encountered a very different view of adolescence, one that permeates our culture and
the mental health community. It is a negative, frightened
view of adolescence, a view that adolescence is a time to be
dreaded for families, a time when children become wild and
disconnected. What's more, in this view, adolescents should
shun their parents in order to find their identities. Boys'
growth will be stunted if they continue looking to their
parents for guidance rather than to their peers. Girls must
develop adversarial relationships with their mothers. Adolescent clinical research over the last decade challenges these
notions. My clinical experience in a wide range of settings—
in an urban general hospital psychiatric emergency room and
outpatient clinic, a suburban private practice, a private inpatient hospital with a separate adolescent unit, and a community clinic in a poor, insulated urban neighborhood—has
led me to believe that adolescents fare better if they maintain connection, if their parents continue to hang in with
them, if they feel close to their families during their exploration of a separate identity. My work in doing family therapy
and in writing this book is informed by this premise: adolescent work can be approached with a respect for, and a belief
in, family connection. I hope this book will offer clinicians new
ways of using family therapy as a context for inspiring adolescents and their parents to grow separately and together.

# Acknowledgments

I feel deeply appreciative of the time and support given by my friends, family, and colleagues.

Thanks to my colleagues who generously shared with me their clinical experiences with adolescents and their families: Steve Durant, Ed.D.; Ken Duckworth, M.D.; Tom Frank, M.D.; David Herzog, M.D.; Jeffrey Kerr, LICSW; Lise Motherwell, Ph.D.; Ann Munson, LICSW; Steve Nickman, M.D.; Ava Penman, Ph.D.; Bethany Montgomery, LICSW; Dennis Norman, Ed.D.; Martha Straus, Ph.D.; and Larry Selter, M.D.

I also wish to thank the adolescent family crisis team at Massachusetts General Hospital, who offered invaluable insights and clinical input: Cathy Conboy, Psy.D.; Marianne Findler, M.A.; Jodi Gastfriend, LICSW; John Julian, M.D.; Rob Muller, Ph.D.; and Julia Reade, M.D.

Judy Smith, Ph.D., professor of film at the University of Massachusetts, helped me think about film from a cultural and historical perspective.

Donna Healey, Ph.D., and Audrey Tolman, Ph.D., provided crucial feedback to me in their readings of early drafts of this book. My editor, Cindy Hyden, offered incisive suggestions that helped make this a much better book.

I also want to thank "The Ladies" (so named by my sons)—Nancy Bridges, LICSW; Beth Harrington, Ph.D.; Chris McElroy, Ph.D.; Paula Rauch, M.D.; and Sue Wolff, M.D.—who have provided peer supervision, comfort, and laughs every other Thursday night for the last fourteen years. In addition, they helped with many aspects of this book: from reading chapters to sharing their extensive clinical experience. Several other friends were especially helpful, each in her own way—Laura Weisberg, Ph.D.; Ginger Chappell, Ph.D.; Eva Schoenfeld, Ph.D.; and Rachel Bricklin.

In the course of writing this book, I have been both teacher and student. I remain indebted to several teachers. Frances Taliaferro, my beloved schoolteacher and good friend, first taught me the power of stories to give meaning to one's life and more recently inspired my thinking about adolescent literature. Sunny Yando, Ph.D., first introduced me to the study of psychology and has remained a mentor and friend for the past twenty-five years. Kathy Weingarten, Ph.D., a brilliant teacher and family therapist, connected theory and practice while also opening the world of family therapy to me.

Special thanks to Rob Abernathy, M.D.; Chris Gordon, M.D.; John Herman, M.D.; Michael Jellinek, M.D.; Crystal Moore; Kathy Sanders, M.D.; George Tesar, M.D.; and Nancy Wilcox, Ph.D., who have actively and enthusiastically supported my teaching of psychiatry residents and psychology interns. I am also grateful to my trainees over the years at Massachusetts General Hospital for their probing, thoughtful questions, which have pushed me to articulate what I think and why.

None of this work would have been possible without the many families who have come to MGH for treatment.

Finally, I owe the greatest thanks to the loving support of my own family. My sister Elizabeth Fishel, a gifted writer, by her example and support let me believe that I, too, could write a book. In countless transcontinental conversations, she offered insights, advice, and humor. My two sons, Gabe and Joe, made room for this book and kept me in good spirits throughout. To my husband, Chris Daly, an accomplished teacher and writer, who read every word, cheered me on, and took our sons on many Saturday outings to give me "booktime," I offer my boundless love and appreciation.

And I am deeply grateful to my mother and father, Edith and James Fishel, who have always believed in me and taught me the meaning of connection in families.

# Introduction

This book offers a developmental and narrative perspective to family work with adolescents. I am interested in the meaning that is made of adolescence—by the luminaries of the past who have written about their work, by the family therapists who currently treat them, by the writers and filmmakers who reinvent adolescence, and most of all by the families who struggle with the dual pull to separate and connect.

This book is not a manual or a work that clusters adolescent problems into different diagnostic groups. Instead, it offers a practical approach to the clinician who is confronted with adolescent patients, an approach that challenges the traditional practice of banishing parents from the room.

Each chapter presents a series of responses to questions that my students and I have raised over the years about practicing family therapy with adolescents. The chapters have been prompted by a set of trainee's questions. Each chapter begins with clinical material, followed by treatment approaches, and then anchored by relevant research findings and theory.

In the next two chapters, I present a full range of family therapy schools, though certainly not an exhaustive compen-

dium, that are currently being practiced and taught in the
United States. This range includes seven distinct varieties of
family therapy—Psychodynamic and Object Relations, Experiential, Behavioral, Structural, Strategic, Systemic, and
Narrative. In order to make the distinctions among different
schools more vivid, I will introduce a family with two adolescents and two middle-aged parents whose family treatment
will be approached by each school in turn. This family, the
Peaces, is a composite of several families I have worked with.
I have chosen them because I think they will be recognizable
to any clinician who has worked with adolescents and their
parents. While not a "typical" family, they are not unusual
either.

For each of the major approaches, I will delineate the primary theoretical ideas and major proponents associated with
that school. In my discussion, I will highlight the main contribution made by each school to the study of adolescence.

While the family is being treated, I hope that the reader
will be treated to the rich variety of clinical approaches that
are available. I wish to demonstrate, too, that what we think
and believe about such topics as change, generational conflict,
the nature of adolescence, and the role of parents in control-
ling or guiding adolescent behavior will dictate what we look
for, what we ask about, and how we assess and treat a family with adolescents. In these two chapters, there will be seven
different pathways traveled between a therapist's beliefs and
the resulting clinical interventions.

While I have tried to be fair in my depiction of each school,
I do, of course, have my own bias, which I wish to disclose at
the outset. Over the last twenty years I have received formal
training in each of the schools discussed here, but my teaching and practice of family therapy falls at one end of the continuum—with systemic and narrative family therapy. I wish
I could say that my choice of theoretical orientation was based
on my doing or at least reading about a comprehensive out-

come study that compared the efficacy of these seven treatment approaches. It does not, nor do I know of any such body of literature. My theoretical orientation is derived from a complex blend of deeply held beliefs about change, from experiences in my own family of origin, from contact with inspiring teachers of family therapy, and from twenty years of clinical experience.

I have separated my theoretical discussion into two chapters: the first contains the five schools of family therapy, which will anchor the family therapist in the history and scope of the seminal ideas in the field: psychodynamic, experiential, structural, behavioral, and strategic. The second chapter explores systemic and narrative family therapies, which are the orientations used throughout the rest of the book. I will start the discussion of all seven schools by introducing the Peace family, beginning with the initial phone contact and the first five minutes of an opening family interview. This material will be cited throughout these first two chapters. Subsequently, from the perspective of each school of family therapy, I will describe the rest of the first interview with the Peace family, an initial formulation, and a trajectory for further treatment.

Chapters 3, 4, and 5 grow directly out of my fifteen years of teaching at Massachusetts General Hospital and several years of running a team in the hospital's Emergency Room to help families with adolescents in acute crisis. These chapters were prompted by very immediate, pressing clinical questions and dilemmas: At what point should we include parents when the adolescent is the one in trouble? Won't the adolescent refuse to come in if her parents are there? How should we conduct an initial interview? How should we end it? What happens after the first interview, in those murky middle sessions? In Chapter 3, I lay out the issues and dilemmas of beginning therapy with adolescents and their parents. In Chapter 4, I discuss five clinical interventions that are particularly useful in crisis or short-term work, with a clinical story to illustrate each intervention. Chapter 5 offers two additional interventions, again with clinical illustrations, that are more applicable in an open-ended therapy or as a consultation.

The next two chapters address common developmental variations in the presentation and treatment of adolescents and their families. Chapter 6 focuses on the adolescent who is having particular difficulty with leaving home. This chapter was prompted by the question: What do you do with an adolescent who is refusing to grow up? Is that a case for family or individual therapy? In this chapter, a family with six children (ranging in chronological age from adolescent to young adult) is presented, in which all members are having trouble moving on to the next stage of development.

Chapter 7 looks at a couple with adolescent children and a situation in which marital issues are more at the root of family difficulties than are parent–child or individual adolescent problems. This chapter tries to answer such questions as: How do you talk to the couple about their marriage, without violating their privacy, in front of the adolescent? How do you know whether the adolescent should be seen at all? Maybe his behavior would improve if his parents figured out what they wanted to do about their marriage? In this chapter, a couple's case is presented, followed by several suggested guidelines for doing couples' work when the adolescents are absent from therapy.

The next two chapters address the cultural and clinical discourse within which family therapists do their work. After learning from the questions of my students and the stories of my families, I explore in Chapter 8 the stories of therapists who are drawn to this work. Based on an exploratory study of clinicians, I grapple with such questions as: What distinguishes these therapists from others? How does aging affect their work with adolescents and the parents of adolescents? Finally, in this chapter, I discuss training and supervision.

Chapter 9 lays out the different, sometimes contradictory, stories offered from cultural sources such as novels and films and from scientific sources such as public health data and mental health research. The overarching question asked in this chapter is: What is the discourse on adolescence within which we, as family therapists, conduct our work?

For our society, the fullest solutions to easing the transition from childhood to adulthood must lie in many systems— schools, courts, television portrayals, community-based programs, and federally funded anti-poverty programs. This book looks at the kinds of interventions that can be made in the context of family therapy. It asks several questions: How can families, in the context of therapy, change the dominant story about adolescence, which is so often portrayed as a time to disconnect? What are the ways that adolescents can "become someone" without summarily rejecting their families as part of the process? How can therapists help parents be strengthened and stretched by living with adolescents? Can families absorb recent clinical research suggesting that adolescence seems not to be a time of increased risk-taking, increased emotionality, and tumult? And when adolescents *do* engage in dangerous behaviors, how can families stick by their teens and not give up on them? This book is intended as a practical guide for therapists working with adolescents and their families. At the same time, it challenges our well-worn beliefs about adolescence as a time when separation from family is the only developmental current to uphold. Instead, the approach offered here honors the dual and simultaneous pulls to become someone distinct from family and to grow up within the context of family relationships.

# PART I

# OVERVIEW OF FAMILY THERAPY WITH ADOLESCENTS: SEVEN APPROACHES TO A CASE

# 1

# Psychodynamic, Experiential, Behavioral, Structural, and Strategic Approaches

## INTRODUCING THE PEACE FAMILY[1]

Mrs. Peace called the clinic to request help for her 16-year-old son, Bert, who had been truant from school for about a month. She also suspected that he had been experimenting with drugs for about the past three months. When asked if there had been any other changes in the family, she admitted that a few months earlier her husband had announced that he planned to relocate the family from Boston to Tampa because of a new job opportunity. Anticipating the next question, Mrs. Peace stated that Bert had been very upset about this impending change. She added that she feels very sympathetic toward Bert about his upset feelings but she knows better than to second-guess her husband. She then mumbled something about having panic attacks when there is a lot of yelling going on at home but quickly changed the subject to ask whether Bert should come alone or if she and her husband should come to the first meeting. When asked if there

---

1. Names of families and identifying details have been changed to protect the confidentiality of my patients.

was anyone else in the family, she sounded a bit surprised and mentioned Sally, her 13-year-old daughter, who is quiet, "no trouble," and a straight-A student. I suggested that the whole family come initially, since it sounded like everyone was being affected by the upcoming move and by Bert's truancy.

In one week, the Peace family came to my office. I asked each member to tell me his or her own view of the problem and anything that he or she would like to be different in the family. Bert, slumped in his chair and intently investigating his right shoelace, muttered to the floor, "I'm here, man, and that's all you're going to get from me. Shrinks are stupid and I'm not talking here." Mrs. Peace, hiding a smile but casting a look of reproach at Bert, said: "I think that the real problem is that Bert doesn't want to move to Tampa. Now, I don't want to cast aspersions on my husband, but I don't think he fully realizes the impact of this move on a 16-year-old. Of course, *I* don't mind where we live." When asked, "What is your view of the current situation?" Mr. Peace looked me right in the eye and declared: "The problem is that everyone is in their own tree. No one listens to me. There are too many chiefs in this family and not enough Indians, and that's starting with Bert. If he doesn't want to be part of this family, he can try living on his own." And then, with less bravura, he said, "I guess I'm just not good enough for anyone to listen to." Sally's answer to what she would like to see different in the family was a soft response: "I just try to stay out of everyone's way. I wish there were more peace at home, just not so much screaming."

Although this is just a clinical sketch, it raises many questions that can be answered in a variety of ways, depending on one's theoretical orientation. Who should be seen? Is this a family or an individual or a couple's case? What is the problem? What kind of change can be effected? How do people change? Are the clinician, the parents, or the whole family responsible for making change happen? What is normal adolescent behavior?

Each of the seven family schools discussed in this chapter and the next one offers different answers to each of these questions. As seven distinct lenses are applied to the Peace family, the reader is invited to locate his or her own reactions to these varied approaches to family therapy. What we each believe is important about the centrality or marginality of parents to adolescent development, the role of the therapist as expert or collaborator, and the nature of change (for example, must a therapeutic relationship be in place? Does insight precede behavioral change?), will dictate what we ask about, what we look for, and how we enter the families we work with.

## PSYCHODYNAMIC AND OBJECT RELATIONS FAMILY THERAPY

### Basic Theoretical Assumptions

In this view, the goal of family therapy, as it is in individually oriented psychodynamic therapy, is more self-awareness, gleaned from rendering unconscious material conscious. Change may also occur when mutual projections between husband and wife, and between parents and their children, are reclaimed so that individual members are no longer burdened with distorted perceptions and expectations. Emphasis is placed on the power that secrets hold over a family, secrets that are often handed down across generations. Consequently, the family therapist tries to help family members disclose secrets and express the associated feelings of anger or grief.

At the heart of psychodynamically oriented family therapy is the notion that current problems in the family or in the marriage are due to unresolved issues with the previous generation. A primary goal of therapy, then, is to free the family from excessive attachment to previous generations. The therapist is much like a lead-test scientist who helps a gardener decide what to plant today by first digging up the soil and making manifest the legacy of past lead chips and gas fumes. Only with accurate information about the status of the old layers of soil does the current gardener know whether it will be safe to plant carrots and potatoes, or only fruits and flowers. The past, when unexamined, has the power to harm family members through unwitting projection of previous hurts and maladaptive patterns. The examined past, by contrast, enables parents to raise their children knowing which toxins are real and to be avoided and which are merely imagined. The family therapist's unearthing is aided by several tools, most of which have been adapted from object relations theory.

The first of these tools is *projective identification*, which Zinner and Shapiro (1974) define as the process "by which members split off disavowed or cherished aspects of themselves and project them onto others within the family group" (p. 179). This process occurs in order to grant intrapsychic peace at the expense of interpersonal conflict. For example, if impulse and superego were not well integrated in the parents' own development, then in the family unit, one family member can become the bearer of impulse gratification, while another takes on the role of controller and punisher of those impulses. To complicate things further, these unconscious projections take place reflexively so that each member behaves in such a way as to elicit the disavowed function of the other. For example, the parent of a delinquent adolescent covertly endorses his son's truancy while the son, for his part, unconsciously welcomes and invites his father's harsh criticism.

Maggie Scarf, in her book *Intimate Partners* (1987), eloquently describes projective identification as it occurs between spouses, as a process that transforms intrapsychic pain into interpersonal struggle: "What was once unacceptable within the self is now what is so intolerable in the partner. The war within each member of the couple has been transformed into a war between them" (p. 227). Thus, in the Peace couple, each partner may have unconsciously agreed to take over the parts of living that were difficult for the other person. For Mr. Peace, it was the expression of tender emotion that he disavowed after learning in his family that it was forbidden for men to emote. For Mrs. Peace, what was verboten and therefore projected was the pursuit of autonomy and ambition. Their collusion allowed Mr. Peace to carry out their shared wish for drive and independence while Mrs. Peace kept up her end by expressing wishes for closeness and intimacy. Over time, these mutual projections became too polarized, and each found unbearable in the other what was hated in the self. Mrs. Peace accused Mr. Peace of being too self-centered and preoccupied with his work to the exclusion of his family. Mr. Peace reciprocates, finding his wife "too damn emotional." In short, the characteristics that had initially drawn the Peaces to each another became repellents. This transformation, from what was once appealing to what is now an antagonism, is a by-product of projective identification. Along the way, however, projective identification serves many psychic functions.

Zinner and Shapiro (1974) elaborate on some of the purposes of these mutual projections: they serve to keep alive relationships with members of previous generations by reenacting conflicts that parents had with their families of origin; the current generation of parents and children is spared the intrapsychic pain of integrating impulse and control by instead externalizing the conflict. Family members, then, are often involved in an unconscious collusion with each other to sustain these mutual projections: by so doing, parents get to hold on to lost relationships from their family of origin, with the bonus of achieving a comfortable defensive arrangement. Meanwhile, adolescents comply with their part of the bargain out of fear of losing their parent should they reject their parents' projections. The family therapist must provide some accepting land for the meteoric showers of projections to crash into, land that won't explode but will merely absorb. A family therapist's capacity to tolerate family members' multiple projections, while holding on to her own sense of effectiveness, is referred to as *containment* (Smilansky 1994).

Another important tool for digging up the past is *transference*. In both individual and family therapy, the here and now of the therapy session stirs up memories of past relationships and offers an opportunity to clarify and understand earlier distortions and disappointments. In family therapy, however, the transferential objects are in the room and, consequently, interpretations can be made more directly rather than waiting until they show up in the relationship with the therapist. For example, the therapist might ask Mr. Peace about the antecedents of his opening remark regarding his family, "I guess I'm not good enough for anyone to listen to." Who made him feel that way in his family of origin? When he reveals that his mother often told him that he was a good-for-nothing boy who would never measure up to his perfect older brother, we are on our way to understanding an important distortion— that is, the way that by using an old lens, he misperceives any current criticism of him as being an all-out repudiation of him as a husband, father, and provider.

## Contribution to Adolescent Work

The psychodynamic family therapist looks at adolescence in a three-generational context and exposes to the light secrets, unresolved difficulties, lost relationships, and disavowed feelings. Because adolescence brings to the fore aggressive and sexual feelings, it can heat up the whole family. This therapist wonders what is making the parents upset about their adolescents' burgeoning sexuality and push for independence. The answer may have more to do with the parents' inner life and unresolved issues from their own families of origin than with the child in question. This therapist cautions us not to take an adolescent's behavior and presentation merely at face value. A girl's outrageous rebellion may be a signal that the whole family is anxious about growing up. A boy's reluctance to apply to college may express a father's longing to be loved for more than his achievements. In each of these instances, the psychodynamic therapist asserts that adolescence is a time when powerful unconscious forces are at work, which stir up family members on both sides of the generational divide.

## Major Proponents

James Framo (1976) concretely brings past distortions into the present by requesting that parents and adult siblings come in person to individual or couples' meetings. This "family-of-origin" work is typically brief and intensive, with family members attending two lengthy sessions on consecutive days. The goal of these meetings is for the adult child to become less reactive to his parents and to learn what his parents had to contend with during childrearing years. The meetings may focus on unresolved issues and secrets, with the concomitant intent of promoting increased honesty and forgiveness on the part of all family members.

Norman Paul (1969) applies Freud's notion of repression to the issue of unresolved loss in the family. He believes that most symptoms in the family can be connected to a previous loss that has not been properly mourned. In family therapy, then, each member mourns an important previous loss while other members look on with a stance of increased empathy.

Murray Bowen (1978) emphasized the importance of differentiating the individual as a separate entity while maintaining that person's connection to the family. In an effort to help a family member become more independent, he would coach that member to return to his family of origin and try to extricate himself from problematic triangles. This could be done through letter-writing, phone calls, or actual visits. In any case, the therapist demands that the patient focus on dyadic relationships without getting distracted by a third party. Patterns of relationships are identified through the use of a genogram. Key triadic arrangements that repeat across the generations (for example, an intensely close mother–son relationship with conflicted sibling relationships) become the target of intervention.

Ivan Boszormenyi-Nagy (Boszormenyi-Nagy and Sparks 1973) is known for the idea of a *family ledger*, which consists of multigenerational accounting of obligations incurred and debts repaid over time. *Payment* is made over several generations and not necessarily by the person who acquired the original debt. Problems occur when there have been too many injustices accumulated without proper retribution made. Symptoms are explained in terms of individuals making sacrifices in their own lives for the sake of family loyalty. Therapy focuses on forgiveness of previous generations' mistakes.

## Psychodynamically Oriented Family Therapy of the Peace Family

The psychodynamic family therapist would need to pay attention to the intergenerational transmission of unresolved issues, problematic triangular relationships, and secrets. She would begin this task by constructing a genogram, a visual picture of at least three generations of the Peace family. She might be struck by a triangular configuration that repeats across the generations: a distant marital couple alongside an intense opposite-sex parent–child bond. The therapist might hypothesize that parent–child bonds were forged at the expense of the marital couple. Mr. Peace could be coached to return to his family of origin and have dyadic conversations with each of his parents, actively blocking attempts made by his parents to bad-mouth, complain, or gossip about the other parent.

The therapist might suggest other tasks that Mr. and Mrs. Peace could carry out with each family of origin that could help diminish the intensity of mutual projections now flying between them. Having identified the damaging effects of Mr. Peace's parents' harsh criticism of him, Mr. Peace could be instructed to go talk with his parents about how hard he had tried to measure up to their standards and to ask them why their standards were always so unattainable. Mrs. Peace might be asked about her tendency to avoid direct conflict with her husband by triangulating in Bert when a marital difference arose. That triangle might be traced back to similar triadic arrangements from the family of origin, in which wives, fearing for their safety, deflected their husbands' rage onto their sons.

The projective identifications that allowed Mr. Peace to abdicate emotional expressiveness and allowed Mrs. Peace to renounce her own drive and ambition could also be challenged and explored in the therapy session. In these explorations, the therapist might choose to leave Bert and Sally out of the sessions, trusting that change in the marital relationship would ultimately help the children.

One area that would be fruitful for the psychodynamic family therapist to take on with the whole family is the way that impulse control is not integrated within each member of the family but instead is split off into separate functions among family members. The therapist would want to know how sexual and aggressive impulses were expressed and contained in each of Mr. and Mrs. Peace's families of origin. Questioning might reveal that both Mr. and Mrs. Peace came from families in which compliance to parental authority was rigidly maintained. Through Bert's acting out, they have the opportunity to reenact with him the kind of freedom that they were forbidden in their own families. For his part, Bert, by projecting his self-criticism onto his father, gets to avoid the messy business of integrating impulse control and expression. No matter what the focus, insight into unconscious processes would be championed.

## EXPERIENTIAL FAMILY THERAPY

### Basic Theoretical Assumptions

In contrast to the previous model's concern with antecedents, the emphasis in experiential family therapy is on the here and now. Change takes place in the immediacy of the therapeutic relationship. This therapist tries to disrupt comfortable and socially circumscribed interactions among family members so that something new and unrehearsed can happen. It is a model of therapy in which expression of affect and spontaneous behavior are valued over insight. This therapist is a kind of folk artist who takes everyday objects and transforms them into works of art. The viewer is surprised to find that a set of old spoons could unexpectedly become the wings of a rooster. Finding the unexpected in the routine, and using playful techniques to do so, are two of the earmarks of experiential family therapy.

Experiential family therapy has its roots in the Human Potential Movement of the 1960s. In its embrace of experience, it is a way of doing therapy that is adamantly atheoretical and therefore does not easily lend itself to explanations of psychological constructs. The ideas embedded in this school can best be conveyed by describing how proponents practice— what they *do*, rather than what they *think*. The focus is on experience rather than on the making of meaning. This therapist believes that here-and-now experiential change also produces deeper changes.

## Contribution to Adolescent Work

The experiential model has a particular resonance in working with adolescents. The experiential therapist underscores the validity of being real in an effort to precipitate something more authentic happening between family members. Similarly, no matter what their theoretical orientation, most of the two dozen family therapists interviewed for this book (see Chapter 8) emphasized the importance of being genuine and self-disclosing in their work with adolescents. The use of humor and playfulness, earmarks of experiential therapy, also were highlighted by this group of family therapists, regardless of theoretical orientation.

## Major Proponents

Virginia Satir is generally regarded as one of the early luminaries in family therapy and one of the founding mothers in a field dominated by charismatic men. Initially a school teacher, she came to understand the role that the family played in influencing a child's self-esteem when she paid home visits and got to know her students' families. She believed that good communication among family members and the self-esteem of individuals within that family are inextricably connected and that both should be goals of therapy. She had a great interest in revealing individual differences within a family and encouraged family members to feel self-confident enough to voice their own opinions of a family situation (Haley and Hoffman 1967, Satir 1964).

Satir is remembered for her strong emotional presence as a therapist and for her capacity to focus on what was positive in a family, joining with them around their hopes and pain. She made emotional connections to families in part through her sensitivity to nonverbal communication, a sensitivity that depended on all the senses; she believed that if families could learn to hear, see, and touch more, then they would have more resources available to solve problems.

Satir developed several techniques to make something new happen in the therapy session itself (Andreas 1989). Early on in each therapy, she would coach families to talk about what they wanted right now that would make life better, and she would interrupt any communication that was negative or blaming. She asked detailed questions about small interactions to get a sense of repetitive patterns and to let the family know that she was interested in each member's perceptions and views.

She is also known for more dramatic, action-oriented techniques that spurred new opportunities for growth. She might have family members assume symbolic postures (called *sculptures*) to concretely demonstrate rules and roles within a family and then even use ropes or blindfold members to graphically represent the constricting nature of these roles. Sometimes she worked within the context of group therapy and had an individual use group members to stand in for family members in a technique called *family reconstruction*, a blend of body sculpting, guided fantasy, and psychodrama. The individual, termed the Explorer, would enroll group members to play each side of his or her family in a multigenerational drama that enabled the Explorer to view the family with new eyes.

Since most experiences occur outside awareness, Carl Whitaker (1975) believed that we can best gain access to them nonverbally or symbolically. To do this, he tried to engage family members in encounters that were free of social constraints. He practiced "therapy of the absurd," a method that accesses the unconscious by using humor, boredom, jokes, vulgarity, free association, speaking in metaphors, even wrestling on the floor. From these unusual encounters, rigid patterns of thought and behavior are disrupted or, as Whitaker put it, "the whole process of therapy is breaking the mask" (Haley and Hoffman 1967, p. 320).

Therapy is a potent mixture of controlled and uncontrolled moves. Initially, Whitaker would set the therapy up so that he had a lot of control, establishing obstacles and playing hard-to-get to see if the family would mount a campaign to declare their engagement in therapy. He believed that he must win at establishing the rules of the game before therapy could really begin. But once he had established that he was in charge, he hoped that the family would take over. He likened this process to pole vaulting—as the therapist, he got the family to the top of the pole and then expected gravity to take care of the rest.

This process of therapy is one of looking for something unforeseen and unexpected in the session: this surprise element is the change agent that Whitaker termed the "growing edge" (Haley and Hoffman 1967). The unexpected is most likely to crop up when anxiety is stirred up in family members other than the identified patient. He tried to highlight covert family conflict that was being obfuscated by the scapegoating of one family member.

Whitaker liked to practice with a cotherapist to help him steer clear of entanglements with any one member. He described the division between the two therapists as one playing while the other administrates. Where the pychodynamic family therapist sees his role as a transferential one in the therapy, Whitaker saw his stake in the therapy as similar to that of the family: he wrote that his reason for doing therapy was "to experience some more of myself."

## Experientially Oriented Family Therapy of the Peace Family

Since the use of the self is the primary theoretical construct of this model, it is easier to describe the treatment of the Peaces by highlighting the personality of the therapist. At the risk of being hubristic, I have chosen to approach the Peaces' therapy as I think Virginia Satir might have.

A Satir-like therapist, careful to address each member by the name he or she preferred, would have asked members how they found out about the meeting.

"Sally, how did you find out about the meeting?"

*Sally*: "From my mom and dad. They said we'd be talking about problems in the family."

And then the therapist might say, "Bert, how did you hear?"

*Bert*: "From my sister."

The therapist, summing up so far: "So Sally got her information from both parents and Bert got his information from Sally. So you have different ways of transmitting information. What happens if Mr. and Mrs. Peace give information to Bert together? Why don't you try it right now?"

This brief exchange captures Satir's emphasis on the here and now and the linkage of the family's communication patterns to each member's capacity to speak of his or her own views and opinions. In other words, good communication among family members depends on Bert, Sally, and Mr. and Mrs. Peace being able to speak about their individual differences regarding how they heard and felt about family therapy.

Next, this therapist might ask the family members what they would wish for right now that would make their life better immediately. Again, the emphasis would be on eliciting each member's point of view in a context that allowed the hearing of those disparate wishes. She would capitalize on any moments of communication that were warm or indicated a wish for more closeness. Conversely, she would interrupt communications that were antagonistic. For example, if Mrs. Peace said she wanted her husband to really pay attention to her when she spoke, the therapist might ask her if she was willing to risk going out on that limb right now. She would then interrupt any of Mrs. Peace's musings on past attempts that failed at getting his attention and instead would keep bringing Mrs. Peace back to the present moment. She might ask Mrs. Peace to hold her husband's hand and look into his eyes and then ask what that felt like. In turn, she might ask Mr. Peace how it felt to be touched and gazed at by his wife.

This experiential therapist would puzzle about Bert's symptom of acting out and try to figure out how Mr. and Mrs. Peace are trying to settle family-of-origin issues through this symptom. In particular, Mrs. Peace doesn't feel she is valued by her husband—in much the same way her mother was belittled by her father. Bert's truancy and drug use might be seen then as his attempt to make his mother feel more central by undermining father's authority.

The Satir-like therapist might then "sculpt" this triangle of Bert and his parents by trying to bring the mother into the center of the family by enlisting her aid with his acting-out behavior. She might ask Bert to reach for his mother with one hand while blocking his father with the other. She would then ask Bert if this is how he feels in his family. Then she might resculpt the family, placing one of each of the mother's and father's arms around each other with their free arms reaching out to touch Bert and Sally. The therapist would then continue to ask about how this sculpture felt, trying to unearth more positive roles for the Peace family and trying to unmask the constricting family patterns that had prevented the parents from getting close to each other. For example, after this revised family sculpture, Mr. Peace might have said that he felt uncomfortable in this position with his and his wife's arms around each other because he believed his children wouldn't respect a father who had an equal relationship with his wife. The therapist might then challenge this family rule by saying that, divided, the parents had lost almost all control over their son, so maybe it wasn't such a powerful position for a father to stand alone. She might ask the father to check in with his son about how *he* felt in this sculpture. In this way, the Satir-like therapist would continue to challenge the family rules about power and would be promoting a new and more intimate pattern in the family.

## STRUCTURAL FAMILY THERAPY

### Basic Theoretical Assumptions

In this way of working, the formal structural properties of the family, rather than affect or insight, are the focus of change. Structure, in this sense, is the pattern of interaction rather than the content. Structure is defined by rules (e.g., Whose words are listened to? Who sits where at the dinner table?); by boundaries within the family (e.g., Do the children stay out of fights that the parents have? Do the parents have a separate relationship as a couple? Do the siblings have their own relationship and is each afforded special privileges and tasks according to age and gender?); by boundaries between the family and the outside world (e.g., Does the family talk to outsiders about their problems or are they very insulated and closed to outsiders?); and by the generational hierarchy (e.g., Are the parents in charge or is the adolescent running the show? Is there a grandparent to whom the parents defer for advice about parenting?).

The structural therapist approaches a family case with a notion of normalcy based on these rules, with some allowance offered for cultural, ethnic, and economic variations. A well-functioning family should have distinct generational boundaries, with parents clearly in charge; well-defined parental, couple, and sibling subsystems; and flexible but robust lines of communication with the outside world. By contrast, problems with a child often occur when children are caught in power struggles between the parents. The therapist is alerted to such a problem by a child wielding too much control or by the presence of a cross-generational triangle that involves a secret kept from one parent but shared between another parent and child. The structural therapist, armed with this blueprint and a therapeutic stance that focuses on the present family context, is ready to intervene.

This therapist is like a building inspector who marches in without any concern about the furnishings or the history of the house. Instead, he asks, does the building need a large-scale renovation or just a few touch-ups? Are the walls solid? Do the doors have locks but easy access? Does each room have a specific function? Are there separate stories for bedrooms and a common living space? Is there a safe outdoor play space? If the house is built well, that is what counts. Or, to translate the metaphor: if the structure of the family is intact, symptoms will disappear.

## Contribution to Adolescent Work

The structural family therapist brings a confidence and authority to families with adolescents that is enviable. In response to acting-out adolescents, particularly substance-abusing and truant ones, this therapist has a plan that involves each and every member of the family. This is a model that engages the family to alter behavior through action and asks that every member of the family be accountable and present.

## Major Proponents

Salvador Minuchin is widely regarded as the founding father of structural family therapy. While head of the Philadelphia Child Guidance Clinic, he worked extensively with psychosomatic families and inner-city families (Minuchin 1974, 1978). In his work with families, Minuchin typically followed several steps in his interviews. First, he would "join" with each family member, making a relationship with each that would later become important in terms of restructuring the system and empowering different family members. In his initial joining moves, he would be careful to support the existing rules of the family; for example, if the father were an authoritarian head of the household, Minuchin might ask the father's permission to speak with other members. He would try to immerse himself in the particular culture of the family, imitating the family's use of language (metaphoric or concrete) and mirroring individual members' posture, speech tempo, and mood.

Next, Minuchin would conduct an assessment to determine whether the parental, couples, and sibling subsystems were well defined. Boundaries would be evaluated according to how rigid (Are outsiders prohibited from visiting, as in many alcoholic families where family members are too ashamed to invite others over?) or how diffuse they are (Are outsiders constantly passing in and out, offering advice?). The family would also be assessed along the disengagement–enmeshment continuum: in an enmeshed family, differentiation of individual members is forfeited in exchange for constant vigilance and sensitivity to everyone else's moods and actions. In a disengaged family, members are so separate that it takes a major catastrophe for family members to take notice of each other.

Following the assessment phase, Minuchin would employ a variety of techniques aimed at restructuring the family. These techniques might begin with the manipulation of space—as when two parents who have lost control of their children are asked to sit together while the children are segregated in a corner of the office. He might also impose some communicational rules on the family, such as, "Speak only for yourself, not for others," or "Instead of talking about your spouse, speak directly to each other."

Another type of intervention that Minuchin made was an enactment of the problem in the therapy session itself. So, for example, with an anorectic girl refusing to eat, Minuchin had both parents try to get the girl to eat a hot dog, and then each one tried alone (Minuchin 1978). When together they attempted to get their daughter to eat, their daughter's triangulation in their power struggle with each other was revealed. When they tried and failed individually to get her to eat, Minuchin was ready to unite them in defeat and extricate their daughter from the couple's relationship.

Stanton and Todd (Stanton et al. 1978, Stanton and Todd 1982) are known for their work with drug-addicted and alcoholic adolescents and their families. In their work with substance-abusing adolescents and their parents, they came to view the adolescents' substance abuse as inextricably tied to marital difficulties. That is, as the addict became more competent and able to function independently from the family, the parents' marital problems increased and the addict would often revert to self-destructive behaviors that would ensure that he would not leave his parents alone with their marriage.

Their treatment plan for enabling adult children to leave home began with recreating a family structure that was more appropriate for an earlier stage of development, a stage in which parents are in charge and family members are more closely connected to one another. Stanton and Todd argue that this structural move has the effect of precipitating separation by the adolescent, who bristles at this infantilization. The therapist also redefined the drug abuse as "misbehavior" rather than "illness," since the former definition allows the parents to be experts and, therefore, in charge. The parents are encouraged to work together; at the same time, any alliances between one parent and the adolescent are discouraged. Siblings may be brought into treatment for their own session to delineate more clearly the boundaries between the generations. Parents will be asked to negotiate appropriate rules and consequences for their adolescent's misbehavior. Finally, the therapist searches for strengths among individual family members to facilitate the adolescent's developmental need to be different from the rest of the family.

## Structurally Oriented Family Therapy of the Peace Family

The structural therapist would focus first on assessing the formal structural properties of the Peace family. Addressing Mr. Peace first, since he sees himself as the head of the family, this therapist would be struck by the shaky alliance between husband and wife, the covert support between Mrs. Peace and Bert, and the lack of well-defined marital, parental, or sibling subsystems. The boundaries within the family would be assessed as disengaged: it took Bert's truancy from school and his substance abuse for his parents to realize that something was awry in the family. Between the family and the outside world, the boundary appears to be rigid, since there is no mention of visits from friends or relatives, nor have the Peaces asked for any help or advice from extended family or school personnel. This family therapist would view Bert's drug abuse and school truancy as symptoms of a poorly demarcated parental subsystem. His substance abuse, in particular, would be seen as Bert's misguided attempt to stave off escalating marital tensions that might really explode without his deflecting behavior.

As assessment becomes treatment, the structural therapist might impose the communication rule that each member should speak only for himself or herself. Thus, the therapist would interrupt Mrs. Peace when she asserts that she doesn't dread the move to Tampa but knows that Bert does. The therapist might also manipulate space in an effort to shore up the parents' relationship with each other—for example, by asking Mr. and Mrs. Peace to sit side by side on a couch while instructing Bert and Sally to read quietly in a corner of the room or even to leave for part of the interview. Bert's substance abuse could be redefined as misbehavior, with Mr. and Mrs. Peace being coached in monitoring this behavior more closely, just as they had kept track of Bert when he was a latency-age child. This intervention would be aimed at reconnecting the parents as the tighter unit they had been as the parents of younger children. In addition, the reframing of Bert's substance abuse as misbehavior rather than an illness puts them in charge, since parents can be experts on bad behavior whereas doctors are needed for their expertise on illness. Mr. and Mrs. Peace would be asked to plan together what the consequences should be for Bert's truancy from school. Finally, Bert and Sally might be invited in for their own sibling meeting to explore and shore up their relationship, which at present seems almost nonexistent.

## BEHAVIORAL FAMILY THERAPY

### Basic Theoretical Assumptions

The advent of applying behavioral techniques to families with children and adolescents can be traced to the launch of the journal *Child Behavior Therapy* in 1979. (The journal soon changed its name to *Child and Family Behavioral Therapy*, reflecting the emphasis on parents as essential social reinforcers.) Of course, behavioral therapy as a whole has a much longer history, stretching back to the 1920s with Skinner and Watson, but the focus here will be on its more recent applications to family therapy.

Over the last twenty-five years there has been an evolution in thinking among behavioral therapists, from their original espousal of techniques that adhered strictly to observable behavior to their adopting methods of newer, cognitive behavioral therapy with its inclusion of invisible, internal states. Several principles, however, were consistent over time: that the focus of treatment should be on the present situation; that interventions, derived from learning theory, should be operationalized; and that treatment goals should be objective to allow monitoring and evaluation of therapeutic progress.

Behavioral therapy begins with a rigorous assessment phase in which target behaviors are objectively defined and the contextual factors, (i.e., at school and at home), related to their occurrence and severity, are identified. Assessment techniques include direct observation of the family at home or in the clinic, rating scales, role-playing, and interview inventories. Assessment is a continuous process that repeatedly allows the clinician to measure changes in behavior throughout the course of therapy.

Behavioral interventions cover a great range of techniques, some of which will be discussed in more detail in the following sections. Briefly, these techniques include respondent conditioning (Morris and Kratochwill 1983), operant conditioning (Weathers and Liberman 1978), social learning and imitation (Bandura and Walters 1963), cognitive behavioral interventions (Meichenbaum 1977), and the training of parents as stand-in behavioral therapists (Falloon and Liberman 1983).

## Contribution to Adolescent Work

Behavioral therapists offer a critical way of working with adolescents and their parents, when therapist and family alike feel hopeless and are overwhelmed by the intensity of affect and conflict. This approach favors a systematic, methodical approach to problem-solving that conveys to all parties involved that there is a safe path to be negotiated here and that the therapist can be their guide. With the emphasis on equitable negotiation, this approach conveys, at a meta level, that there are at least two perspectives and that each side requires respect and accountability.

## Major Proponents

The work done by Weathers and Liberman (1975, 1978), using *contingency contracting* with adolescents and families, represents an important contribution to this field. Contingency contracting is an operant conditioning technique used to promote cooperation and positive behavior when negative behaviors prompting angry attention have spiraled out of control. It introduces very structured interaction into a family system marked by conflict, in which family members have difficulty speaking about or listening to each others' needs.

Weathers and Liberman identify six steps to making a contract with adolescents and their families: First, the therapist identifies rewarding behavior for the adolescent and the parents—that is, for the parent, "What does my child want that I can offer?"; and for the teen, "What does my parent want that I can offer?" Second, each identifies what is desired but was not initially offered. Third, each side figures out priorities on a wish list. Fourth, the adolescent and parents are each guided toward empathizing with the other's position, with the therapist asking each member, "How does the other feel about doing this for me?" The fifth step is setting the costs on providing the desired rewards, for example, how hard would it be for us or for me to do what the other wants? Finally, there is a bargaining step in which family members are asked to sort out what each is willing to exchange with the other to get what is desired for the self. The authors caution that this approach is most effective with parents who have maintained control over the major reinforcers in their adolescents' lives and is minimally useful in more deviant, disorganized families, particularly those with delinquent adolescents. The behavioral therapist is like a federal mediator, hammering out a fair agreement between labor and management in a process that requires a commitment on everybody's part to gradual, step-wise, goal-directed movement and a willingness to value group harmony over absolute personal gain.

Gerald Patterson (1982) in Oregon is well-known for his work with conduct-disordered adolescents. Coding behavior in the home, he focused on those parental responses that encourage aggressive behavior among adolescents. In particular, he discovered that parents' irritability, intermittent punishment, and threats with no follow-up action reinforced their children's aggressiveness. In addition to his work with aggressive teens, Patterson and Forgatch (1987, 1989) have written books for families with adolescents that are consistent with the behaviorist notion that the tools of change should lie with parents since they are the major reinforcers of their teens. In these books, the writers focus on the need for planfulness and consistency on the part of parents to promote responsibility and autonomy on the part of their teens.


**Behaviorally Oriented Family Therapy
of the Peace Family**

The behavioral therapist would begin by performing a functional analysis of the Peace family: Mr. and Mrs. Peace would be asked to keep track of their responses to Bert's truancy in a diary. The therapist might ask: "What would happen if this truancy were not paid so much attention? What would be gained if the truancy disappeared?" These questions would be asked to figure out how the target behavior is currently being reinforced, perhaps through negative attention. The larger social context would also be assessed with questions like these: "Under what circumstances does Bert's problem increase or decrease? What is the school's response to his truancy? Has the school determined any consequences for Bert's truancy? If so, what is the effect of these consequences on Bert's behavior?"

The family could also be engaged in contingency contracting. Perhaps Mr. and Mrs. Peace would be willing to offer Bert something he wants, such as permission to use the family car on the weekend. Bert would also be asked to volunteer something his parents would like, for example, agreeing to make his bed every morning without needing a prod. Subsequently, the therapist would ask Mr. and Mrs. Peace what else they would like from Bert. They might answer, "The truth about whether or not Bert has gone to school that day, for him to stop using drugs, to help out more around the house, to talk to us about what he does each day." Bert would be asked the same thing and might answer, "I'd like for my parents not to interrogate me about my whereabouts, to let me stay out as long as I want at night, to give me a bigger allowance, and to stop comparing me to Sally." Then, each party would be asked to set priorities about its wants, with the parents asserting that stopping drug use was most important to them and Bert stating that not being interrogated was most important to him. Mr. and Mrs. Peace would be asked what they think it would be like for Bert to comply with their wishes, and Bert would be asked how his parents would feel about agreeing with his wish. The therapist would then ask Mr. and Mrs. Peace to speak about the difficulties they anticipated in not questioning Bert about his whereabouts, and Bert, in a symmetrical way, would be asked to talk about the difficulties he thought he would have in abandoning all drug use. Finally, they would all be helped to bargain with each other: "Mr. and Mrs. Peace, what would you be willing to offer Bert in exchange for his not abusing drugs anymore? And Bert, what can you give your parents in exchange for their not bugging you about your whereabouts?" Throughout this contract-making process, family members would be coached in effective communication skills, such as maintaining eye contact, keeping their bodies turned toward each other, and using nonverbal indicators, such as nodding the head, to show that they were listening to each other.

Most likely, this process of contingency contracting would

not go off without a hitch. It requires more open communication and more talking about personal wants than has occurred in this family in a very long time. It could be expected that Bert would resent the invasion into his privacy that would result from opening up negotiations, that Mr. Peace would bristle at the egalitarian premise of the contracting process, and that Mrs. Peace would falter when asked what she wished for herself. In other words, inherent in this exercise is a fundamental challenge to the present status quo, and the family members might well offer up some protest that could derail forward movement.

## STRATEGIC FAMILY THERAPY

### Basic Theoretical Assumptions

In this model, change takes place by interrupting maladaptive behavioral sequences. The therapist tries to determine how solutions to initial difficulties have themselves become unsolvable problems. This therapist differentiates between two kinds of change, first order and second order. First-order change refers to commonsense solutions that sometimes work, though at other times have the effect of making the problem worse. Second-order change refers to random events or therapeutic interventions aimed at interrupting or disrupting first-order solutions. An example will illustrate.

A couple came for a consultation to a couples team I direct because they and their therapist had arrived at a formidable impasse in the marital relationship. The husband, who had been drinking to excess for the previous ten years, had recently stopped drinking because he wanted a more satisfying sexual relationship with his wife and blamed his drinking for his impotence. He was then perplexed to find that he and his wife still had serious sexual difficulties even after he stopped drinking, and he concluded that she must be having an affair. Initially, he interrogated her about her whereabouts, and she would answer. But over time, he became more convinced that she was lying and started to follow her around. She found this surveillance intolerable and became more evasive and secretive. He, in turn, stepped up his efforts to catch her in an infidelity, even taking a job leave so that he could watch her around the clock. She responded with increased secretiveness and anger.

This case contains several examples of first-order change, in which the solution becomes the problem. The husband's watchfulness prompts secretiveness in his wife, which in turn causes the husband to become more suspicious, which has the effect of making his wife more secretive, and so on. Seen this way, the couple is locked into a sequence of behaviors whose internal logic results in more of the same.

Enter the strategic therapist, who has elicited a description of the sequence of behaviors surrounding the presenting problem. This therapist might suggest that the wife choose two times during the next week to tell a lie. Every night the partners are to talk together, with the husband guessing whether today was one of the two days that the wife lied. The wife is to tell her husband whether it was a lying or a truth-telling day. In this way, the strategic therapist explains, the wife can teach her husband to distinguish between her lying and her truth telling. The strategic therapist would expect that this paradoxical intervention—an example of second-order change—would disrupt the couple's own escalating, dead-end, commonsense solutions. The strategic therapist relies on the use of paradox for making interventions because paradox is aimed at the central dilemma that families present with: get rid of the symptom but don't ask us to change.

This type of therapist is like a master chess player who maps out each move but who also has an overall game plan. The strategic therapist has an idea about the goal of each individual session and has an overarching picture of the outcome of this problem-focused therapy. There is a notion that a small change in behavior in one part of the system will set off other changes elsewhere in the system, changes that are largely predictable by the therapist.

## Contribution to Adolescent Work

The particular significance of the strategic approach to work with adolescence is its ability to make paradoxical interventions that are a fitting match for the paradoxes inherent in adolescence. Adolescence is a time of connecting and separating, of being not quite an adult and not quite a child, of needing to criticize one's parents and yet also needing to demand acceptance for one's own unsteady self-discoveries. The strategic therapist appreciates these dilemmas and offers a positive way of reframing the developmental struggles that can occur between adolescents and their parents.

## Major Proponents

The entire school of strategic therapists has been heavily influenced by the work of Milton Erickson (Erickson and Rossi 1981), who emphasized the pragmatics of therapy: actual behavioral change, rather than insights about change, is the goal. Erickson's active, optimistic stance and his use of indirect suggestion through stories, riddles, and metaphors find their way into the work of strategic therapists.

The California Mental Research Institute (MRI) family therapists, which at one time included Jay Haley, Paul Watzlawick, John Weakland, and Gregory Bateson, were the earliest proponents of strategic family therapy. They posited that families are fundamentally homeostatic: that is, families will do whatever they must to maintain the status quo even at the expense of symptomatic members. Thus, insofar as the therapist tries to change the status quo, a power struggle between the therapist and the family will ensue. The therapist must manipulate and take charge to interrupt the homeostasis.

This focus on power led these therapists to their work with paradox, which indirectly confronted families' resistance to change. One such paradoxical intervention is "prescribing the symptom," in which the family is asked to continue with the problematic behavior or some aspect of that behavior. For example, in a family where the mother has frequent panic attacks, the strategic therapist might suggest to her, "You should panic first thing every morning because panicking makes your husband feel in charge, which you both know is very important to him. You should continue with this behavior every day because it is so important to the welfare of your family." This prescription is a kind of "therapeutic double bind," an intervention that mirrors the paradoxical binds in the family. If, in this example, the mother resists the suggestion to panic daily and tells the therapist that she is being ridiculous, then change occurs. If, on the other hand, the wife does not resist the suggestion, then she has made a choice to continue with the symptomatic behavior and change takes place anyway because now the symptom will be seen as being under voluntary control, whereas previously it had been out of control.

Chloe Madanes (1981) is an innovative strategic therapist whose work with children is particularly instructive. Like her strategic colleagues, she takes as her starting point the literal presenting complaint and tries to make changes as quickly as possible without concern paid to the family's understanding of the problem. When children are part of the clinical picture, she assumes that their symptoms are in the service of helping the family. In addition to helping the family, however, a child's acting out also reverses the generational hierarchy, placing the helpful child in a superior position to his or her parents. Madanes suggests the use of paradoxical techniques to restore the parents' authority while simultaneously honoring the benevolent meaning of the child's misbehavior. Her techniques include having the parent ask the child to pretend to help out and having the child pretend to have the problem. In each of these instances, a playful, benign context is introduced that makes overt what had been hidden: that the child was in control of the parents. These paradoxical techniques allow the child to continue being in charge, but now in a childlike way. These techniques respect the child's desire to be helpful while at the same time they put the parents back in charge. There is an extra bonus to the reframe of the child's acting out as a helpful if misguided effort: it allows the parents to experience their children's love for them and to respond by taking responsibility as parents.

## Strategically Oriented Family Therapy of the Peace Family

The strategic therapist would begin by asking the Peaces about the behavioral sequence that occurs around the presenting problems of Bert's school truancy and the parents' chronic and covert disagreements. For example, the therapist might ask, "When Mr. and Mrs. Peace are on the verge of an argument, what happens next?" Mrs. Peace says, "I start to cry." The therapist asks, "And then what?" Mrs. Peace reports that her husband looks very angry and that she goes into her room, closes the door, and lies in bed. The therapist would ask the other family members what they are doing when this happens. Father then relates that "Bert starts mouthing off about what a bully I am and before I know it, he and I are going at it, verbally, I mean." "And what then happens to you, Mrs. Peace?" the therapist asks. "Well," she sighs, "I feel like such an ineffectual mother because my retreating has led to Bert and his father getting into a big fight that will end with Bert's car privileges being taken away. I feel so bad, I just stay in bed." The therapist asks, "How does this sequence end?" Bert states, "My father tells me I'm to blame for my mother being so unhappy and I say, 'Screw it, I'm leaving,' and I take off for a few days, skip school, and go hang with some friends." The therapist asks Mr. and Mrs. Peace what happens to them. Mr. Peace says, "I feel so mad at everyone that I don't know what to do, so I do nothing, just slam the door and smoke in my study." "And you, Mrs. Peace?" questions the therapist. "I usually go to sleep, sometimes take a Valium, and when I wake up I go looking for Sally."

The strategic therapist would be struck by several examples of first-order change embedded in the behavioral sequence that was elicited around the presenting problem. Over and over, family members respond to anger and conflict by withdrawing, retreating, or leaving the field. Mother absents herself when she senses an argument coming on with her husband. Bert leaves the house after a fight with his father, a leave-taking that in turn makes the father retreat to his study and causes the mother to tune out completely with Valium and sleep. The only exception to this pattern, in itself another type of first-order change, is Bert and his father having a shouting match following the couples' avoidance of a marital fight.

The strategic therapist, interested in introducing a second-order change, might begin by seeing Bert's acting-out—particularly, his fighting with his father and his leaving home—as being helpful to his parents because it distracts them from full-fledged fighting, which could be dangerous to their marriage. The strategic therapist might ask Bert to pretend to act up so that his mother and father would be kept apart and thus be prevented from engaging in disastrous fighting. In this way Bert's misbehavior would not be seen as being so antagonistic and perhaps his father would respond to Bert's "mouthing off" in a gentler way. Similarly, this therapist might ask the father to enlist his son's help in an overt way the next time the mother started to cry or withdraw to her room. In this way, the generational hierarchy of the parents being in charge would be maintained, while the son could continue with his helping behavior, now in an overt and perhaps more childlike way. Or the therapist might comment to the family that everyone is afraid of conflict in this family except for Bert and that three times a week he should give the rest of the family lessons in fighting. With this reframe, the strategic therapist would expect that the mother and father would not so automatically retreat from each other and that Bert's acting out would be regarded as a more benign activity, both of which would be new perceptions that would interrupt the behavioral sequence in question.

My clinical path has led me to practice within the systemic and narrative schools, the subject of the next chapter. But I have also found great comfort and nourishment in the collective therapeutic wisdom contained within the five theoretical approaches discussed in this chapter.

A brief anecdote will locate the special, though not central, place these schools of therapy hold in my work. I remember my first big conference presentation, which I had nervously practiced so often it was virtually memorized. As it happened, the subject of this first talk, now fifteen years ago, was family therapy with adolescents. Despite my dogged preparation, I flooded myself during the talk with unwanted religious allusions and biblical anecdotes. As a minimally observant person, I was initially puzzled and annoyed by these intrusions. On the ride home, I came to understand the associations this way: that in working with adolescents and their families, one sometimes would like to appeal to a higher authority because the work is so often difficult and confusing. For me, the five schools of family therapy reviewed in this chapter are like sages sitting on the sidelines of my work, connecting me not to a higher authority but to an esteemed body of elders. In upcoming chapters I will occasionally turn to these ancestors for help. But for now, I want to discuss systemic and narrative family therapies that comprise the therapeutic bedrock of the book.

# 2

# Systemic and Narrative Approaches

This chapter is a continuation of the previous one and also a departure from it. As with the five theoretical schools already discussed, I will be reviewing the theoretical underpinnings and major proponents associated with systemic and narrative family therapies. Similarly, I will step into the role of family therapist and treat the Peace family yet two more times. But, unlike my treatment of the five previous schools, the ideas set down here will be referred to and elaborated on throughout the book, as these are the schools of thought that I am most steeped in as a clinician and teacher.

The section on systemic family therapy will focus on its hey-day—the late 1970s and early 1980s when the Milan School family therapists, the members of the Ackerman Institute, and Karl Tomm were busy publishing, teaching, and training. Subsequently, I will outline the contributions of the newer narrative therapists such as Michael White, David Epston, Tom Andersen, Harry Goolishian, and Harlene Anderson, whose work can be regarded as a direct outgrowth of the earlier systemic thinkers.

Both systemic and narrative therapists focus on meaning and beliefs as the locus of change. The systemic therapist tries to introduce new information that family members can use to effect their own solutions. New information is introduced by systemic therapists in the form of innovative questioning techniques, such as circular questions (Penn 1982) and interventive questioning (Tomm 1988), as well as powerful messages told to the family at the end of sessions. These messages acknowledge the patients' dual request for change and stability. The narrative therapists introduce new information by altering those stories that family members have created with one another to give meaning to their experience. Both schools embrace constructivism as a philosophical underpinning for therapy. Constructivism supplants scientific knowledge with the postmodern belief that there is no objective truth. Instead, there is only the reality that is created by our sharing, through language, our beliefs and perceptions. If the commonality between these two schools of thought is their emphasis on changing meaning through language, the differences in technique and style are also important to discuss.

## SYSTEMIC FAMILY THERAPY

### Basic Theoretical Assumptions: Milan School Systemic Family Therapy

The Milan School, or Milan method, refers to a group of four psychoanalysts-psychiatrists (Drs. Mara Selvini Palazzoli, Luigi Boscolo, Gianfranco Cecchin, and Giuliana Prata) at the Centro per lo Studio della Famiglia in Milan, Italy, who collaborated from 1971 to 1980 in developing systemic interventions using a team approach for helping families. The focus here will be on this enormously productive decade (Selvini Palazzoli et al. 1978a,b, 1980a,b).

Milan school therapists, much like their international colleagues at the Mental Research Institute, were initially struck by the paradoxical bind that families were in. Families said, in effect, "Help us with this symptomatic member but don't make us change as a family." Interventions, then, were aimed at freeing family members from their own paradoxical strait-jackets by introducing counterparadox—therapeutic moves that put the family in a therapeutic "double bind" by pointing out positive reasons for maintaining the status quo and positively connoting all behaviors in a homeostatic pattern (Hoffman 1981).

Later, these therapists supplanted the notion of the family as homeostatic with a view of the family as in constant flux but erroneously seeing itself as stuck. In construing the family as an evolving, naturally changing entity, the Milan school therapists found that they no longer had a clear idea about what the family should look like in the future, at the close of treatment. Instead, they would identify the place of "stuckness," where there were redundant interactional sequences, and push on it without concern for the family's next destination. This process is like seeing a mobile that has stopped moving in the wind and giving it a shove, without any expectation of how the pieces will resume movement.

In this model, change can occur in leaps, rather than in mapped-out incremental steps. Change tends to be introduced through two kinds of interventions: directly, by introducing new meanings with a reframe, or indirectly, with new actions in a ritual that allows families to come up with their own new meanings.

With reframing interventions, the behavior of everyone is connected in a therapeutic explanation; problematic behaviors are redefined as neutral or even positive. The presenting problem is construed as a solution to some implied problem that could occur if the symptom were to disappear. The rationale for positive connotation is manifold: it encourages cooperation, introduces the idea of volition when behaviors have been regarded as outside of anyone's control, and adds some confusion and absurdity, which stimulate the family to question tightly held beliefs.

Rituals were introduced not as a behavioral directive but as an experiment, a symbolic gesture or a rite of transition. The Milan therapists did not believe that it was necessary for the ritual to be carried out nor did they regard failure to do so as noncompliance. Rather, it is the introduction of new ideas and beliefs contained in the rituals that brings about change. Rituals enable families to separate out in time two inconsistent behaviors that had been taking place simultaneously. This new prescribed use of time introduces clarity where there had been confusion.

These two interventions, reframes and rituals, typically were introduced at the end of a five-part therapeutic encounter between a family and a team (Tomm 1984b). In the first part, or "presession," the team generated initial hypotheses based on referral information (such as "Who referred the family?"; "Who made the initial call?"; "What was the tone on the phone?"), as well as using theory and clinical experience relevant to the presenting problem. In the second part, one clinician would interview the family while the team watched from behind a one-way mirror. The clinician, seeking to confirm or disconfirm the team's hypotheses, asked circular questions that made implicit connections among family members but did not ask family members to change. During the third part, the "intersession," the team members elaborated their initial hypotheses and generated an end-of-session intervention. This intervention might be a systemic opinion, with or without a prescription for change, a reframing of family beliefs, a ritual, or a declaration of therapeutic impotence. Usually, these messages were succinct and often hypnotic. They were aimed at introducing just enough new information to engender surprise and confusion while at the same time promoting the family's feeling of being listened to and understood. In the "postsession," and last part, team members, in an effort to evaluate the validity of their hypotheses, discussed the family's immediate reactions to the intervention.

The Milan school therapist is like the character Miss Marple in an Agatha Christie novel. She interviews all the suspects about the crime and then at the end of the book gathers them all in the library to tell them how the crime took place. Her new story includes everyone's perspective but is substantially different from any one person's account. The experience for the reader is to be initially confused and then to feel that, of course, it couldn't have happened any other way. That mixture of confusion and fit is what the systemic therapist is aiming for as she collects everyone's viewpoint about a problem and constructs a systemic opinion that will alter perceptions and leave room for change.

In addition to the Milan school's particular view of change and their use of the team, with its emphasis on hypothesis-generating and testing, they also are responsible for introducing two other related ideas: circularity and neutrality. Circularity refers to thinking that emphasizes pattern, recursiveness, and context and is juxtaposed with linear thinking. Linear thinking is about causal connections between parts of a system and leads to intrapsychic formulations and assessments of individuals' intentions and motivations. For example, in an interview with a depressed family member, a therapist guided by linear thinking might ask mental status questions, such as: "How long have you been depressed?"; "What are you depressed about?"; or "Have you suffered any recent losses in self-esteem or in relationships?" A therapist guided by circular thinking might ask instead: "When you get depressed, whom do you show it to?"; or "When that person notices that you are depressed, how do you know?"; or "What do you do in response to that person's showing you that he knows you are depressed?" In short, these questions take depression out of an individual's psyche and place it instead in a relational context in which anyone interacting with the depression could effect a change.

Circular questions are based on two assumptions: first, that the meaning of behavior derives from its context rather than from enduring personality traits of an individual, and second, that all information lies in difference and comparison, which is obscured by our customary use of language. For example, when we say that "Susie is smart," we are really saying that "Susie is smarter than someone else." Circular questions make explicit these implicit comparisons that are hidden by our linguistic habits. A simple substitution of the verb *show* for *be* will unveil circular thinking. For example, the meaning of "Sam is depressed" becomes transformed by supplanting *show* for *is*: "Sam shows his depression to his mother, but not to his father." This linguistic substitution transforms the meaning from a flat clinical description to a more complex contextual one.

In addition, circular thinking will surface with the use of questions that ask about differences in relationships and among ideas and values, that rank traits among family members, and that make comparisons among past, present, and future times. These questions have the effect of making new distinctions, of introducing new information, and of revealing coalitions in the family, since people who are aligned with each other tend to agree. The therapist is not only interested in looking at recursive patterns among family members but also looks at the patterns of interaction between the therapist and the family as important clinical information (Keeney 1983).

Circular questions, in their focus on pattern and their avoidance of individual intentions, allow the therapist to be curious about the web of interaction that is making everyone a victim. This nonevaluative, curious stance on the part of the therapist is what is meant by neutrality. It is a therapeutic attitude conveying respect, acceptance, and admiration of the system. There is no blaming of any individual or any investment in changing the system. As Tomm puts it: "The therapist's goal is metachange; that is, a change in the family's ability to change" (Tomm 1984b, p. 23).

## Other Major Proponents

From our side of the Atlantic came systemic thinkers who enlarged the field with their innovative use of questioning techniques and bold new applications of systemic theory. The therapists at the Ackerman Institute in New York City, including Peggy Penn, Peggy Papp, Virginia Goldner, Olga Silverstein, Gillian Walker, Don Bloch, and Marcia Sheinberg, are an enormously productive, creative group of people who are known for their group research projects such as the AIDS Project (Walker 1987, 1988) and the Gender and Violence Project (Goldner et al. 1990). It is beyond the scope of this chapter to review their illustrious history as an organization. Instead, I want to mention the work of Peggy Penn, whose two classic papers on questioning techniques (1982, 1985) represent an elaboration of the Milan systemic theory.

In the first of these papers, on circular questioning, Penn uses a transcript of a family therapy session to show how the asking of circular questions is directly related to defining the presenting problem, revealing hidden alignments among family members, and developing a systemic intervention. Several types of circular questions are identified, including questions that ask clients to offer their explanations for the onset of the problem and questions of classification and comparison.

In the second of these papers, on future questions Penn constructs new questions that require clients to imagine their relationship at some hypothetical later point in time. She argues that these questions have a loosening effect on people "since the maps for the future are not yet set" and therefore "the family are free to construct or imagine a different set of alternatives to their dilemma" (Penn 1985, p. 299). These questions include those that ask clients to imagine an alternative explanation or solution to their problems that might occur to them in the future. Whatever the content of the future question, Penn argues that it implicitly conveys the message that change is possible and challenges any notions of being stuck in a present state that is preordained by the past.

Karl Tomm, a family therapist in Calgary, Canada, is known for his articulate, elucidating writings on Milan systemic theory. In his paper "Interventive Interviewing" (1988), he classifies questions into four main groups: lineal, circular, strategic, and reflexive. He differentiates among these four along two continua. The first is the intended locus of change that underlies the question, either toward changing the therapist's own perceptions or changing the clients'. The second variable has to do with contrasting assumptions about the very nature of change—at one end of the continuum are questions that belie cause and effect or lineal assumptions, and at the other are those with cybernetic or circular assumptions. Regardless of the subtype, questions allow clients to come to their own solutions and are an antidote to a therapist's possession of special expert knowledge.

## Contribution to Adolescent Work

Adolescents are usually very self-conscious about being in therapy, particularly in the company of their parents. Usually, too, before coming to therapy, they have repeatedly been told about the myriad of ways that they are falling short. Likewise, parents may be disgusted with their own negative reactions to their children, yet feel stuck about how to interrupt this position. Systemic therapy, with its explicit commitment to nonblaming neutrality and to the active gathering of multiple viewpoints, can be an antidote to a pattern of mutual negativity between parents and adolescents. The use of the reframe and ritual also seems particularly well suited

for this population. The reframe, in effect, says that there is
no victim or villain in this family. Instead, all members are
caught in an interconnected web. Rituals, which tease apart
two simultaneously occurring behaviors and ask family members to perform them at different times, are developmentally
well suited to adolescents. Adolescence is a time of contradictions—of being a child yet imagining a future as an adult,
of parents setting guidelines and encouraging independence.
When these different sets of expectations, both internal and
familial, cause undue confusion, rituals help by introducing
clarity.

## Systemically Oriented Family Therapy
## of the Peace Family

The systemic therapist, working with or without a team,
would enter the first interview with a few hypotheses she
wished to confirm or disconfirm using circular questions. One
hypothesis is that Bert's acting out serves to keep the parents distracted from their own marital conflicts, which might
escalate if they didn't have Bert to worry about. A second
hypothesis is that the process of adolescent separation is so
painful, given Mr. and Mrs. Peace's own history of growing
up, that the family wants to hurry up and expunge Bert in
order to get it over with.

   To test out the first hypothesis, linking Bert's misbehavior to marital tension, the following circular questions could
be asked of each family member: "Which dyad in the family
fights the most? Then who fights the next most often, and so
on"; "If Bert and his dad should stop their fighting, who do
you think would have the most fights in the family?"; "When
Bert becomes an adult and moves out of the house, how do
you think the parents' relationship will change with each
other, and with Sally?"; "If there is no change in the fighting
in this family, how will the parents be getting along in five

years? And how will Bert and Sally be getting along with each other and with their parents?"

To check out the second hypothesis, which connects Bert's symptoms to the parents' anxiety about adolescence, one might ask these questions: "Mr. and Mrs. Peace, what do you think Bert knows or has surmised about each of *your* adolescent experiences?"; "When each of you was Bert's age, how did your parents respond when you misbehaved in some way?"; "Who in the family most strongly believes that the family will function more smoothly once Bert is out of the house? Then who?"; "Who in the family sees Bert's truancy as a sign that he needs firmer limits and stricter consequences and who sees it as a sign that he is worried and confused about how to grow up in this family?"

In trying to assess the validity of any particular hypothesis, the therapist would pay attention both to the verbal responses by each family member and to the nonverbal indices of interest in the questions. If family members seemed impatient, bored, or distracted with one series of questions, that hypothesis would most likely be discarded as one that would not be useful to pursue. If, on the other hand, family members seemed interested in listening to each other's responses and if their answers seemed thoughtful, rather than rehearsed and automatic, the therapist would try to construct an end-of-session intervention based on that hypothesis.

If the members of the Peace family were more compelled by the first hypothesis, connecting Bert's acting up to protection of the marital dyad, than by the second, the following end-of-session reframe could be offered: "I am impressed with the way this family works together to keep everyone separate. I want to encourage this kind of cooperation with one another even though it may mean that certain individuals have to sacrifice getting their own needs met." In this intervention, the family is being told a story about itself, one that connects everyone in the family, that gives a positive connotation to their behavior, and that introduces a piece of new information: that the constant disagreements between Bert and his father are a form of cooperation. The therapist hopes that the next time the father and son argue or the next time Mr. and Mrs. Peace disagree covertly, there will be a new perception of these conflicts, and something new will happen— something that the therapist cannot predict.

## NARRATIVE MODES OF FAMILY THERAPY

### Basic Theoretical Assumptions

*Story, restorying, narrative,* and *discourse* are all words used by narrative therapists. Narrative therapists believe that families get stuck because they lack the emotional vocabulary or narrative skills to make a story that is not constraining. These therapists identify the dominant stories that limit the family's repertoire, and they try to amplify minor narratives that contain in them more possibility. Dominant stories include beliefs that the family holds about itself as well as any cultural stories that may be influencing a family, for example, that midlife must be a time of crisis or that adolescence should be filled with *Sturm und Drang*. The dominant discourse on adolescence, which identifies this period of the life cycle as a time of turbulence, heightens parental fears of their children and "may restrain parents from seeing possibilities in and for their youngsters" (Dickerson and Zimmerman 1992, p. 344).

Cultural discourse, a postmodernist concept, refers to the historical specificity about what is said, and left unsaid, in conversation. Rachel Hare-Mustin (1994) defines a discourse as "a system of statements, practices and institutional structures that share common values" (p. 19). She asserts that discourses uphold particular cultural views and reflexively that "the ways most people hold, talk about, and act on a common shared viewpoint are part of and sustain the prevailing discourses" (p. 19).

The narrative therapist believes that the cultural discourse about adolescence informs the stories that family members tell about themselves and each other. The discourse about adolescence includes the notion that for all children adolescence is a time to be dreaded by the adults who love them. Another widespread view is that adolescents must disconnect from their parents in order to effect a proper individuation process. A corollary is that boys are at risk of not growing into men unless they achieve a considerable distance from their mothers. Mothers and daughters are expected to endure a period of constant fighting before daughters can be considered independent women. Another paradoxical part of the discourse is that adolescence is a state that is simultaneously highly revered and envied, and resolutely feared by adults. For the narrative therapist, the cultural discourse may be every bit as constraining as the unique psychological beliefs held by family members about each other. The content of the cultural discourse can be found in a variety of contexts, including films, books, advertisements, and scientific research. (Chapter 9 lays out the different, sometimes contradictory, stories rendered from these cultural sources.) The narrative therapist will challenge the dominant cultural views on adolescence with the same curiosity that she has about family dynamics.

In addition to the new ideas about story introduced by narrative therapists, these therapists have also contributed a new type of team to aid in treating families and training therapists. With this approach—called the "reflecting team"—a group of clinicians observes an interview with a family from behind a one-way mirror. After the interview, the lights and sound go up in the room with the reflectors, allowing them to be seen and heard by the family; then the family and interviewer listen to the reflectors, who have an unrehearsed conversation about their observations of the interview. The reflectors offer comments, questions, homework tasks, and hypotheses about the therapist and the family's verbal and nonverbal behavior, all couched in nonblaming and tentative terms. The family is encouraged to take what is useful to them and discard the rest. The narrative assumptions underlying the reflecting team are many (Miller and Lax 1988): that the abundance of ideas generated by the team will help loosen a family whose members have a limited range of meanings ascribed to their world; that the relationship between therapist and clients should be nonhierarchical, with an emphasis on sharing rather than giving information; that people cannot change under a negative connotation; and that there are no right or wrong perspectives, only ones that are more or less helpful to a family.

The narrative therapist is like a biographer who takes the basic story of a family and transforms it with different organization; with a richer grasp of language, tone, and nuance; and with a highlighting of overlooked anecdotes.

## Major Proponents

Narrative approaches have been espoused clinically by Harlene Anderson and Harold Goolishian (1988) at the Galveston Institute, Galveston, Texas; Michael White and David Epston from Australia and New Zealand, respectively (1990); Steven De Shazer (1994) in Milwaukee, Wisconsin; Tom Andersen of Norway (1991); as well as by social psychologist Kenneth Gergen (1985), who applies narrative to the development of the self, and Jerome Bruner (1990), a cognitive psychologist who studies narrative as it applies to mental activity. In general, these therapists and thinkers emphasize the power of stories to lend meaning to family members' experience of themselves and each other.

One of the earliest examples of therapeutic storytelling is the work of Richard Gardner (1971), who is not generally included as a narrative therapist. His mutual storytelling technique invites the child patient to make up a story, using fantasy and adventure. The therapist then tells a story back to the child, using the same characters and themes and elaborating on the unconscious material provided by the child. The therapist's story also offers alternative solutions to the problems raised by the child. The telling of stories is both a collaborative venture shared by therapist and client and an opportunity for the therapist to introduce higher-level problem solving to the child's internal dilemmas. Milton Erickson is another therapist who raised the telling of tales to a high art but who, like Gardner, is not typically included as an ancestor of narrative therapy. Erickson is known for his use of introducing new story ideas into the unconscious through hypnosis or trance (Erickson and Rossi 1981). For Erickson, like Gardner, the power to construct a meaningful story lies solely with the therapist; by contrast, the narrative therapist's earmark is to collaborate on a story with the therapist and client.

Anderson and Goolishian, from the Galveston Institute, are known for their writings about problem-determined systems (Anderson et al. 1986). They argue that a problem is nothing more than what we choose to call a problem. All those individuals who talk about a problem constitute a system; the system's membership is in flux and is not necessarily synonymous with a family unit. The therapist's job, then, is to engage all individuals who define the problem as a problem and talk with them in such a way that the problem dissolves. This therapist offers small shifts in language to alter the way a problem is talked about. Unlike the techniques of the Milan School, in which the interventions are unique and powerful, these interventions are small and numerous throughout the session—the difference between offering a whole new suit of clothes and making multiple, almost invisible stitches.

Michael White and David Epston (1990) are probably the best-known proponents of the narrative approach. They have introduced a political and social context in which they conduct their work, paying close attention to who has the power to speak and the power to define a problem. Relying on the work of Foucault (1980), they critique the mental health profession's linkage of power and knowledge. For example, they do not use diagnosis or rely on medical records kept private from their clients. Instead, they may write a letter to a client at the end of the session and include that letter in the record. At the close of therapy, the record may then be given to the client to be shared, if so desired, with other clients who might benefit from learning about similar experiences.

White and Epston use story to *deconstruct*—that is, to separate problems from the people experiencing them—and to *reconstruct*, that is, to help families reauthor the stories they tell about their lives. These complementary processes of deconstruction and reconstruction are captured in their technique of externalizing the problem. Here, the therapist and client collaborate on a name for the problem and attribute negative intentions and mischievous tactics to it. For example, in working with a woman who is dragging her feet on completing a book on family therapy, a narrative therapist might ask the following question: "How long has perfectionism been spoiling your pleasure in your writing and tricking you into thinking he is your best friend?" The therapist also asks about the extent of the damage that this problem has been wreaking in the client's life. Then she asks about *unique outcomes*: times when the client resisted the problem's pull, when the client's life was not dominated by the problem. The client is also asked to speculate about what made it possible at those times to resist the dictates of the dominant story. Subsequently, these unusual moments of resistance are amplified and added to by more stories that feature the client as competent and free of the stranglehold of perfectionism. Finally, the therapist and client find or create an audience for these new stories, featuring a perfectionist-free identity. For example, at the end of therapy, the client may make a tape about the new knowledge she has acquired that could be shared with friends and family or with others who are struggling with that demon named perfectionism.

Another incarnation of narrative therapy is the work of Steven De Shazer and Insoo Berg, known for their *brief solution-focused therapy*. In his book *Words Were Originally Magic* (1994), De Shazer offers lengthy transcripts of therapy sessions he has conducted. Several techniques, representing new contributions to the field, are contained in those transcripts. The thrust of the interviews is toward finding some behavior or attitude, already in the client's repertoire, that can be expanded upon to make a solution to the presenting complaint. Each interview is constructed with the emphasis on what the clients will find helpful in constructing a solution, on what experiences they have already had that are in the direction of a solution, and on how they will know when the therapy is over once they have found a solution.

One intervention, aimed at discovering solutions, is called the *Miracle Question*. De Shazer (1994) asks his clients, "Suppose that tonight after you go to sleep a miracle happens and the problems that brought you to therapy are solved immediately. But since you were sleeping at the time, you cannot know that this miracle has happened. Once you wake up tomorrow morning, how will you discover that a miracle has happened? Without your telling them, how will other people know that a miracle has happened?" (p. 95).

These questions help focus the clients, from the outset, on success and on the end of therapy. De Shazer makes the less obvious point that a "miracle can be defined as an effect without a cause" (De Shazer 1994, p. 96). A miracle question thus also introduces the notion that there is an important distinction between the problem and the solution. In other words, he is suggesting that the finding of a solution may not be directly linked to the presenting problem. He further distances solution from problem by actively asking about exceptions to the problem, much the way White and Epston do with their unique outcome questions. De Shazer explains that the more clients can talk about the exceptions, the more real they become. For example, in response to a mother who complains about how remote her teenage son is, how he never listens to a word she says, a De Shazer question might be, "Tell me about the last time your son *did* listen to what you had to say?"

Another De Shazer tool, which can be very useful with recalcitrant adolescents who do not want to talk in therapy, is his application of scales. He asserts that numbers are as magic as words and that numbers can make concrete and real what words render vague and amorphous. Speaking in numbers is a less disclosing place to begin if family therapy is the last place an adolescent wants to be. Specifically, De Shazer asks, "If 10 is the solution to your problem and 1 is no change at all, where do you see yourself?" This question allows the therapist and family members to settle on mutually understandable terms. Also implicit in a scale is a repudiation of all-or-nothing thinking: a scale of 1 to 10 allows for a lot of gray area. Even a family member who is very pessimistic about ever achieving a 10 can be asked, "When you move from 3 to 4, what will be different in your life, and who will be the first to notice the changes in you, and what will your parents and your siblings and your teachers do differently when they notice these changes in you?" These questions are similar to White and Epston's, in that they are aimed at eliciting more optimistic expectations.

Dickerson and Zimmerman (1992) offer a narrative approach particularly tailored to families with adolescents. Their premise is that adolescents and their parents have problems with each other because they do not make important distinctions, namely, between what parents want for their children and what these children want for themselves. Not making this important distinction leads to unproductive reciprocal behaviors and misunderstandings: parents are unwilling to let adolescents make their own decisions, and adolescents are confused in figuring out what they want. Furthermore, these lapses in making distinctions constitute a restraint that prevents parents from being respectful of their children and that keeps the adolescents rebelling against their parents' ideas for them. Both the adolescents and their parents lose the ability to notice what they both hold in common: parents do not notice when their teens are engaging in grown-up behavior, and the teens miss the times when their parents support the teens' own wishes.

## Contribution to Adolescent Work

As with systemic therapy, narrative therapy resolutely shuns any mention of blame or pathology, a position that can be a relief to adolescents and their parents, who often have been mutually assigning blame with no satisfying outcome. The narrative therapist also introduces humor and play into the conversation about problems, a childlike spirit that is still available to most adolescents. Asking about numbers or miracles, telling family stories, or turning a problem into a pesky intruder is simply more fun than being asked to talk explicitly about painful feelings. The narrative therapist does not believe that change has to be hard and serious to be effective.

Many of the interventions, particularly genogram work, challenging the cultural discourse, and externalizing the problem (see Chapters 4 and 5), require collaboration and creativity on the part of adolescents and their parents. In the process of doing these interventions, families' common initial presentations of withdrawal or heated conflict are fundamentally challenged.

## Narrative Approaches to the Peace Family

The therapist might start with the problem description and identify the reciprocal restraining patterns of behavior. For example, Bert's not performing well at school could be seen as part of a reciprocal pattern: Mr. and Mrs. Peace treat Bert as if he is unable to think for himself, which in turn invites him not to take responsibility for himself and to fight against his parents rather than for his own future. As with White and Epston, the presenting problem is externalized, with relative influence and unique outcome questions asked. Once a new story has been shared by family members, a wider audience is sought, either in the school or from the adolescents' peers.

This therapist could also introduce questions to the Peaces about how they would know when the therapy was over. More specifically, this therapist could ask the De Shazer miracle question: "If there were a miracle that took place overnight and Bert were no longer taking drugs and no longer truant from school, what else would be different? How would he be acting instead? How would each of you be responding to him differently?"

The narrative therapist would listen for any metaphors or emotionally charged words used repetitively by family members. For example, if Mr. Peace talked about Bert's truancy as "a monkey on my back," this metaphor could be used to start to differentiate Bert from his problems: "Is this monkey on anybody else's back?"; "Do you think you need to throw this monkey off yourself, or get someone else to pry him off?"; "If that monkey slipped off and you were feeling less stooped and burdened, how do you think your relationship with Bert would change?"

More questions could be generated to deconstruct the presenting problem, using the metaphor of the monkey: for example, "What effect does this monkey have on other relationships in the family?" Bert might offer that the monkey makes his father very suspicious of Bert, which in turn makes Bert act sneaky. The narrative therapist would elaborate on this metaphor by asking questions about Bert's "sneakiness," in an effort to externalize the problem. "How long has sneakiness been spoiling your relationship with your father? Where else has sneakiness been causing mischief?"

Deconstruction of the presenting problem is only part of the narrative approach. There also needs to be a rewriting of Bert's story of himself, a story that can counteract the dominant story of him as a no-good, truant, substance-abusing teen, on his way to a lifetime of no-good, delinquent behavior.

Bert would be encouraged to rewrite this story through the answering of the therapist's questions. The therapist would try to elicit from Bert what hopes he has for himself, visions that may have been obscured by the parents' dominant story about him: "Five years from now, how important do you think school will be to you? If you were living on your own, what would be most important to you in terms of relationships with others, daily routine, how you make a living?" The parents could be asked to contribute to this new, future-oriented story, which is so different from their problem-saturated story of him. They could be asked: "What do you notice now about how Bert is taking care of himself that will be useful to him when he is out on his own? When does Bert say no to sneakiness and behave in a way that supports his own hopes for a future?" And to Bert: "Who in your life now or in the past would be least surprised to hear that you have turned your back on sneakiness and are taking charge of your own future? What stories could they tell us about you?" With these last two questions, the therapist would be expanding the audience for Bert's new story about himself.

Another narrative tack to take with the Peaces is to ask about the influence of family-of-origin stories and cultural stories about adolescence on the presenting problems. "Tell us some stories about your own adolescence, Mr. and Mrs. Peace, about how you became adults. What did you learn about coming of age that you most wanted to teach your own children?" Mrs. Peace then tells a story of how she was expected to do for herself at a very young age and never felt protected by her parents. As a result, she says, she got herself into a great deal of trouble, particularly a teen pregnancy, and then had to hide it from her parents and arrange a secret and unsafe abortion herself.

Father tells his story about growing up in poverty and, as the oldest son, going to work after school at age 13. He felt that this early responsibility was what gave him character and without it he would have turned out like all his siblings, who have never been able to hold a steady job. His adolescence taught him the importance of doing hard work and contributing to the family as the path to manhood.

The narrative therapist might be struck by the similar association in both stories between hardship and adolescence juxtaposed with divergent views on how to transcend this hardship: Mrs. Peace believes that more protection and guidance was and is needed, while Mr. Peace values independent work and loyalty to the family.

The narrative therapist would be curious about the intersection of these stories with cultural stories. For example, do the Peaces endorse the dominant story that boys need to reject their mothers in order to grow into men? If so, does that mean that Mrs. Peace believes that Bert can derive guidance only from his father? Is this a story that could be challenged in order for Mrs. Peace to reforge a connection with her son? In general, the narrative therapist is trying to uncover the stories that currently give meaning to the Peaces' beliefs about Bert and his growing up. Once the therapist has revealed these stories, she will try to introduce some new plot shifts or a twist in language to an old story so that new meanings and possibilities emerge; alternatively, the therapist may elaborate on a forgotten but intriguing anecdote so that it can gain the status of a new story.

## Summary

The metaphors associated with each school are perhaps the best shorthand way to summarize the differences among the seven schools of family therapy discussed in this chapter and the previous one. The psychodynamic family therapist is like a lead-test scientist who checks the soil to assess the legacy of previous generations' use of paint and fumes. Only with such an assessment can the present inhabitants make sound decisions about what to plant in their gardens. The experiential therapist is a folk artist who takes everyday objects and transforms them playfully and spontaneously into an original work of art. The structural therapist is like a building inspector who must assess the frame of the house to determine whether the foundation is solid, the walls and floors sturdy, the wiring up to code. He finds out if this is a house that will need major renovations or a few cosmetic touch-ups. The behaviorist is like a federal mediator, negotiating a fair contract between labor and management, a negotiation that requires each side to compromise for the greater good of harmony. The strategic therapist is like a master chess player who plots each move while keeping in mind an overall game plan. The systemic therapist is like the detective who interviews all the suspects about the crime and then at the end, gathers them all in the library to reveal the solution to the crime. She tells them a story that includes each suspect's individual perspective but is, at the same time, substantially different from any one person's account. The narrative therapist is like a biographer, who transforms the basic story, with the use of more finely nuanced language, a new organization, the highlighting of previous overlooked anecdotes, and attention paid to larger social and cultural contexts.

Throughout this chapter and for the rest of the book, I have begged the question of matching the model of therapy with a particular type of family. The notion of matching only makes sense if one thinks diagnostically about families, which I don't. Matching would be practical, too, if there were a body of research demonstrating the relative efficacy of one model compared to another. But there isn't. Given the absence of comparative outcome studies, I think it is important to choose a mode of working that is intellectually and emotionally compatible with oneself. For example, a therapist who feels easily overwhelmed by the expression of strong feeling would probably be quite uncomfortable as an experiential therapist. Conversely, a therapist who is facile with words, enjoys playing with metaphor, and feels most at home in a nonhierarchical relationship with clients may be drawn to the narrative approach. Strong beliefs about the nature of change may also determine the choice of orientation. A clinician who holds the deep conviction that present dilemmas grow out of unresolved problems in the past will be most drawn to the psychodynamic school, with some tolerance for the systemic and narrative therapies. A belief in the centrality of observable, gradual change will lead to an interest in behavioral and strategic family therapies.

While I have stressed the differences among theoretical schools, there is some intriguing evidence (Duncan and Moynihan 1994) that the commonalities among approaches best explain treatment efficacy. Miller and colleagues (1995) delineated four factors that cut across treatment modality, theoretical orientation, and length of treatment. The first is doing something that requires the clients to help themselves. Expectancy, or the increased hope for change occasioned by merely going to treatment, is the second factor. The treatment relationship, particularly one based on empathy, respect, and genuineness, is the third factor. Finally, the authors state that the most potent factor predicting positive outcome concerns the makeup of each particular client and is defined quite loosely as "the total matrix of who they are—their strengths and resources, the duration of their complaints, their social supports, the environments in which they live" (p. 57). They urge that to make use of this factor, clinicians should focus on clients' areas of competence and strength and use their existing social supports. Miller and colleagues' conclusions regarding these four factors would be difficult to quarrel with: "At the heart of the four factors that characterize all good therapy is the desire and the capacity to form helpful and healing bonds with troubled people who have, for the time being, lost their way and need some directional signals back to their own best selves" (p. 63).

This book is not a defense of a particular model, although familiarity with a theory certainly has a centering and calming influence on clinical work. At times, the interventions presented will be informed by my experience and intuition as much as by the theoretical constructs embodied by systemic and narrative therapies. In the two chapters that follow, I will apply the systemic and narrative principles laid out in this chapter to the evaluation (Chapter 3) and treatment (Chapters 4 and 5) of adolescents and their parents. Throughout the book, whenever possible, I have placed the clinical work in a developmental context, a perspective that is elaborated in each of the subsequent chapters.

# PART II

## PRACTICAL APPROACHES TO CLINICAL WORK

# 3

# How to Start Up the Work

## WHEN IS FAMILY THERAPY INDICATED?

The question of when, and even whether, to involve families in the treatment of adolescents has long been a thorny one. It is particularly problematical if one subscribes to the theory that this is the very stage of life when teenagers are trying to form their own separate identities. Seen this way, family therapy becomes a regressive treatment, pulling adolescents back to a time when they were dependent on their parents. As family therapists, we may ask ourselves, "What business do we have asking teens to bare their souls to their parents in a stranger's office, when they don't even want to be seen walking down the street with their parents?" Isn't it then always contraindicated to ask teenagers to get closer to their parents just at the point when they are struggling to forge a life outside the parameters of the family?

There are two answers to these questions. The first is the critique offered by several family therapists (see for example, Apter 1990, Hauser et al. 1991, Silverstein and Rashbaum 1994) of the traditional notion of adolescence as a time of singleminded separation. These therapists, and I include myself among them, argue that adolescence also requires a new connectedness with parents, an engagement and mutual sharing of life experiences that can be encouraged through family therapy.

Second, even within the more traditional framework that sees adolescence as a stage requiring separation, there are several instances when it is indicated that it is best to stem this developmental tide. What follows are some guidelines for therapists, both traditional and revisionist, for deciding when family treatment of adolescents may be helpful.

## The Assessment of the Suicidal Adolescent

A family therapist begins with the premise that a suicidal act or gesture by an adolescent is a powerful communication to the family, dramatizing problems among family members. Therefore, a family meeting is usually imperative to make sense of this communication, to assess safety issues, and to discuss the need for hospitalization. Of course, it is also important to meet with the adolescent alone to discuss certain topics—such as abuse by parents, concerns about homosexual feelings, disclosure of a pregnancy or rape—that may feel too private or dangerous to raise with parents present in an initial crisis meeting. The disclosure of these topics will need to be negotiated with the adolescent privately. Perhaps in some instances, the adolescent will later agree to share this material in a family meeting.

In an initial family crisis meeting, there are three areas to explore with an eye toward assessing the adolescent's immediate safety and the need for hospitalization: first, the decoding of the meaning of the suicide attempt; second, the expressed wish on the part of family members that the adolescent be out of the family; and third, the presence of other problems and losses in the family.

In regard to the first area, decoding the meaning of the suicide attempt, the therapist wants to know if the family can listen empathically to what the adolescent was trying to express in self-destructive action. For example, was the suicide attempt about revenge or punishment, about asking for help, or trying to reunite with a deceased loved one? Then, family members' reception of their adolescent's explanation of the suicidal behavior must be observed. If they respond with support, asking clarifying questions, demonstrating some understanding of the adolescent's intense feelings, the immediate risk of another suicide attempt is diminished, and this information (along with other assessments, such as the seriousness of the attempt, the secretiveness of the attempt, the adolescent's ability to contract convincingly for safety, the ability of the family to be vigilant for their child, the availability of immediate outpatient services) is put in the column of a home disposition. Conversely, if the parents respond by being dismissive or by becoming enraged at their child, the risk for a subsequent attempt is increased. Accordingly, these responses point to opening a case for hospitalization.

Second, one must keep an ear open for any suggestion that family members think they would be better off if this suicidal adolescent were no longer in the family. Sometimes this is a very subtle message, and other times it is an overt command that the teen should be expunged from the family. Whether overtly or covertly, if an adolescent feels that the family would like to see him or her out of their lives, this is a risk factor and hospitalization should be seriously considered.

Third, an adolescent's suicidal behavior can often be linked to deaths and losses in the family and may even be a preemptive act to signal that someone else in the family is in distress and needs help. Therefore, it is useful to ask about other losses in the family that the adolescent may be consciously or unconsciously reenacting. Past suicidal behavior on the part of other family members, including those from previous generations, should be explored as well. It is important to ask the adolescent and other family members if they are worried about anyone else in the family to determine whether the suicide attempt was in any way sacrificial or intended to get help for someone else. For an excellent, more elaborate discussion of family assessment and treatment of suicidal adolescents, I refer the reader to Judith Landau-Stanton and M. Duncan Stanton (1985) "Treating Suicidal Adolescents and Their Families," in *Handbook of Adolescent and Family Therapy* and to the chapter "Suicidal Adolescents," in *Violence in the Lives of Adolescents*, by Martha B. Straus (1994).

## The Physically Abused Adolescent

When an adolescent reveals that there is ongoing physical abuse or when abuse is suspected, family therapy may be indicated. As with the suicidal adolescent, it is imperative that an individual meeting be conducted to assess safety issues and to inquire about possible sexual abuse that the teenager may not be ready to disclose to all family members. However, a family meeting can be enormously useful as well.

An important distinction should be made between families in which the abuse commenced at adolescence and families in which the abuse has been long-term, since childhood. Research comparing adolescent-onset abuse and long-term abuse suggests that the structures of the families are significantly different (Galombos and Dixon 1984). The long-term abuse families tend to be characterized by multiple disruptions through separation, divorce, poverty, and frequent moves. Perpetrators of long-term abuse tend to be poorer than their middle-class counterparts, who begin abuse later. In addition, Straus (1994) observes that in short-term abusive families, marital conflict is common and may focus on disputes over how to manage an adolescent's behavior. Often, a wife will feel threatened and endangered by her husband's violence toward their teenager, expecting that the abuse will eventually be turned on her. Sometimes battered wives will abuse their children, explaining that they are doing so to prevent worse abuse of the children by their husbands.

In a family session, the snarled marital web surrounding adolescent physical abuse can begin to be disentangled. The couple can be asked whether they have been contemplating separation or divorce, since this is a very common and often an unspoken threat and wish in these families. In addition, family members can be asked if anyone else is worried about their safety or anyone else's in the family. Often, the treatment of choice is a combination of marital therapy to help a couple discuss their differences more directly and decide whether or not they want to stay married, and individual therapy for the adolescent, who may be placed outside of the home, at least temporarily.

## The Treatment of Specific Disorders

There are several individual disorders of adolescence that are so entwined in family relationships that seeing only the adolescent is like trying to conduct a symphony when only the cellist shows up. While each of these individual presentations—of eating disorders (Minuchin et al. 1978, Selvini Palazzoli et al. 1978a), substance abuse (Elkin 1984, Kaufman and Kaufmann 1979), and a first psychotic break (Haley 1980, Stierlin 1974)—could easily warrant a book or two on family treatment, I want to offer a few general parameters for the assessment phase, using eating disorders as an example.

### Family Work When an Adolescent Has an Eating Disorder

In the assessment phase, two family issues are critical. First, the eating disorder may be a solution to a particular family dilemma that needs to be surfaced. As a symptom, anorexia usually indicates difficulties around growing up, becoming sexual, trying to be perfect, and conflicts regarding the needs to be both self-sacrificing and self-interested.

In a family context, anorexia can be a shorthand expression of a family dilemma. For example, a family presents with a youngest daughter of three sisters who has started restricting her eating soon after her menarche. The weight loss also coincides with the death of her maternal grandfather, a man who lived with the family in the last stages of his illness. There is an 18-year-old sister who is so debilitated by obsessive compulsive disorder (OCD) that she finds it almost impossible to complete her daily rituals and go out of the house. The mother in this family, by profession a nurse, has sacrificed a job promotion and individual leisure time to monitor her oldest daughter's OCD and to care for the grandfather before he died. The father, while well-meaning and devoted to his family, is demanding and largely unavailable due to his busy law practice.

In this family, the girl's anorexia may be a way of asking, now that she is biologically a woman, whether it is safe to grow up in a family where there have been recent losses and where an oldest sister is blocked in her ability to go out of the house, let alone move out. If she grows up, will her mother's and father's conflicts with each other be highlighted? Will she upstage or humiliate her older sister? Or is the anorexia a way of raising the dilemma in the family about how self-seeking women are permitted to be, particularly in light of her mother's numerous acts of self-sacrifice? Anorexia may be a way of saying, "I have a powerful will, but I'll undo it by expressing it through going without." Or she could be saying, "This is the only thing I can control in my life."

To check out hypotheses about the meaning of an eating disorder within the family context, there are several questions that can be posed. Family members can be asked to reflect about the onset of the disorder and its confluence with other life events in the family. They can be asked, "How will the family be different once the anorexia goes away?" or in a more externalizing fashion, "How does anorexia get in the way of your relationships with your family?" And each member of the family can be asked, "If anorexia had a voice, what would it be trying to say to your daughter and to the family?"

Once an eating disorder sets in, family relationships shift to try to get rid of the disorder. Part of the family evaluation should be directed at determining how the marital, sibling, and parental relationships have changed since the onset of the eating problem and how well-intentioned "solutions" may be making additional problems. This is a very different perspective from trying to figure out how the family *caused* the eating problem. The clinician may want to ask each parent, "What have you tried to do already to get Susie to eat again? What is her reaction to these efforts? Could you show me in here how you talk to each other about your strategies?" It is also important to find out what the pediatrician or internist thinks about the eating disorder and what medical strategy, if any, is in place.

## Therapy with Families Having Difficulty with Life-Cycle Transition

This category is the largest and most encompassing, and includes families struggling with normative issues as well as those further off the track. There are three prevalent overlapping presentations that point to developmental issues as being of primary importance—vague parental complaints about communication difficulties with their adolescents, dissatisfaction with how one or more children are making the transition to adulthood, and marital difficulties.

The first presentation is the parents who come in with vague complaints about communication difficulties with their teens. These complaints often mask a fear that they are losing their relationship with their child because of what they see as the inevitable disconnecting force of adolescence. To counterbalance the perceived problems in communication may come a tendency to enforce the rules of latency and thus propel their adolescents into an all-out rebellion against them. Some parents may feel so excluded by their children's new outside interests that they start reading their mail and diaries. Or, some of these may be families in which there are so many preconceived notions about adolescence as a time of total disconnect that the parents and adolescents are feeling frightened about impending relationship losses.

With these families, a thorough exploration of their beliefs about adolescence is in order. The parents and the adolescents should be asked about cultural myths about adolescence—for example, who in the family thinks that it needs to be a time of rebellion or a time when mother and sons, in particular, don't listen well to one another?

In addition, parents can be asked in front of their children to describe their own adolescence and the beliefs they hold based on these experiences. For example, one parent may feel that she was left too much on her own to make her own mistakes, to pay for college, to care for younger siblings, and has decided to make adolescence for her own child a time of freedom from responsibility. Meanwhile, her husband may feel that he was overprotected and not prepared for adulthood by having everything done for him—laundry folded, lunches packed, bed made. He, by contrast, has vowed to step back and let his child learn about growing up without parental intrusion. These differences in experience may present as a parental tension centered on how to manage their child's burgeoning steps toward independence.

Another developmentally driven presentation is the complaint that an adolescent is not preparing to leave home at the expected time. This is such a frequent and complicated presentation that I have devoted an entire chapter to it (see

Chapter 6). The complaint needs to be considered in a cultural and a three-generational context. In other words, the clinician needs to understand the family's particular cultural dictates about leaving home as well as the family's experiences with leave-taking across the generations. For example, in a case that will be discussed in greater detail in Chapter 6, a mother presented with her six adolescent and young adult children with the grievance, "We're a family that doesn't want to grow up," referring to the fact that five of her children hadn't moved out of the family home. A genogram revealed that the mother came from a second-generation Irish family in which she had been expected to leave home at age 17. The father, who had died a year before the family's clinic visit, was from a tightly knit Italian family in which several adult children never married and he himself hadn't left home until he was in his late thirties. The children's difficulty in moving on was seen as embodying an ongoing debate between their mother and father, fueled by their parents' cultural differences and contrasting experiences about leaving home, and with the volume turned way up following the father's death.

In addition to deciphering the impact of the past on the decision to leave home, it is helpful to explore the family's ideas about the future. For example, the parents may be asked: "When your child is grown up and moved out, what would you like your relationship to be like?" Whereas the adolescent could be asked: "What kinds of things do you expect you will be talking about and doing together when you have your own apartment or are away at college?" These questions implicitly challenge the view that growing up is synonymous with loss of a relationship and can start to plant the idea that adolescence and early adulthood can be a time of intimacy, renewal, and transformation. Parents may also be asked to reflect on how their relationships changed with their own parents in their twenties, thirties, and forties, in order to deintensify the current moment and to suggest that leaving home takes place in many stages and has a concomitant trajectory of reintegration with one's family of origin.

The state of the marriage should be assessed whenever there is a conflict about leaving home. Is the adolescent afraid that the parents' marriage won't survive his or her leave-taking? What are the parents' hopes or dreams for their relationship beyond their active parenting years?

The third developmental presentation is the complaint that begins with a concern about an adolescent and quickly gives way to questions about the survival of the marriage. Because this is such a common and interesting presentation, it is the topic of an entire chapter (see Chapter 7). I think that the resonance of adolescence with midlife issues often propels couples at this stage into therapy. For example, both adolescents and their parents are dealing with changing hormones, shifting relationships with parents, and profound identity questions.

The affinity between adolescence and middle age is lyrically captured in the novel *The Finishing School*, by Gail Godwin (1984), in which a now middle-aged woman, Justin, tells the story of her mentor relationship with Ursula Devane when Justin was an adolescent girl and Ursula an exciting but ultimately flawed middle-aged woman. Ursula tells Justin, "We are both at crucial turning points in our lives. In a strange way, the adolescent and the middle-aged person are neither one thing nor the other; they are both in the process of molting, of turning into something else" (p. 210). It is just this process of molting that often brings couples into therapy, asking the question, "Can we continue the marriage with the old contract, now that one or both of us is changing?"

Clearly, all three developmental presentations can be intertwined and do not represent distinct clinical entities. With any of the three presentations there can be marital difficulties that are the primary clinical focus. With all of them it is important to understand the cultural and familial legacies surrounding adolescence, leaving home, and marriage at midlife. We will return to these issues in much more depth in Chapters 4, 5, 6, and 7, which deal with case material. But before we delve into cases, I want to take some earlier steps in order. Once the clinician has decided to consider a family approach, what happens next?

## SETTING THE STAGE

Just because the clinician has decided on the wisdom of a family approach, it does not follow that all the family members are clamoring for such an appointment. It is quite common for an adolescent to refuse to come to an initial family meeting or, if he or she does come, to make it clear that this is a once-in-a-lifetime appearance. In both of these situations I have a standard statement that I give, either to the parent to give to the adolescent, or directly to the adolescent patient who claims at the outset that he or she will never return to my office.

To the adolescent who has promised never to return, the following message is often quite effective: "I would be really worried if you had been eager to come here today. I would know that there was something seriously wrong with you if you thought that this was a great place to be. I mean, no self-respecting teenager should want to be here. And I will be really perplexed if you want to come back. However, I don't think your parents should be meeting without you and possibly making decisions that will affect your life, without you being here to offer your version. I think that you are too old to let changes in your life happen behind your back. So if you decide to return, I will never mistake that as a sign that you like being here or want to be here but only as a sign that you don't want your parents to go too far off the track in making changes that will affect you."

This policy statement, which is offered in the spirit of preserving the adolescent's dignity and appealing to his or her wish to be heard and regarded as a responsible, important member of the family, often opens up negotiations. The adolescent might then agree to come to a handful of appointments and later recontract for a few more. This is enough. One doesn't need a lifelong commitment to treatment in order to proceed.

There is at least one caveat to this approach. In those instances in which it is imperative for the child to return, as when there has been a suicide attempt or serious substance abuse, the policy statement cannot be delivered with equanimity. Then the therapist might still express skepticism about the child wanting to return but would add the expectation that he must return. If the adolescent does not come back, then he and the family are letting the therapist know that outpatient family therapy is not the treatment of choice and hospitalization must be considered instead.

Almost as common as the reluctant teen is the one who requests a private meeting. This is a request that usually is granted. It often means that there is a secret that the teen wants to test out before telling the rest of the family. If at all possible, the child should be encouraged to share the secret in a family meeting, explaining that to keep one secret will probably make the therapist untrustworthy in the child's eyes. After all, how will she then be sure that the therapist is not keeping secrets with her parents that exclude her?

There are some secrets involving safety that need to be told to family members even if the adolescent is in disagreement. They include a suicide attempt, sexual abuse, and serious substance abuse. There are other confidences that an adolescent does not want to disclose but is clearly troubled by. Examples of these are questions about sexual identity or a fear about going crazy. In those instances it may be best to refer the adolescent to individual therapy and leave open the possibility of family therapy down the road.

## THE EVALUATION

The opening moves in therapy with adolescents and their families require more flexibility than most other assessments. When evaluating couples, for example, I have choreographed the first steps like an orderly square dance—meet with the couple together, then an individual appointment with each member of the couple, then sashay back to the center with a final feedback session. By contrast, family assessments with adolescents seem more like improvisational hip-hop.

As a general rule, it is wise to meet with the adolescent alone, the parents alone, and the family as a whole, but there are many variations on this general pattern. One must consider the initial presentation, the setting, and who is requesting help for whom, to compose a suitable evaluation. A few clinical vignettes may suggest the complexity of thinking that goes into deciding whom to see and in what order. Later these vignettes will provide a springboard for looking at an array of issues that must be considered in the first few interviews.

## Case #1: First Psychotic Break:
## A Long Way from Home

A pediatrician called me in the emergency room of a major city hospital with a request that I see a family whose 18-year-old daughter was "very depressed, probably psychotic" and now refused to come for appointments. The family, composed of a mother, a father, and three adolescents, had recently emigrated from India, giving up a very comfortable life to come to the United States and pursue educational opportunities for the children. The pediatrician had prescribed Haldol, which the father had been giving to his daughter for several months, telling her that it was for an ear infection that was causing her to hear voices.

When I called the father at his workplace, he was adamant that his daughter would never come to see a psychiatrist because in India, mental illness was a terrible taboo that resulted in complete ostracism. He confided that he was becoming increasingly worried about his daughter who, though a straight-A student last year, had just flunked out of college and was complaining of being followed. He wondered whether we could meet somewhere outside the hospital so that she wouldn't suspect that I was a psychologist.

From this initial presentation I was very concerned that the daughter had a psychotic depression. Worried, too, that she would not come in on her own, I offered to send an ambulance to bring the young woman to the emergency room. To this suggestion, the father responded, "My father, who is in poor health, lives with us. If you send an ambulance to take my daughter away, that will surely cause my father to have a heart attack and die."

## Commentary

The initial presentation contained a strong warning to take note of cultural differences regarding the role of outside helpers and the nature of mental illness. The case also posed a very difficult dilemma. On the one hand, the father told me that he and his family regarded psychiatric help as dangerous. On the other hand, his daughter sounded as though she might be in need of immediate hospitalization if she were both psychotic and suicidal. The challenge of this initial assessment was to make a speedy evaluation to ensure the daughter's safety without completely trampling on the family's cultural beliefs about psychiatric intervention.

I decided to meet immediately with the mother and father to learn more about their cultural beliefs and to see if there was some bridge that could be made between the family and the pediatrician, who had effectively been fired. The parents emphasized the terrible shame associated with mental illness and their wish to avoid psychiatric hospitalization, as it would mean a lifelong stigma for the daughter and the entire family. When asked what would be helpful, they disagreed. The mother thought they should return to India, where a marriage could be arranged. The father believed that their daughter needed medication and should return to college as soon as possible. I was struck by the tremendous loss of culture and family that they had incurred by moving to the United States. Privately, I wondered what kind of burden this put on the eldest daughter, who was expected to achieve great heights to justify this emigration.

In the meeting with the parents, I used language that was nonpsychiatric in an effort to describe their daughter's distress in a way that we could all agree on. I suggested, for example, that she needed help to be able to concentrate better and to feel less sad. We agreed that this was an explanation the daughter would understand, and the father was amenable to using this language to bring her in to the emergency room later that day.

The daughter came in with her younger brother by her side. She didn't want to meet with me alone and asked if her brother could accompany her, which I readily acquiesced to. The young woman was trembling. She wept as she described how difficult it was to concentrate on her school work and how disappointed her family was in her for failing at college. She said she wished she could return to India for her own sake and for the sake of her mother, who was terribly homesick. However, she believed that the family couldn't return to India until all three children had completed college, a goal that was unreachable, as she was too tired, sad, and distracted to attend classes. She told me that she was preventing the family from ever returning to India, and this thought was unbearable.

The goal for the family meeting was to take pressure off this child and unite the family in an effort to get her help. The father was enlisted to assure her that the family would return to India in five years, regardless of who had or hadn't completed college. In addition, I suggested that as the oldest child, she had been shouldering a tremendous burden since the move to the United States and that she really needed a vacation from college for at least a few months. I asked the parents to help her get some rest and find some unpressured activities for her to do. Mother suggested that the daughter take some art classes and make the family's dinner meal. I underscored the importance of follow-up at the hospital with a psychiatrist who, in deference to the family's distrust of psychiatry, I referred to as a medication specialist. Father agreed that he would bring his daughter to these appointments so the doctor could help her with her difficulties concentrating and her sad feelings. Finally, the parents agreed to rally the extended family to keep their daughter company at all times, "in case her sad feelings took over." Hospitalization was avoided and the parents agreed to call us if the daughter became suicidal.

## Case #2: A Midlife Marriage
## Churned Up by Adolescence

A married woman, Mrs. Sanders, with a 16-year-old daughter, Polly, and a 10-year-old son, Larry, called requesting family therapy for help with her daughter. She told me that she couldn't bear the frequency of the bitter fights she was having with her daughter and the feeling that Polly no longer respected her. Although she wanted to come in just with her daughter, I suggested an initial meeting with the whole family.

The family meeting was full of surprises. Polly told me, choking back tears, that it was her relationship with her father, not her mother, that most upset her. She maintained that her father had changed since Polly's bat mitzvah and now felt "unfamiliar." Polly agreed that she and her mother fought a lot but didn't think the fights were as important as all the things they enjoyed together, like going out to dinner, gardening, and enjoying the same movies. The father said that he had undergone a spiritual transformation based on his participation in a weekly men's group at the synagogue, a transformation that no one in the family really understood. Mr. and Mrs. Sanders sat at opposite ends of the room, rarely exchanged glances, and never once spoke directly to each other during the interview. Polly and her brother Larry dominated the session, using the time to declare the changes in privileges they would like made and challenging their parents to make new rules about such things as TV watching and sleepovers. Each parent presented his or her own position on these issues, which was subtly but definitively at odds with the position of the other. At the close of the session, Polly asked when she could return and told me how much she enjoyed the meeting. The parents looked frightened when I suggested a couple meeting.

## *Commentary*

From the start, I was struck by the difference between the children and the parents in this family. Polly and Larry were unusually comfortable for a first session, talking openly with me and unabashedly sharing their complaints with their parents. That Polly wanted to return and said so in front of her parents was further confirmation of the relative ease she experienced being open and disclosing. By contrast, the tension between Mr. and Mrs. Sanders was palpable, though unspoken. I wondered how they had provided a family environment that was so welcoming of emotion and conversation for their children but so strained between the two of them. This discrepancy in presentation was my first tip-off that this family's difficulties were concentrated in the marital arena.

The couples meeting confirmed my initial impressions. Mr. and Mrs. Sanders reported that they had been on a "low simmer" of anger for many years, with a long list of slights, hurts, and indignities visited on each by the other. When asked, they told me they had not had sexual relations for over a year. By the end of the meeting it was evident to all of us that couples therapy, rather than mother–daughter meetings, was indicated.

The children, however, were not so eager to be excluded. They frequently asked their parents when they could return. Perhaps this eagerness was propelled by concern for their parents, whose distress was certainly not lost on these bright and sensitive children. In any case, the children came to family meetings every few months, using them to hammer out a negotiation with their parents regarding privileges or discipline. These meetings continued to be strikingly lighthearted and jovial compared to the painful and painstaking couples therapy. I never felt a need to meet with Polly individually; she was so emotionally accessible in the family meetings. Also, the only problem definitions offered were dyadic or triadic in nature and so could best be tracked in joint meetings. In other words, no one ever said that they were concerned about Polly's ability to do schoolwork, avoid drugs, make friends, tell the truth, or shun danger. Problems were cast in terms of relationships within the family and since Polly seemed free to comment on those in the presence of her parents, it didn't seem necessary to meet with her separately.

## AREAS TO ASSESS IN EVALUATION

Whatever the configuration is in the first few meetings, there are several important bases to touch before offering a summary and a set of recommendations to a family. These areas can possibly be covered in a single meeting, although usually it takes three or four to offer thoughtful and convincing feedback.

### Resources of Parents and Adolescents

Since families' strengths are the key resource in solving whatever problems brought them to therapy, it is here that evaluations begin. The therapist might open with "Tell me something you like about yourself, something that you would miss if it disappeared one night" or, "Tell me what you admire about your mother, father, son, sister." If a family is in the midst of an acute crisis, this part of the evaluation can be postponed, since it feels disingenuous to ask people to reflect on what is positive about their lives when they are feeling overwhelmed by a tragedy or crisis.

Sometimes a family member is stumped by this line of questioning. Most often, when this occurs, it is an adolescent who feels embarrassed "blowing his own horn." Then other family members can be asked to describe the adolescent's strengths and check with the teen to see if they were on target.

It is important to be specific when asking about capabilities. For example, if a man states that he has "a good sense of humor," one must ask more. What kind of humor are we talking about? A dry sophisticated wit, a prolific punning tongue, a capacity to see the absurdity in any situation, a knack for the hilarious story? Or if an adolescent describes herself as "caring," one wants to know the particular flavor of caring. Does she show her caring at home as much as at school? Does she anticipate others' needs, or is she someone whom friends seek out for advice? Could she give an example of her caring behavior?

It can be very telling to see the reactions of other family members to these strengths. It is heartening when family members want to elaborate on their relative's capabilities, offering additional examples or amplifying the strength so that it becomes an extraordinary trait. Conversely, it is distressing when family members are sarcastic or discredit the strengths, saying that they never see these things at home. Often, if an adolescent and a parent are very angry and hurt with each other, they will initially find it difficult to talk about the other's fine points, but such a conversation can also begin to melt entrenched adversarial positions, as each becomes reacquainted with the other's better self.

Of course, a family has other resources besides those of its individual members. The therapist will want to know how cohesive the family is as a unit. Do they enjoy participating in any activities with one another, such as planting a family garden, playing Scrabble, volunteering at a soup kitchen, or going to the movies? What are mealtimes and vacations like? Is there anything that organizes this family around pleasure, fun, and relaxation, or do they come together only to fight with one another? If it is the latter, one may ask about an earlier time when family members did enjoy spending time with each other and then try to build on those earlier experiences.

Besides exploring their capacity to enjoy each other, it is instructive to know something about their history of coping with adversity. One can learn a great deal about a family's ability to meet obstacles by asking about a time in the past when a change was required. If outside help was useful at a previous juncture, what was most useful? Is there anything the family therapist can learn about how to be helpful now, based on how they were able to use professionals before? Were extended family members a resource then or now? Family members may differ in their approaches to asking for help— a man may want to gather information for problem solving while his wife wants someone to listen to her without offering any advice. Such differences can be a source of rich collaboration or the stuff of repeated misunderstandings.

## Meaning of the Future

The future holds special meaning for adolescents and their parents. Whereas for younger children, future time has an almost mythic quality—a long, long time from now when you are all grown up—for an adolescent, it is within reach. During this phase of the life cyle, families are preparing adolescents for that time when they will be living on their own.

Typically, adolescents fantasize about their adulthood and spend many hours sharing those fantasies with their peers. Sadly, many adolescents are deprived of this imaginative freedom by witnessing the violent deaths of friends and relatives, a knowledge that precludes the belief in an open-ended future.

Dr. Steve Nickman, a psychiatrist specializing in adolescent work at Massachusetts General Hospital, told me in an interview that he believes that future-oriented questions are the single most telling ones in talking with adolescents. He asks teens, "What is lying ahead for you?" by which he means something broader than "What do you want to do when you grow up?" How adolescents respond is indicative of their current symptom formation. For example, a depressed youngster will find it difficult to answer future-looking questions. In general, Nickman argues, whatever gives adolescents confidence in the future will lessen their entrenchment in current symptomatology.

This line of questioning can be taken one step further. It is enormously powerful for *parents* to speak with their adolescents about the future since this is a topic that is often fraught with pain and misconceptions. One 16-year-old boy announced to his parents at our first family session that he planned to move out on his own within the year. His parents were furious and hurt, interpreting his anticipated leave-taking as a rejection of them. As it turned out, there had been little if any conversation among them about John's future plans, because the parents had been so distracted with the illnesses and deaths of the mother's siblings. John had made up his mind that the sooner he got away from his parents, the better—they seemed so preoccupied with their own sadness that he didn't think they would even notice that he was gone.

I suggested that, in between sessions, the father talk to his son about the son's future educational and career plans, and their conversation took off. In a later meeting, when I asked each family member how they envisioned their get-togethers after John moved out, he burst into tears, stating that he had never imagined any contact after he moved out. In their silence about the future, intensified by so much conversation about death and illness, this family had developed profound misunderstandings about John's plans for himself. John had assumed that his parents were not the least bit interested in his plans for the future. His parents were so mired in mourning a series of losses that they had been unavailable to John. Everyone had construed his leaving home as just another unbearable loss that was best not spoken about. In fact, by discussing John's plans for the future, relationships were strengthened, and the family felt less like they were in mourning and more like they were working together on a shared effort to help John reach manhood.

## Problem Definition, Including an Answer to "Why Now?"

The therapist should never assume that she knows why the presenting problem is a problem, nor should she assume that there is a single shared understanding of it. One of the first clinical challenges is to ascertain the multiple perspectives of the problem in a family and to establish oneself as someone who can hold and keep track of many points of view simultaneously. The clinician thus needs to draw out each family member to define the problem and any wishes for change.

It is critical, too, to figure out the precipitant for the call for treatment. Stress is family-specific. What breaks the camel's back in one family will roll off the back in another. To identify this family's entry into therapy, one can ask, "Who had the idea to call for therapy?" and "When did you have the idea? Why today and not two weeks ago?" Locating the final indignity, or the last straw, will provide a beginning point for the evaluation and will tell a great deal about the vulnerabilities of this family.

Frank Pittman (1987), in his book *Turning Points*, delineates four kinds of stress. The first he terms "bolts from the blue," in which the stress is obvious, specific, and arises from forces outside the family. The stress could not have been anticipated, has never happened before, and probably will never happen again. Examples are the rape of an adolescent daughter, a natural disaster, or exposure to a Chernobyl-type accident. Pittman states that the danger of bolts from the blue is that family members will try to assign blame when only bad luck is involved. The best scenario is that the intensity of emotion unleashed and the coming together around a crisis will allow for open communication and the healing of past hurts.

The second type are developmental crises, in which the stresses are universal and predictable, resulting in permanent changes in roles. Examples are getting married, a first child entering adolescence, a last child making plans to leave home, a couple retiring. While these are all normal changes, they become crises when the structure of the family cannot adapt and accommodate because the system is overloaded with multiple changes or because this particular transition is charged with unresolved conflicts from a previous generation or a previous life stage.

The third kind of stress is a structural one, in which there is actually no obvious precipitant. Rather, there seems to be a perpetual volcano raging just below the surface of the family that can and does explode at some point. These families present with chronic problems as well as an acute crisis. It can be difficult to get a foothold in as a therapist because focus on long-term issues may prompt the family to redirect her to some pressing current concern. However, if the therapist tries to resolve a problem in the here and now, the family may inform her that their problems are long-standing. Pittman suggests that ongoing structural crises may serve to prevent the resolution of a developmental transition.

The final kind of stress is that prompted by a family member who is dependent or nonfunctional because of a chronic disability or a medical or psychiatric illness. Often these families will come in for treatment when a member has been recently diagnosed—for example, when an adolescent has had a first psychotic break, or when there is a disagreement among family members about how to manage this individual.

Naming the stress can be very calming to a family in crisis. Moreover, identification of the stress provides a fairly neutral entry into the family system, not obviously fraught with blame and accusation. For example, the therapist may summarize at the end of an evaluation, "It's no wonder that you come to family therapy now. John is getting ready to leave home, which is a stressful time for any family. But you have been dealing with terrible losses for many years, and his imminent leave-taking seems like just another unbearable loss."

The problem does not get defined, however, just by figuring out the stresses in a family or by asking each family member to offer his or her perspective. In the evaluation phase the definition of the problem should be expanded and loosened. One method of broadening the definition is to shift the focus from an identified patient to the idea that family members are interconnected and that everyone will be needed to solve the problem. Circular questions (Penn 1982, 1985) go a long way in making this shift. Examples are "Who is the most/ least affected by the problem?" or "When John says he can't wait to leave home, what does Father say?"; "When Father says nothing but goes to his room and shuts the door, how does John interpret that?"; "What does Mother do?"; "When she tells John that he can't even wash his clothes, how will he ever live on his own, what does John do?" And so on, so that each family member begins to see the impact of his or her actions on the others and each sees that a change on any one person's part could change the whole pattern of interaction.

Another way to loosen the problem definition is to offer a new way of thinking about the family's difficulties. During the course of the evaluation, the therapist tries out a few new ways of looking at the problem to see if she can offer a reframe that leads to new possibilities for interaction.

A family, the Stanleys, came to the psychiatric emergency room in an acute crisis. Their only child, Harry, now a young adult, had been maintained well on antipsychotic medication for several years, until he suddenly took himself off his medication and began chasing his mother around the house in a threatening manner, declaring that he was the Antichrist. In the first interview, the father revealed that his brother-in-law had died a month before. This man, Harry's uncle, was beloved by Harry and was the one person in the family able to cajole him back on his meds when he had gone off them in the past.

The mother was furious at Harry for threatening her and told him, "You're killing me with those threats. Get back on your pills," to which he responded, "I'm an adult and I'll do whatever I want." To this family the following reframe served to loosen the grip of the presenting problem. "I think that Harry's not taking his medication is an act of mourning, a way that he ensures the family will not forget the uncle's role in this family as a helper and a guide. This is an extraordinary burden of mourning that Harry has taken on his shoulders because it has meant sacrificing his job, his girlfriend, his relationships with his parents, all to make sure that his uncle's memory is kept alive." Then I suggested that Harry's parents could share in this burden by bringing in some stories and memories of the uncle to our next session.

The reframe was aimed at disrupting the repetitive cycle of the mother seeing Harry as a good-for-nothing who was out to harm her and Harry using his denunciation of his medication as proof that he was a grown man who didn't have to listen to his parents. The reframe offered a benign way of looking at Harry's behavior that transformed the context and ultimately allowed Harry to resume his meds, while saving face.

## Intersection of Current and Past Stresses

It is not enough to understand the precipitating stress and the particular normal vicissitudes of a family's life transition. It is also important to explore how these current difficulties reverberate and are underscored by difficulties from previous generations. McGoldrick and Gerson (1985) differentiate between present and past stresses with their use, respectively, of horizontal and vertical anxiety. Horizontal anxiety "emanates from current stresses on the family as it moves forward through time, coping with inevitable changes, misfortunes, and transitions in the family life cycle," while vertical anxiety "derives from patterns of relating and functioning that are transmitted historically down the generations, primarily through the process of emotional triangling" (p. 6).

Only by looking at the intersection of these two "flows of anxiety" can one make sense of a current difficulty. So, for example, while all families may expect some bumpiness around the time that a last child gets ready to leave home, a family marked by emotional cut-offs in previous generations will be particularly stressed by a leave-taking. In the next chapter we will be looking at the genogram as a tool for reading the relative contributions of vertical and horizontal anxiety.

## Understanding the Family's Style

In order to enter the family's world and be accepted as a respectful, knowledgeable guest, it is imperative that one appreciate the way they perceive and process their world. This stance cannot really be choreographed in advance but flows primarily from an open, nonjudgmental, curious attitude on the part of the therapist. It helps, too, to pay attention to the family's use of language, their cultural milieu, rules around the expression of feeling, and decision-making.

A family's unique use of language reveals a great deal about what they value and believe in. Do they describe problems with specific examples, lyrical analogies, or philosophical musings? Do their explanations of the problem focus on moral character, immaturity, craziness, or lack of opportunity? One pathway in is to pay attention to any highly charged and idiosyncratic words that repeatedly crop up in the interview. For example, a family consulted me for help with their two young-adult sons who had both withdrawn from college after a series of academic failures and uncompleted courses. One son described his difficulty completing college work this way: "If someone would put me on the roller coaster and slam down the bar, I'd be fine. But I can't get on that roller coaster myself, knowing how scary the ride will be." That metaphor was so evocative and unusual, speaking both to his inner world and the dynamics in the family, that I took special care to remember it and use it later in my conversation with the family. I wondered who in the family has slammed that bar for him, and does he still need that service performed and would it work to lower the bar more gently, and was the ride always as scary as he anticipated or does he sometimes scare himself unnecessarily? The family's language ushered me into a far richer, more complicated world than asking about "academic failure," "fear of success," or "underachievement."

Attitudes toward mental health professionals, expectations of adolescent behavior, developmental changes, and gender roles are all mediated by culture. When a family has a cultural background that differs from the therapist's own, it is important to ask, rather than assume that one knows the foreign terrain.

The therapist must also gauge the extent and intensity of emotional expression that is allowed in a given family. Pushing too hard or too soon for self-disclosure in a family that views such behavior as a sign of weakness can drive a family out of treatment prematurely. Rather, interventions should be made that are not too discrepant with the family's own tolerance for emotional expression.

## FEEDBACK TO THE FAMILY

At some point, usually within the first four sessions, it is useful to comment to the family on what the therapist has observed and now recommends. If the family presents in the midst of an acute crisis, this feedback may happen at the end of the first session. If there is the luxury of time, the therapist may wait until there have been meetings with the couple, the adolescent, and the family, before trying to summarize impressions. The process of delivering feedback has developed into a kind of therapeutic ritual with its own set of steps.

To heighten its impact, one can forecast from the start that formal remarks will be offered at the end of the session or the evaluation process. If the therapist tries to construct feedback in the midst of a crisis, it is wise for her to leave the room for a few minutes in order to think more clearly away from the emotional fray. Otherwise, the therapist can take time in between sessions to write a message to the family.

The message typically has four parts to it (Fishel and Gordon 1994). The first is a comment on the family's strengths, aimed at diminishing defensiveness, eliciting cooperation, and promoting an openness to the rest of the message. In addition, by emphasizing the coping abilities of the family as a whole, the therapist tries to shift attention away from the identified patient to family relationships in a way that is tolerable and nonblaming. So, for example, if family members have barely said a word to the therapist or to each other, one might comment on how attuned they are to respecting each other's privacy.

Second, when possible, the presenting problem can be normalized by identifying external stresses and situating the problem in a developmental perspective. For example, "It is no wonder that you come to family therapy now when your daughter is getting ready to leave home and as a family you are trying to sort out this leave-taking from the multitude of losses you have incurred over the last two years. Any family would feel confused about this next transition, not knowing whether to mourn it as yet another loss or celebrate it as a sign that you have successfully ushered your daughter into adulthood." By normalizing the presenting problem, one hopes to interrupt a cycle of blame, anger, and guilt, which so often characterizes a stressful situation but which rarely leads to constructive problem solving.

Third, it is a powerful intervention to redefine the family's difficulties in a way that points them in a new direction.

Thirteen-year-old Sarah was experiencing severe separation anxiety when she was home from school and her mother, Louise, was still at work. The anxiety had started after Louise was late one night returning home from work and Sarah had imagined that her mother was in a car accident. The anxiety also coincided with Sarah's starting a new junior high school that was larger and farther away from home than her small elementary school had been.

Louise was a highly accomplished doctor and devoted mother of four. She described herself as someone who was hard on herself in all arenas of her life, who strove for perfection as a mother, daughter, wife, and doctor. She seemed to have boundless energy and managed to give prodigious amounts of it to her work and her family. The mother and daughter, the only females in the family, enjoyed each other tremendously, and the session was punctuated by laughter and warm exchanges. At the end of the session I redefined Sarah's separation anxiety in the following way: she was a daughter who had no experience with her mother screwing up and therefore became alarmed when her mother slipped up even in small ways, like tardiness.

To follow up on the reframe, I offered some new actions the mother and daughter could take with each other during the intervening week. To Louise, I suggested that she go out of her way to point out things that she had not done perfectly during the week and to try to model a relaxed attitude toward those transgressions. To the daughter, I suggested that she practice telling her mother some small thing that displeased or disappointed her about her mother so that she would learn another way to respond to her mother's shortcomings without full-fledged anxiety. My reframe was aimed at giving them a way of navigating the increased separations brought on by adolescence by underscoring their deep connection to each other and keeping them in conversation with each other.

Finally, at the end of the feedback session, the therapist will negotiate a follow-up plan, one that is reasonable and tolerable to all parties involved. The therapist may suggest something for the family to work on in the intervening week. For example, each family member can be asked, "What is the smallest change you could make in the next week that would indicate that something positive has begun to occur? And why don't you tell me how that goes when you return next week." The therapist also tries to give a rough estimate of how long these meetings should continue and makes any suggestions for adjunctive couples and individual work. It is important to leave time for the family to process these recommendations in the session before they leave.

If the family returns, then what? One is into the more ambiguous middle stages of therapy; it is to this murkier, less well-defined phase that we now turn our attention.

# 4

# The Middle Phase of Therapy: Interventions for Adolescents and Their Parents

Although an evaluation tends to be time-limited and structured, the rest of therapy meanders in a more amorphous manner. This chapter and the next are a partial answer to the question, "What does the family therapist do and say now that the evaluation is over?" The reply is a distillation of several techniques that have proven helpful to me over the years in working with adolescents and their families. This chapter focuses on five interventions—life-cycle messages, developmental reframes, rituals, challenging the cultural discourse, and externalizing the problem—that are particularly useful in crises or short-term family therapy with adolescents. The subsequent chapter discusses two interventions—genogram work and reflecting teams—that are better suited for more long-term therapy or for consultation.

These two chapters are not meant to be a comprehensive manual for conducting family therapy. Rather, seven ways of interacting with families will be explored that enhance the family's own creative problem-solving capabilities. Each way of interacting is the offspring of a developmentally informed, systemically based, narrative approach.

These seven ways of interacting represent approaches that I have found to be a good match for adolescents and their families. They are not meant to be an exhaustive list or an exclusive one. These techniques can be expanded on, used repeatedly, or used consecutively. They do not prohibit the use of other interventions, such as making clarifications or acting swiftly and decisively in the case of an emergency. Any one of the interventions, in its broadest contours, could be applicable to families other than those with adolescents; however, each has been tailored to the particular developmental pulls of adolescents and their parents. For each way of interacting, a clinical vignette is offered. In subsequent chapters, vignettes will give way to full-blown case studies in which the evaluation and intervention phases will be integrated.

Since each of these techniques has a developmental underpinning, a review of family life-cycle theory is a fitting introduction. Broadly stated, family-developmental theorists (Carter and McGoldrick 1989, Preto 1989, Preto and Trevis 1985) propose that the family is a unit having its own developmental tasks and identifiable transitions that occur in sequence and are accompanied by some degree of stress. Symptoms in individuals are regarded as a signal that the entire family is having difficulty moving to the next stage of development (Coopersmith 1981, Haley 1973). While these transitional crises are normative and predictable, several factors can complicate and exacerbate these turning points. First, when a transition happens at an unusual or unexpected time (Harkins 1978), such as a teenager not moving out of the house at the same time that his peers do, ordinary stress may cross over into a crisis. Second, if several stressors coincide with a transition point, the shift to another stage will be made more difficult, as when the death of a parent coincides with an adolescent leaving home. Third, if the current transition shift resonates with a comparable difficulty in the previous generation (Carter 1978), the family may be overly constrained by the legacy.

Developmentalists take note of different stages within the larger rubric of adolescence. The breakdown of phases is early adolescence (ages 11–14), middle adolescence (ages 15–18), and late adolescence (ages 18–21), a phase that may overlap with the next family life-cycle stage of launching children from the home and into the world. That said, there is this caveat: adolescence is also not a stage defined solely by chronological age. Teenagers often leave home by 15 or 16, or jump ahead a few stages and have babies. Then, too, many stay home well past the age of 21.

When the family with adolescents is regarded from a developmental perspective, two views have predominated. One view (Blos 1962, Erikson 1968, Freud 1958) emphasizes the conflict, while the other (Farrell and Rosenberg 1981, Preto and Trevis 1985, Prosen et al. 1981) stresses the similarity between the two generations. The first view is that middle-aged parents and their adolescent children are working at developmental cross-purposes; the aggressive and sexual drives of adolescence are on the rise while their parents' energies are waning. There is some evidence, for example, that in families where mothers are ending their reproductive years just as their daughters are entering puberty, mothers and daughters have increased difficulty with each other, particularly around the issue of eating (Paikoff et al. 1991). In addition, the different views of time and mortality held by parents and adolescents are seen as colliding with one another: adolescents often feel that their time on this earth stretches ahead without end, while their parents have often received jolts to their mortality through their own parents' deaths and the disquieting knowledge that time is limited. This perspective, emphasizing generational conflict, lies at the heart of the *Sturm und Drang* view of adolescence.

The other developmental view is that parents and adolescents are confronting similar life issues, such as hormonal surges, the challenge of negotiating new relationships with parents, and piercing questions about identity, such as "Will I choose to be the same person in the next stage of life as I have been in childhood [for the adolescent] or in young adult-hood [for the middle-aged parent]?"

Each of these developmental viewpoints—generations clashing and generations in synchrony—has validity. It is important in working with families to know if one of these beliefs predominates among family members, or if there is a difference in opinion within the family about the meaning of this stage. When one view predominates, it may be helpful to bring up the other one. Where there are differences, it may be helpful to explore and clarify them. Both views contain the acknowledgment that parents and adolescents have a mutual impact on one another. Erikson, in *Challenge of Youth* (1965), eloquently captures this process of mutual parent–child transformation. He writes:

> In youth the table of childhood dependence begins slowly to turn: no longer is it merely for the old to teach the young the meaning of life, whether individual or collective. It is the young who, by their responses and actions, tell the old whether life as represented by the old and presented to the young has meaning: and it is the young who carry in them the power to confirm them and, joining the issues, to renew and to regenerate, or to reform and to rebel. [p. 24 ]

Family life-cycle theorists have defined the tasks that adolescents and their parents must grapple with as a family in order to move on to the next stage of development. Some of these tasks require mutual, complementary involvement, while others are really individual tasks that the adolescent is in charge of but that can be promoted or thwarted by parents. Still others are marital tasks that do not involve the adolescents.

The individual tasks of adolescence are many and varied. They include dealing with biological changes brought on by the onset of puberty; choosing a peer group to associate with; figuring out, through experimentation, one's sexual identity;

developing a coherent value system; and preparing for a future as a worker and marriage partner.

In describing a healthy family, developmentalists offer the following parameters. There is a greater need for flexibility to allow the adolescent to move out and back in; seen this way, the adolescent is an explorer having new experiences with peers and with other families, and discovering new ideas, music, values, and language. Repeatedly, the voyager returns, enlivening the family by sharing these new experiences and lending a critical eye that often comes from comparing a new world to an old one. The parents, for their part, try to be open to these new experiences, willing to listen to their child's critique of them while also maintaining a parental stance of monitoring their whereabouts (Fuligni and Eccles 1993). The other major family task that culminates at the end of the adolescent stage but that must be built upon from early childhood is the family's ability to negotiate the departure of its adolescent members.

Several researchers have studied the effects of different parenting styles on adolescent development. The combination of parents setting high standards, staying involved, and being responsive to their children's demands is associated with the most positive outcomes (Darling and Steinberg 1993, Lamborn et al. 1991, Maccoby and Martin 1983).

Hauser and colleagues (1991), in their extensive research on adolescents and their families, offer several crucial ways that parents can foster the individual development of their children. They advocate that parents "hang in," through repeated engagement, regardless of the rejection and insults hurled at them and that parents try to reveal more of themselves by telling about their own experiences as adolescents and some of their inner lives. In addition, these researchers urge parents toward tolerance—of new ideas, of an adolescent's experimentation, and of intense, often unwanted emotions, such as anger and mood swings.

Not only do the family as a whole and the individual adolescent members experience myriad changes, but the couple may find that they, too, are changing. Several studies suggest that parents of adolescent children report higher marital dissatisfaction than parents of younger children. This dissatisfaction may arise from the couples' own midlife issues, from the stresses of parenting adolescents, or from an interaction of the two. With the advent of their children's adolescence, the couple is looking ahead to a future alone, without the distractions, triangulating possibilities, and shared passion that childrearing has entailed.

## FAMILY THERAPY INTERVENTIONS: WAYS OF INTERACTING

### Life-Cycle Messages

These are descriptions of family difficulties designed to resonate with expectable developmental issues. They are messages aimed at putting family struggles into a different emotional context that lessens defensiveness, reduces shame, and promotes cooperation. The messages may be aimed at the family as a whole, to a parent–child dyad, or to the couple. In any case, the spirit of the message is the same: to honor the normal developmental significance of an interaction that has been obscured by the particular struggle of the moment. The reframes redirect family members to the key developmental tasks confronting them: for example, how do we maintain our connection to one another, on the one hand, while, on the other, help our adolescents move toward having a distinct sexual, moral, and social identity that will soon enable them to live on their own?

Let me offer a few clinical examples of life-cycle messages, beginning with one directed at a father–son dyad, both of whom complained of incessant and vicious verbal fights.

The father, Mr. Gibbs, who initiated family therapy, said that for the previous year he and his 14-year-old son, Alfred, had been incapable of civil conversation. Mr. Gibbs attributed the change in their relationship to his own switch from a steady managerial job to the riskier position of starting his own business. The trigger for the fights was usually something to do with Alfred's schoolwork and Mr. Gibbs's thinking that Alfred was not trying hard enough or taking on enough challenging courses and extracurricular activities. Both of them expressed sadness for the relationship that they used to have, one that in retrospect was close, effortless, and based on doing sports and making projects together, such as a tree house. To this pair, I said: "I know this fighting is hard on both of you, particularly after years of enjoying a close relationship where you shared many activities together. But I think if you can bear these disagreements, they are an opportunity for you, Alfred, to find out more who you are as a young man. Every time you fight, you, Mr. Gibbs, give your son the chance to find out how he stands in relation to you, and you help him define who he is, how similar and how different he wants to be. Alfred, by fighting with your father about what is important to you, you give him a chance to really know you."

With this message the fighting is reframed as another joint project, this time aimed at a normal developmental task—Alfred's forming a separate identity, which he lets his father know about. By normalizing the fighting, perhaps Alfred and his father will come to see each other differently the next time they fight. The fight might be less vicious and more playful, or perhaps the father and son will be more forgiving of each other when the disagreement ends.

There is another type of life-cycle message, one aimed at loosening up a silence. When an adolescent is present in body but will not speak, this life-cycle message, directed at the adolescent, is also meant to make the parents feel less embarrassed by their child's stonewalling. In the face of a sulky silence that is saying, "I might be here physically but I'm sure as hell not going to speak," the therapist might refrain from cajoling or barraging the teenager with questions that get answered with shrugs. Instead, the therapist can say: "It's fine if you choose not to talk right now. In fact, your not talking reminds me of something I meant to say to all of you, which is, if I ask a question that anyone doesn't feel ready to answer, please let me know. That way, I will feel free to ask whatever questions I think would be helpful. I see that Sarah already has a clear understanding of the importance of privacy and autonomy, and I'm glad to see that. Please, Sarah, don't feel like you have to talk before you really size up the situation. After all, you don't know me at all yet."

This life-cycle message positively recasts Sarah's recalcitrance as normal, autonomous, even helpful behavior and is aimed at loosening her commitment to this position. After all, it is difficult to be defiant when asked to be so. This message, however, can be offered only if it can be spoken truthfully. A suicidal adolescent, in particular, cannot be given permission to remain silent since assessment of his or her safety depends on a dialogue. Then, too, there are silences that derive not from defiance but from fear or severe depression. A normalizing life-cycle message will miss the mark in these latter situations.

### Developmental Reframes

When the life-cycle messages are aimed at the family as a whole and are largely paradoxical, rather than normalizing, they are reminiscent of a technique called *developmental reframing*, designed by Coopersmith (1981). Beginning with the premise that all presenting problems indicate that the entire family is stuck at an earlier stage of development, she tells families that they are having trouble growing up. In essence, any presenting problem is redefined as one involving immaturity rather than craziness or immorality. The family is told that their symptomatic adolescent is "not bad, or mad, just young," with this intractable youth explained in terms of misguided thinking or circumstances out of everyone's control. The reframe is followed by a homework assignment designed to help the immature member grow up and is implicitly aimed at getting the whole family unstuck and ready to move on to the next stage of development.

This technique has a pointedly paradoxical intent: typically, the child who receives this reframe bristles at the description of his or her behavior as young. Then, the only way to prove the therapist wrong is to engage in behaviors that do not fit the therapist's description. These reframes are most powerful when they reframe as immaturity something an adolescent was doing that was making everyone in the family anxious. Then the reframe becomes a way for the family to speak about something that had been off limits. Perhaps a clinical vignette can best illustrate how a developmental reframe can be used to open up a topic that the whole family was too anxious to speak about directly.

Mr. and Mrs. White and their 19-year-old son, Danny, were referred to me by Danny's psychiatrist, who was overwhelmed by the barrage of phone calls he was receiving from Mrs. White about her son. Mrs. White called Danny's psychiatrist, imploring that Danny be hospitalized for an operation to cure his "brain disease." Danny, who carried the diagnosis of Tourette's and had tested in the borderline mentally retarded range of intelligence, had been having outbursts since he turned 18. These outbursts consisted of throwing furniture and yelling swear words at his mother. Medication had done little to control these storms.

When I met with the Whites and asked them their ideas about the recent increase in temper outbursts, there was some agreement among the three of them. According to Danny and his parents, the increase had coincided with Danny's quitting his job, dropping out of vocational school, and spending many hours each day gazing out the window in the hopes of seeing his downstairs male neighbor. At this point, the mother added that Danny had a "brain disease" that required surgery while the father told me that the problem was simply that "Danny doesn't like us." Absent from the meeting was Tina, a 17-year-old sister who recently had heart surgery and was "too weak" to attend. Mother volunteered somewhat cryptically that she had given Tina money to join a dating service but that Tina had used it for something else—"I'm ashamed to tell you what."

Just a few minutes into the interview, I was feeling anxious: I was aware of several difficult, shameful topics afoot but also felt that I wasn't allowed to ask about them directly. I wondered silently, "Was Danny concerned about homosexual feelings he was having toward his neighbor?"; "Had Tina spent her dating money on an abortion or drugs?"; "Wasn't it unusual for Tourette's to start right on an eighteenth birthday, be immune to medication, and manifest itself only at home?" I knew I wanted to make an intervention that would somehow normalize the family's difficulties, helping Danny become an adult and make some room for him to talk rather than throw tantrums in the face of anxious material.

Next, I inquired more about the outbursts, since they were the presenting problem. Mr. and Mrs. White told me that they were afraid of Danny when he lost his temper and threw furniture. They also told me that he often forgot to go to his individual therapy appointments and that he sometimes locked himself out of the house and then would wake them up in the middle of the night by throwing rocks up at their bedroom window. When I asked Danny how the family would be different if he stopped having temper outbursts, he told me without hesitation that his parents would yell at each other more, the way they used to.

At the end of the third session I suggested a developmental reframe to the family: "I don't think the problem is that Danny has a brain disease, or that he doesn't like his family. I think the problem is that he's behaving like a 10-year-old—he has tantrums when he doesn't get his way, he can't remember his keys or his doctor's appointments, which is what you'd expect from a young boy. Also, a 10-year-old wouldn't be able to keep a job or attend vocational school, and I think that's why Danny dropped out—he's behaving as though he's very young. Now, I don't know the reason for this. I think he may have the idea that the family needs him to be younger than he is. Maybe, he's afraid that if he grows up, his parents will start fighting too much with one another. Or, maybe he's afraid that if he grows up, his sister's secrets might come out in the open. Or, maybe Danny is trying to protect his parents from grown-up information about himself that he thinks will worry them. I don't really know why he's acting younger than he is, but I feel sure that you need to help Danny grow up." To this, Danny stood up and said, "If I'm only 10, then why am I thinking about h-o-m-o-s-e-x-u-a-l-i-t-y?" With that secret out in the open, the family was able to start talking about what they had all known was in the air. On follow-up a few months later, the tantrums had virtually disappeared. This reframe, aimed at the entire family's difficulty in helping Danny grow up, couched in language that emphasized immaturity, allowed the family to talk about what had previously been too charged to discuss.

## Rituals

In the literature, the use of the word *ritual* refers variously to religious celebrations such as bar mitzvahs (Davis 1988), everyday interactions like family dinners (Imber-Black and Roberts 1992), rites of passage like a leaving-home ceremony (Quinn et al. 1985), therapeutic rituals like the Milan odd-even day ritual (Selvini Palazzoli et al. 1978b),[1] and symptoms viewed as attempted rituals aimed at leading a family through a difficult transition (Lax and Lussardi 1988). Its first usage in the family therapy literature appears in 1978 by Selvini Palazzoli in her book *Paradox and Counterparadox.* There, she offers a definition that is as good as any that follow. A ritual is "an action or series of actions usually accompanied by verbal formulas or expressions, which are to be carried out by all members of the family. The ritual is prescribed in every detail: the place in which it must be carried out, the eventual number of repetitions, by whom the verbal expressions are to be uttered, in what order, etc." (p. 95). Furthermore, rituals convey multiple meanings, rely on symbols and symbolic action, and require that the family create some of its own content, as well as adhere to a cultural or therapist's script (Whiting 1988).

Each of the applications found in the ritual literature, from religious celebrations to symptoms, is relevant to work with adolescents and their parents and perhaps more relevant than at any other developmental stage. Lax and Lussardi (1988) make the compelling point that if rituals are useful in reducing confusion and clarifying roles, then adolescence, which is itself a paradoxical state, is a time of life highly receptive to

---

1. In an odd-even day ritual, families who are giving their children contradictory messages are asked to perform two different actions or behaviors—one on Monday, Wednesday, and Friday, and the other on Tuesday, Thursday, and Saturday.

ritual. It is a paradoxical state, they argue, because adolescents are neither children nor adults and they are both children and adults.

Rituals can work by introducing time into a paradoxical system. With rituals, one can prescribe two different times to do contradictory behaviors that the family previously had been performing simultaneously. By suggesting that there is a specific time for a particular behavior, relationships between all members become more clearly delineated. Consider, for example, members of the Banks family, who were treating their 17-year-old diabetic son as though he were both an immature adolescent and an antisocial adult. In this case a therapeutic ritual was offered to tease apart these tangled messages.

## *Ritual 1: The Adolescent as Child and Adult*

Mr. and Mrs. Banks brought their taciturn, angry son Tom, age 18, to see me. Mrs. Banks explained, through clenched teeth, that her son had become verbally abusive toward her and his sister following his girlfriend's breaking up with him three days earlier. He had also been throwing furniture at them and had left home for two days. Complicating this presentation was Tom's diabetes, which had been diagnosed at age 14 and had been under good control until quite recently, when he had stopped taking his insulin. In addition, a month earlier he had stopped going to his after-school job, where his boss was a close friend of the family. Though Tom was now in his senior year, it was doubtful that he would graduate, as he often skipped class and rarely did his homework.

In the first few interviews, it became apparent that Mr. and Mrs. Banks each used very different language to describe Tom and had competing strategies for getting him to shape up. Mr. Banks, the oldest child in a large family, saw Tom's behavior as bad and as a sign that he was a young man who would be in perpetual trouble with the law unless he were thrust out into the world where he would get some sobering hard knocks. Mrs. Banks, on the other hand, who didn't leave her home until she got married, talked about her son as being immature. She thought that Tom's diabetes had interfered with his growing up: therefore, he needed some extra time at home with supportive parents to compensate for the difficulties incurred from having a chronic illness. I saw Tom as making it quite clear by his actions that he was not ready to move out on his own and yet I felt that he was daring his father to throw him out on his ear. And the testing ground was growing by the day.

The family also described an unusual pattern of communication: as differences heated up, family members left each other notes around the house with affect connoted by the use of bold face and a rainbow of magic markers. By the time they came to therapy, Mr. and Mrs. Banks were so angry they had stopped talking to each other. However, their house was annotated with dozens of Post-Its, each one written on in a different color to connote a narrow range of emotions—red for anger, purple for fury, black for despair.

During the fourth session, I suggested the following odd-even-day ritual. On Monday, Wednesday, and Friday the family was to think of Tom as a young child who needed help growing up. In their bedroom, for fifteen minutes in the evening, Mr. and Mrs. Banks were to talk together and write down their ideas with a felt-tip marker, using whatever colors were most suitable. These ideas were to address how best to help Tom grow up, including remedial tasks for him to do to make up for time lost due to his illness. Then, on Tuesday, Thursday, and Saturday, they were to construe Tom as someone who had gone off track and who was on his way to becoming an irresponsible young man, in trouble with the law. On these evenings, again for fifteen minutes, Mr. and Mrs. Banks were to talk together and write down any ideas about how to get life to teach Tom some important lessons. On Sunday, they were to do whatever they wanted.

At the next session, the parents reported that they had difficulty with the experiment because Tom had hardly misbehaved. Instead, they had talked and written about past transgressions. Even so, each parent had managed to learn something new from the exercise. Mr. Banks talked about how little protection he had gotten from his parents, since he, as the oldest, had been expected to grow up quickly. He realized that he felt envious of Tom when his son was "babied" by his wife. Mrs. Banks admitted that she agreed with some of her husband's ideas about expecting more from Tom. Tom, for his part, thought the experiment was off the mark completely—the problem wasn't that he was too immature or too irresponsible; he was just plain spoiled and he was getting tired of that role.

According to Richard Whiting (1988), there are several elements that a therapeutic ritual should contain: symbols, symbolic action, open and closed aspects, and the prescribed use of time and space. The Banks ritual illustrates these four elements. The symbol was the colored magic markers, here transformed from something the family used to connote anger and discord to something meant to capture a spirit of playful cooperation. The symbolic action was the writing down of the two different conversations about Tom. The open part of the ritual was all that was not dictated to the family—that they could use whatever incidents they wanted and come up with any solutions. The closed aspect was the way the ritual was scripted for them—that they were supposed to think of Tom as alternatively immature or irresponsible. Time was introduced to separate out by day the two contradictory ways of perceiving him. Finally, the ritual was located in space: it was to take place primarily behind Mr. and Mrs. Banks's closed bedroom doors.

This ritual allowed Mr. and Mrs. Banks a way of moving out of the position of competing with each other over whose view was better and into a stance of cooperation. The parents became joined in their approach and Tom had the benefit of responding to one set of expectations at a time. The ritual allowed the parents to see that both points of view were valid and that each one complemented the other. Where Tom's dilemma about whether he was still a child or almost an adult had been further exacerbated by his parents' disagreements, the ritual helped to clarify his developmental issues. Such a ritual not only addresses the different opinions in a family about the adolescent's readiness to become an adult but can speak to the family as a whole regarding their ripeness for moving from a child-focused system to a more fluid and flexible system featuring adult relationships.

### Ritual 2: A Therapeutic Rite of Passage

Sometimes a therapeutic ritual may take the form of a rite of passage and here again the ritual addresses contradictions inherent in the family system. This time the paradox to be grappled with is this: How do parents stay connected while the adolescent physically separates? In other words, we all know that it is a positive move for an adolescent to separate, but we fear that it will have dire consequences for the rest of the family.

The Barrett family, whom I saw in an emergency room, provides an example of a rite-of-passage ritual designed to address the dilemmas this family faced in helping their 24-year-old son, Tony, move out of the house for the first time. When I saw them, one hot August night, they had been to the emergency room five times in the last four days, each time with the parents complaining that Tony's behavior was out of control. Mrs. Barrett accused her son of chasing her around the apartment with pots and pans. Mr. Barrett grumbled that the yelling between his wife and son had to stop. Tony admitted to both the yelling and the chasing but stated that he had never hurt anyone and never would. His behavior, while objectionable, was not cause for commitment.

Mr. and Mrs. Barrett were a retired couple who had recently sold their family home and moved into an assisted-living apartment. Tony, who had been diagnosed with manic-depressive illness five years earlier, had managed to stay out of the hospital, hold a job, and have a girlfriend since starting on medication at the time of his diagnosis. Periodically, he went off his medication but could usually be cajoled back onto it by his father. He had just come through such a period of being off and going back on his meds, and his parents had hoped that his behavior would improve with his resuming his lithium, but it hadn't. In fact, the verbal altercations had increased.

I soon discovered that Tony's taking his medication heightened the family's real crisis, which had begun a month earlier when he had applied to live in a halfway house. Now that he was on his meds, he would be able to take more steps toward leaving home, such as getting a special-needs bus pass and going for an interview.

To myself, I puzzled about what this family would risk by Tony's moving out. In light of the recent move to the apartment for the elderly, I hypothesized that the family was concerned about the advancing age of Mr. and Mrs. Barrett. I also couldn't fail to notice that as long as Tony was chasing his mother around the house, he was keeping her rather youthful. As long as Tony was unable to live on his own, his parents were needed to stay alive to care for him. I asked the family several questions to check out my hypothesis and to determine how receptive they might be to an intervention that derived from this hypothesis.

To Tony, I asked, "If in the next few years you were to move out, how would your parents get along?" Tony responded, "My mother would drive my father crazy." Then I asked Tony, "If you stayed at home forever, what would your parents' relationship be like?" To this question Tony answered, "I don't know, it would be about the same." But when I asked Mr. and Mrs. Barrett how their relationship would change if Tony were to move out, I heard a different tune. Mrs. Barrett exclaimed, "Well, we'd get to enjoy our old age more, you know, spend time with people in the building without worrying about getting kicked out." Mr. Barrett added, "I think it would be about the same, except I guess we'd sit around more and watch TV."

Then I really probed the connection between Tony's moving out and his parents' advancing age. I spoke to Tony: "You seem quite worried about your parents getting old. How much longer do you think they will live if you stay home?" But before Tony could answer me, Mrs. Barrett interjected, "He's going to kill us with that behavior before it's our time to die." Tony, pretending to ignore his mother, said, "They'll live longer with me at home." When I asked his father similar questions, Mr. Barrett told me that he didn't know which way they would live longer, but he did know he would miss Tony tremendously if he were to move out. Because the family responded to these and other related questions with a lot of intensity and interest in listening to each other, I decided that this hypothesis about the risks for the parents' survival if Tony left home had hit a chord.

At the end of this session I suggested a rite-of-passage ritual. I introduced the ritual by offering an interpretation of the family's recent escalation of fighting: I thought that Tony was having trouble making the next move in his life because he was afraid that his parents couldn't survive without him there. Furthermore, I proposed that the fighting they were doing was in the service of helping Tony leave home because it would be easier for him to leave if home life was unpleasant rather than nice and calm. I asked the father to keep track of the fights, timing them and announcing when they were over. At the end of the first one, he and his wife were to leave the house for a couple of hours. When they left, they were not to tell Tony where they were going, and when they returned home, they were not to tell him where they had gone. They should try to assess Tony's reaction to their being apart and to test out whether they could survive without him. At the end of the second fight, Tony was to leave the house, also without announcing his destination. When he returned, he was to assess how his parents had managed without him. Tony and his parents were to alternate in this way throughout the week. I explained to them that the fighting would then help them practice being apart from each other.

Not surprisingly, only Mr. and Mrs. Barrett showed up at the next appointment. They explained that after a fight, Tony had left and gone to spend the night at his girlfriend's house. He had called his parents the morning of our appointment to get a ride, but they had told him to come on his own. I heard this information as direct feedback to the intervention linking fighting with leaving home. Choosing not to comment directly, I inquired about the past week's experiment.

Mr. Barrett, who was much more active and talkative during this meeting, reported that he and his wife had gone out on their own after the first fight. He thought that Tony had been able to handle his parents being on their own and had made calls to friends during their absence. The second fight, which resulted in Tony's departure to his girlfriend's house, stemmed from Tony feeling slighted by his cousin and asking his mother to intervene on his behalf. The description of this incident led to a discussion of

Tony's immaturity, and specifically to the mother's complaints about all the tasks she was still doing for him, like his laundry, cooking, and bed-making. When I asked her what would happen if she stopped doing so much for him, she made a slip and said, "He'd be gone," and then quickly corrected herself with "He'd hurt me." I think the slip spoke to how intertwined Tony's leave-taking was with his abusive behavior.

Instead of making an interpretation regarding the unconscious meaning behind Mrs. Barrett's slip (an interpretation I thought she would reject), I asked the parents how old they thought Tony was acting. When they agreed upon age 12, I wondered with them what tasks they thought a 12-year-old was competent to take on. I suggested that if he were to leave home, he would need to learn to do more for himself. I encouraged Mr. and Mrs. Barrett to discuss between themselves what tasks they thought Tony was ready and able to do for himself. Then, I asked Mr. Barrett to have a heart-to-heart with Tony to tell him that he and his wife had decided that they would help Tony get ready to move out by letting him do more on his own. This intervention, a developmental reframe, elaborated on Mrs. Barrett's shift in language from describing Tony as a good-for-nothing son to an immature young man who needed help growing up. This reframe was designed to further shore up Mr. and Mrs. Barrett's connection to each other, in an effort to prepare them, as well as Tony, for the next developmental stage—Tony on his own and Mr. and Mrs. Barrett as an independent dyad.

At the next session, also our last, Mr. Barrett and his son argued about car privileges. I commented that this fight was typical of those that transpire between teenagers and their parents, a sign that they must have been working hard as a family to help Tony grow up if they were having battles like this one. I learned that two months later, Tony did indeed move into a halfway house.

The developmental reframe, piggybacking on the rite-of-passage ritual, seemed to offer the family a new way of grappling with their contradictory attitudes toward Tony's leaving home. The ritual disentangled two paradoxical messages: go ahead and leave home, but if you do, we're not sure we will survive. The paradox was expressed in the presenting symptom of fights escalating as Tony got closer to leaving home. The ritual, using the fights to punctuate separation, transformed the symptom by making it at once explicit and more lighthearted. The developmental reframe, based on a benign description of their son, offered the parents something concrete to do as a team and implicitly gave permission to Tony to leave.

### Ritual 3: Time-Tripping

One of the most painful projects of adolescence is envisioning a future in which parents and their children remain connected even as they move physically apart. Anne Tyler's book *Ladder of Years* (1995), about a 40-year-old mother of three adolescents who one day walks out on her family and starts over in a small town, evokes a powerful fantasy: that parents can leave their kids before they are left and, in doing so, bypass the whole painful process of loss.

At the end of the book, the mother, Delia, has returned home to attend her daughter's wedding and decides to stay. Her three children have each managed to leave home during her absence. As she looks back on her year-and-a-half adventure, she calls it a "time trip that worked. What else would you call it when she'd ended up back where she'd started . . . When the people she had left behind had actually traveled further, in some ways" (p. 325). She reminisces about the moment she left her family and realizes that it was when her children were "poised to begin their journeys." Suddenly, we understand the mystery of why she left home: it was not, as it seemed in the beginning, because she felt taken for granted by her family; rather, Delia left because she didn't know how to say goodbye to her children or how to be with them when they were moving toward a future without her.

This book is a parable about separation between adolescents and their parents. Most important, it captures how mutual the process is: both adolescents and their parents are leaving and being left. Delia's solution to the ambiguity of the separation process was to remove herself from her almost-grown-up children, a solution that other families resort to, though not usually in such a literal and dramatic fashion. This story raises the clinical question: What other solutions to the pain of adolescent leave-taking are possible? Can families with adolescents take a "time trip" without resorting to Delia's drastic measures? A therapeutic ritual can be used.

When families come for help in negotiating their children's leave-taking, time travel is a powerful tool. Families can be asked to travel backward as well as forward. In going backward, the family is asked to consider what was left undone as a family and what they might still like to attempt with each other to prepare for the next developmental stage. In time-tripping ahead, families can be asked to envision a future in which they are physically separated but continue to have relationships with each other. Sometimes, therapy requires time-tripping in both directions. This feat was required with the Kleins, a mother and daughter pair who presented for help around recurring fights regarding the 18-year-old daughter's readiness to leave home.

Jane, the youngest of the four Klein children, 18 years old and the only daughter, had been sexually abused by a friend of the family from the time she was 13 until she was

16. A month before coming to family therapy, Jane had told her mother about the abuse. Mrs. Klein, who herself had been sexually abused as a teenager, was very upset by her daughter's disclosure and insisted on family therapy. Her reaction was complicated further by the knowledge of her own drug abuse during the time of her daughter's sexual abuse, activity that had made her unavailable to her daughter at a critical time. Mrs. Klein, now in recovery, wanted to hear about her daughter's abuse, to tell Jane about her own, and to apologize for years of emotional unavailability. Jane wanted none of it. She was angry with her mother and was counting the days until she graduated from high school and could leave home for college. Whenever Jane talked about her future plans, Mrs. Klein became tearful, explaining that she didn't want to lose Jane before they even knew each other, a repetition of her relationship with her own mother, whom Mrs. Klein had gotten to know only in the last years of her life.

The first frame for the therapy was a time-tripping one. I suggested that the constant fighting had to do with trying to live in two time zones simultaneously, a stunt that was next to impossible. Mother and daughter, it seemed, were behaving as if Jane were still 13, with the mother trying to repair the relationship that had gone off track when she herself had been abusing drugs. And they were interacting as if Jane were 18, on the verge of leaving home. The problem was that they could not live in these time zones at the same time. So, a ritual was recommended to give them two different times to explore their relationship together. On odd-numbered days, they both were to pretend that Jane was 13 and they were to talk about what she needed from her mother, about what had been lost at that point in her life, and about her mother's regrets. If Jane felt that she could forgive her mother for anything, she could tell her mother on these days. On even-numbered days, they were both to concentrate on Jane's being 18; they were to talk about Jane's plans for the future and about the kind of relationship they wanted to have with each other after Jane moved out.

The point of this ritual was twofold. First, their fighting was disrupted by offering a more collaborative frame. Second, two covert and painful time zones were made manifest—five years earlier, when Jane's sexual abuse started, and the near future, when Jane would leave home without closure reached about the past. Jane would be unwilling to look back in time with her mother unless her mother were willing to look forward with Jane. Similarly, the mother could not tolerate Jane's leave-taking without some conversation about the past. Both time frames needed to be talked about and lived in, with mother and daughter convinced that each would pay attention to the past *and* the future.

## Challenging the Cultural Discourse

A powerful way of interacting with families is to inquire about their adherence to the cultural discourse regarding adolescence and, when appropriate, to encourage their resistance to this discourse. Sometimes, a family's adherence to the discourse means that they minimize truly disturbing behavior. At other times, adherence to the discourse means that parents push their children away, making them reliant on other peers in the belief that remaining connected to family will stunt their adolescents' growth.

The cultural discourse that regards adolescent turmoil, withdrawal from parents, and extreme moodiness as expectable adolescent behavior encourages some parents to normalize the behavior of their adolescents, who are actually in great trouble. The catch-all phrase uttered by parents, teachers, and therapists—"That's just normal adolescent behavior"—means that some teenagers get overlooked.

Sandra, a 14-year-old, was dragged to see me by her mother, Mrs. Stone, who told me that her daughter refused to eat with the family and had failed all her subjects despite extra tutoring. In the first therapy hour, Sandra was almost completely mute. Her mother informed me that Sandra was not talking much more at home. Then Mrs. Stone apologized for bringing Sandra in to therapy for behavior that was "probably just normal." I suggested to the mother and daughter that they had fallen prey to a dangerous and erroneous cultural belief, prevalent in movies, music, and books, that teenagers are naturally moody and don't want their parents to know anything about them. I told Mrs. Stone that I was impressed with her willingness to stand up to this idea and question it by bringing her daughter to therapy. When she went along with the cultural idea of depression and silence as expectable adolescent behavior, it seemed that her daughter withdrew further. I encouraged the mother to continue to turn her back on this cultural teaching and to voice her many real concerns about Sandra. Once the mother resisted the cultural discourse and spoke at length about her observations of her daughter, Sandra started to talk about her consuming jealousy of an older brother who had recently transferred to a private school and about her terror attending a school where there were gangs.

Another aspect of this cultural discourse is the belief that parents should not talk truthfully about their lives to their teenagers and that teenagers should save their important self-disclosures for peers. Certain topics seem particularly off-limits for parents to discuss—not only their own experiences with mental and physical illness, sexuality, and drugs, but also their own dreams for the future and their own adolescences. Do parents fear that they will burden their children or that their adolescents won't be interested? It seems that it is in the clinical setting that these subjects are first broached. But research (Hauser et al. 1991) on the family's influence on healthy adolescent development suggests that it is good for teenagers if parents talk honestly about their own inner lives and relevant adolescent experiences. In *The Mother's Voice* (1994), Weingarten eloquently weaves together her own experience with breast cancer and mothering, to challenge the cultural message that mothers should silence themselves about their pain.

In identifying beliefs about adolescent development, the clinician may ask family members about their favorite films or books or what stories they find particularly compelling. Or the therapist can ask directly about a family's level of adherence or resistance to cultural beliefs about adolescent development. For example, instead of approaching adolescence with dread, what if families were asked, "What are the wonderful aspects of being the parent of an adolescent, the parts that defy having a 'terrible teen'?" or, a question that challenges the notion that parents need to support their children's separation and do so at the exclusion of ongoing connection with them—"How do parents and adolescents think that a child becomes grown up, *other than* by leaving home or by disconnecting from parents?" And we could ask, "What are the ways that parents and their children feel *more* connected to one another during adolescence than in previous stages?" And to challenge parents and adolescents who are reluctant to talk intimately with each other, "Are there any subjects you have at times wanted to broach with each other but felt somehow at a loss for words, or not so sure that the other was ready for such a conversation?" The conversations that ensue from such questions might very well start to shift the current discourse.

## Externalizing the Problem

Externalization of the problem is a multi-part technique (White and Epston 1990) aimed at detaching the problem from the adolescent so that he or she is no longer the focus of blame and no longer synonymous with badness (previously discussed in Chapter 2, pp. 53–54. Without any concern for why the symptom developed in the first place, the therapist instead shows curiosity about the current negative consequences of the behavior and the ways the problem spreads its tentacles into the family, disrupting relationships. By construing the problem as a meddlesome intruder or a mischievous monster, family members are invited to join forces against the problem rather than fight among themselves. The problems most amenable to change using this technique are those that crop up, with no clear antecedent or purpose, in response to developmental stressors. They may gain a foothold in part because parents expect adolescents to develop negative traits.

This technique does not invite curiosity about why the problem may have occurred in the first place or what it is trying to express. I have found this technique to be most effective when the problem is of fairly recent onset and when the family does not have a lot of ideas about the cause of the problem—in other words, when the problem seems to have come out of the blue and is at odds with the child as the parents thought they knew him. Often, the problem has quickly taken over their view of the child.

The beauty of this intervention is the way that normative adolescent assertiveness is used in the service of preserving connection to the family. For example, the technique relies on the language of rebellion and resistance, on the importance of standing up for yourself and using your power and courage. But instead of using all this energy to fight with each other over whose position is correct, the energy is transformed into a united struggle against the problem.

The technique begins with a shift in language. The problem is labeled as separate from the adolescent. Then, the adolescent and family are asked to describe the problem's effect on their lives and relationships. Subsequently, they are invited to reflect on their own effect on the problem, on the ways that they outfox and resist the problem. Any examples of resistance are then elaborated on to become alternative stories, different from the dominant problem story that the family initially presented with. A brief case example will illustrate the different components of this technique.

### The Boy with a Bad Temper

A pediatrician referred the Jenkins family to the adolescent crisis team after the 13-year-old son, Bob, punched his fist through a wall, breaking a bone in his hand. Bob was the younger of two brothers. His older brother, Philip, age 16, had been in trouble previously with drugs but had been clean for over a year.

Mr. and Mrs. Jenkins stated that Bob's temper had appeared out of nowhere. He had been an easy child, eager to please them, with many friends and well liked by most teachers. A learning disability had been diagnosed at the beginning of that eighth grade year, and Bob was currently in an LD classroom. Although Bob complained about being separated from his friends and about feeling stigmatized by his diagnosis, there had been no reports from the school of impulse-control problems or of difficulty getting along with peers and teachers. Bob's temper outbursts occurred only at home. About twice a week he went into his room and destroyed a piece of furniture or tore a poster off the wall. When asked in therapy what these outbursts were about, Bob said he hadn't taken the time to figure them out and his parents had been too busy to inquire. Bob complained broadly that his parents expected too much of him and that he felt misunderstood most of the time. During Bob's description of his temper, his parents looked genuinely puzzled and concerned: they regarded Bob as an easygoing child in contrast to Phil, the "high-maintenance child," whose moods they had always had to monitor.

Bob's temper had been a problem for about three months. When asked what they had already tried to do, Mrs. Jenkins said that she had made him pay for any property that he destroyed. Mr. Jenkins had lectured him about the dangers of a temper in turning people against you and in preventing you from getting and keeping a job. Mr. and Mrs. Jenkins had started talking to Bob about his being an angry and antisocial boy, although they felt uncomfortable with this description.

Because of the sudden appearance of this symptom and because of how entrenched the problem had quickly become, externalizing the problem seemed a good intervention choice. The first step was to introduce a way of talking about Bob's temper that separated him from his outbursts. I started asking Bob and his family about his "impatient temper," a temper that didn't take the time to find out what was really bothering him or to tell anyone in the family what he was upset about. Then I asked each family member about the influence of this impatient temper on each of them. For example: "How has Bob's temper affected the ways in which your relationships have developed over the past few months?" Bob stated that he is so ashamed of his temper that he avoids his parents even when he is feeling good. Mrs. Jenkins said that she is so braced for Bob's temper that she has stopped noticing anything else about him. Then family members were asked about "unique outcomes" or times when they had resisted the impatient temper or told it to slow down. For example: "Have there been any instances when Bob rebelled against his temper by taking the time to tell someone that he was feeling upset? Was there any time that you, Mr. Jenkins, could tell that impatience was starting to get the better of your son, and even though you were busy with something else and knew that asking about your son's upset would take some time, you decided to do so anyway?"

To expand on these instances or unique outcomes, family members are then asked "how" questions that help to develop an alternative story: for example, "Bob, how did you find the courage to stand up to your impatient temper and tell it to slow down?" To the mother: "What does this power of Bob's to say no to his temper tell you about him that you didn't know before?" Additional questions can be asked that take the alternative story into a larger context of people and into a different time frame: for example, "Of all the people you have known, who would be least surprised to hear that you have been able to take this step? What would you predict about Bob's future, knowing what you do now about his ability to stand up to his temper?"

The therapist, with the family's agreement and then input, can write a letter about the family's progress in resisting Bob's impatient temper and send it to those who had been involved in seeing Bob as having a bad temper. Such a letter was sent to Bob's grandparents, who had been very concerned about his transformation from a "good kid" to a "bad" one. In other cases, a letter is sent to a previous therapist or school principal, or anyone else who had been involved in the old story about the child that focused on the problem.

# 5

# Interventions for Long-Term Therapy and Consultations

The two interventions—story-oriented genograms and reflecting teams—described in this chapter are somewhat arbitrarily separated from the previous five. They are certainly additional examples of developmentally informed, narrative ways of interacting with adolescents and their families. These two interventions, however, in contrast to the previous ones, tend to take place over several sessions and do not include a discrete set of questions or an end-of-session task for the family to take home with them.

## GENOGRAM WORK

The genogram is a visual and symbolic representation of a family tree that charts in one picture the patterns of many generations of a family. Although the genogram has been used by medical physicians (Jolly et al. 1980) and by psychodynamic therapists (Paul and Paul 1975, Wachtel 1982), its use among systemically oriented therapists depends on Bowenian theory. Monica McGoldrick (1995, McGoldrick and Gerson 1985) has written accessible and cogent books applying Bowenian theory to the analysis of dozens of genograms. She draws on Bowen's notions of multigenerational transmission of family patterns, the salience of relationship triangles, and relational characteristics, including distance, complementarity, and balance, to interpret genograms (1985).

Genograms can be put to clinical use in a variety of ways. They can be used as a simple information-gathering tool so that a clinician can garner a great deal of historical data quickly and efficiently, including names, important dates, illnesses, and ethnic background of key family members. The genogram is also a powerful instrument for changing a family climate of self-blame and recrimination. By enabling family members to see themselves as part of a much larger picture, fingerpointing at one individual gives way to awe for the complex intergenerational patterns at work.

The genogram is also an elegant way of tracking what McGoldrick and Gerson (1985) refer to as "vertical anxiety," or the stresses that are passed down through the generations, and "horizontal anxiety," or current difficulties. Families that encounter an intersection of these two axes will experience compounded difficulties. For example, a mother and father came to therapy with concern about their 18-year-old son who, in the previous six months had gained 50 pounds, refused to go out of the house, and dropped out of school. When asked about the parents' experiences of their own late adolescence, powerful information about the "vertical anxiety" in the family was revealed. The mother had had her first manic break at age 18, and the father had not moved out of the house until he married at age 30, at which point his parents had disowned him.

In my work with adolescents and their parents, I have used the genogram in a more interactive, interventive, and narrative fashion, which I will refer to as "the story-oriented genogram." By going beyond the factual genogram data and also asking for stories about a family, the central beliefs and values held by the family are revealed. The therapist's aim is to figure out what the family's central themes, metaphors, and dominant story lines are, and then work like a biographer, helping the family members to write a different version of their story.

By asking for descriptions of family members, the therapist will start to hear an overlap of certain types of adjectives that suggest what is most valued by the family. For example, in one family, members will be delineated according to how selfish or care-giving they are, while in others, marital failures and successes will be highlighted, and in still others, creativity and financial worth will be stressed.

The therapist can also ask directly for stories about family members and around the presenting problem: "What can you tell me about the family you grew up in that will help me understand the difficulties you are having today?" Or to parents of adolescent children, "Tell me the central stories about your own adolescence?" These stories are fascinating and deeply revealing. Consider a family of two parents with two children who, every night at the dinner table, has each person tell one story about the day. Over the course of 18 years, this family will generate more than 26,000 stories, a number that does not include stories told at family gatherings by other family members or stories told at bedtime or on car rides. However, despite this enormous pool of stories, when families are asked to tell their most important stories, typically there is consensus about which handful of stories is most significant and emblematic. The selected stories have particular meaning because they have been told and retold and because they contain some particular message or meaning that is significant to that family. Often, there is a recurring moral to the stories told, such as "Beware of good things because bad things always follow," or "Don't aim too high," or "Those who take risks will be richly rewarded."

In my genogrammatic work, these stories need not be regarded as sacred texts but rather as material to be rewritten; by rearranging stories, or highlighting an overlooked part of the family, or eliciting and then underscoring a nearly forgotten piece of history, one can help families rewrite their own three-generational narrative. The technique and purpose of a story-oriented genogram can best be illustrated through a clinical case. Through this case, involving a middle-aged couple with adolescent children, I will outline an approach that includes the gathering of historical data, descriptions of family members, and important family stories. Using McGoldrick and Gerson's (1985) method of analyzing the abundance of data collected, I will then present a new story that I wrote based on the genogram material.

The genogram usually belongs to the middle phase of therapy, particularly when it embodies more than history-taking. The genogram is an imposing tool, and families may feel that their own initial presentations have been overshadowed if the genogram is introduced too early. Instead, it can be referred to at the end of an evaluation as something that will be used later to deepen their understanding of their dilemmas. The story-oriented genogram can also be used when a critical family member is missing but should be included in the therapy. Then, with the family's permission, a letter based on the genogram material can be sent to the missing member.

Increasingly, I use the story-oriented genogram when I am feeling stuck because the same material or the same fight is repeated, and a dramatic change in context is required. Therefore, it is usually not part of short-term therapy, since it takes a period of time to get mired enough to use this intervention. It was with this urge to interrupt an entrenched pattern that I introduced genogram work to Paul and Karen Brown.

Paul, 52, and Karen, 48, came to see me with concerns about their lack of intimacy, an uneasy feeling about their ability to move forward in their work lives, and worries about their two daughters, one who had taken time off from college and the other who had graduated but had no job.

About a year before coming to therapy, Mr. and Mrs. Brown had uprooted from the south, where they had grown up, raised their children, and left behind all of their extended family. The purpose of this relocation to Boston was to allow Paul to pursue a graduate degree in public health and to liberate Karen from the care-giving role she held in her family of origin. Now, a year later, the move had profoundly unsettled the Brown family. Both daughters were living at home, Mr. Brown was unemployed, and Mrs. Brown had several projects in mind for herself, particularly a trip to the Far East, but couldn't get started on any one of them; she was waiting for her daughters and husband to make the first move toward finding a career direction before she felt that she could. Summing up the family's current developmental status, she said, "Every Brown is in transition."

With the Brown couple, the genogram work was the final piece of therapy we did, following a year of once-a-week couples therapy. In part, the genogram was initiated to include the daughters, who refused to attend therapy meetings. In addition, while the couple's intimacy had improved, they had not moved as a couple or as a family to having any direction in their work lives. The story-oriented genogram was aimed at putting their impasses around work into a three-generational context.

This work generally starts with a basic question: "What can you tell me about your families that will help me understand your current impasse or dilemma?" I asked the Browns to tell me family stories about work and money, how relationships changed after retirement, and about family loyalty. I will relate a sampling of the stories they related to me.

Paul told of his father's father making a fortune early in life in banking and then retiring by age 50 to pursue exotic philanthropic pursuits. These pursuits involved

international travel with his wife and resulted in the neglect of their five children. He then took up flying and
sailing but frequently "had his wings clipped" by hospital-
izations for manic-depressive illness. Paul felt that his
father never really found work that he loved and that
his avocations were all solitary and risky (made more so
by his illness). Paul's mother tried to "control the universe"
in an attempt to keep her husband's manic depression
under control. Paul's sister, Helen, who made a suicide
attempt in her teens, had arranged a rather unconven-
tional life for herself. She and her husband were costume
designers for a community theater. Paul, clearly his
mother's preferred child, had been given the family's second home, an act of preferential treatment that had long
strained the siblings' relationship. Paul's mother had demanded complete loyalty from Paul and discouraged him
from having contact with his sister. During the previous
year, Paul had gone behind his mother's back and visited
his sister and her husband after many years of estrange-
ment.

Karen's father had switched careers at midlife, a move
that made Karen's mother very nervous because her family had lost all their money in the Depression, a loss that
precipitated her mother's father's suicide at the age of 48.
Karen's mother rarely complained directly to her husband,
as that would be seen as a sign of weakness on her part.
Rather, she remained a "loyal wife" by not letting on how
distressed she was by her husband's less lucrative and
more pleasurable mid-life switch. As always, Karen's
mother tried to put others' needs ahead of her own and
suffered alone, a code of femininity she urged her daughter to follow as a wife and mother.

The genogram, along with these stories, generates enough
information to be analyzed by McGoldrick and Gerson's (1985)

interpretive principles. This analysis, focusing on three principles—life cycle fit, pattern repetition, and clustering of life events—is a necessary preparation for the genogram letter that follows.

Life cycle fit refers to the extent to which life events have occurred within normative expectations for the culture and for this particular family. In analyzing the Browns, I was struck by the number of retirements and changes in work lives that occurred in family members' middle age, the age of Karen and Paul. For example, Paul's paternal grandfather retired in his late forties and his father retired at 50. Karen's maternal grandfather committed suicide at age 48 after a financial loss, and her father changed jobs when he was in his early fifties. Karen and Paul made a break from their families, and Paul began graduate school to ready himself for a second career in his and Karen's late forties.

Analysis of "pattern repetition," in functioning and in family roles over the generations, revealed several recurring themes. On both sides of the family there are alternating attempts to find security and to take risks, attempts that are quite bold and extreme. Many males pursue careers in banking, only to forgo them in middle age and pursue risky and daring avocations, including flying and travel to exotic lands. These riskier pursuits seem to tax marriages and families, with children getting neglected and wives becoming overburdened by the freewheeling lives of their husbands. The most disturbing pattern involved several suicides and suicide attempts, including Karen's grandfather and Paul's sister (an attempt as a teenager), and the risk-taking of Paul's father's sister's son and daughter (who died in a motorcycle accident).

A third principle, identifying the recent pile-up of life events, highlighted the profound changes demanded of the

Brown couple in their move to Boston. In June, 1993, Karen's mother was diagnosed with cancer. Within months the Brown couple had relocated to Boston from the South, and two months after their move, Paul's mother had died.

Reflecting on these principles and patterns, stories and themes, I constructed a letter to the Browns that was aimed at recontextualizing their current stuckness around work in a three-generational framework. What follows are excerpts from the letter I read to Paul and Karen and subsequently sent to them.

Dear Paul and Karen,

I wanted to share with you some reflections I've had, prompted by Karen's comment to Paul several weeks ago, "Why don't you just retire? Then you'd be free to do what you want." It seemed that you were posing a dilemma here that has been posed by both your families over the generations: Is it possible to be en-sured security and take risks? Can you be free and loyal at the same time? Your family stories point to an almost unequivocal no. Let me tell you what I've heard about the difficulties that family members have encountered trying to take risks and still play it safe, trying to be loyal to a family and free to be an individual.

When parents were free to pursue their own interests, as with Paul's father's parents, they were grossly neglectful. Paul, when your father got free of his job and was able to pursue his real love of flying, his wings were clipped by illness. There are many in both families who pursued careers in insurance (Paul's father and father's father, Karen's maternal grandfather and sister), perhaps hoping to provide security to others. There are also many family members who pursued bold attempts to fly free, lit-erally in airplanes, motorcycles, even suicide.

Loyalty to family has been highly prized by both families, too, even when it came at great personal cost. Karen learned that it is disloyal to ask for help, put yourself first, ask questions, or com-plain about your spouse, and that the cost of maintaining loyalty is missing out on finding important missing pieces. Actually, you've risked being a bit disloyal, by moving out of your care-taker role with your family and moving out of the south. Paul, you believed for a long time that it was disloyal to your mother to become close to your sister, but you chanced that and began to get to know your sister even while your mother was still alive.

What I see is that each is trying to help the other take more risks. You each give each other advice from the heart: "Paul, go ahead and retire. Make mistakes, the world won't end." "Karen, feel free to take a trip by yourself. Go ahead and complain about what you don't like, voice your own opinions." But what seems to happen is that taking a risk alone is not enough to silence the backlash from family legacies you have both internalized: the legacy that says it is disloyal to your families to put yourself first, to suffer loudly, to complain, to make mistakes. I wonder what would happen if instead of taking turns at taking risks, you traveled together. Instead of encouraging the other to take a chance, you grabbed the other's hand and took off into the unknown to-gether. What, for example, would it be like to plan Karen's trip together, even if she took it alone? Or brainstormed together about a road trip for Paul to take with his sister? Or complained and grumbled together about your families, or took a class in something that neither of you knows anything about? Pursued alone, each of these adventures seems almost certain to crumble under the weight of the previous generations decrying you as disloyal. How can you leave your family even for a week to travel alone, Karen? Paul, what will you and your sister talk about in a car when you've never been that close? This is how I imagine the ghosts of family loyalty rising up to squelch such new plans.

It will take hard work on both of your parts to learn how to relax, if we understand relax as meaning being fully engaged in whatever you are doing. I think that learning this hard work, as it applies to new projects, plans for travel, writing, and having conversations with each other and with your daughters, will be a new legacy to give to your children, a way of teaching them that a child may have multiple loyalties.

In this letter I am trying to say to the Browns, "Look at what you're up against, no wonder it's hard to make a change at midlife to something that is less staid. Let me help you stand in awe of what your legacy is and therefore relax the self-criticism." In fact, I tell them that the legacy of conformity and dire consequences when individuals break with conformity is so powerful that the best strategy is to combine forces rather than urge each other on individually. In addition, I am mindful of a polarity in their conversation with each other that inhibits them: either you work hard at a job or give up, relax, and don't work. These are categories that previous generations have been constrained by, too. In my letter, I try to blur these categories and suggest that one can work hard at relaxing and that relaxation can lead to full engagement.

The Browns were intrigued by this letter and decided to take a break from therapy and see how far they could get on their own, drawing on their new insights and improved capacity for communication. A year later Karen told me that she and Paul were doing well, one daughter had returned to college while the other was launched in a career. The letter remained on their refrigerator so that they could refer to it as needed.

## Use of the Reflecting Team

The history of reflecting teams bears no special relationship to adolescents and their families. The team was first used, quite spontaneously, in 1985 by a Norwegian psychiatrist, Tom Andersen, and three of his colleagues at the Romso University. In observing an interview from behind a one-way mirror, Andersen recalls that the therapist repeatedly got inducted into the family's pessimistic outlook, regardless of the more upbeat questions suggested by the team. Finally, after three failed attempts at redirecting the interview, "We launched the idea to the family and the therapist that we might talk while they listened to us. Our fears made us hope they would not accept the offer, but they did" (Andersen 1995,

p. 17). By having the team speak directly to the family, in many voices, without first screening their comments, the idea of the reflecting team was born.

Since that time, the reflecting team has evolved as a way of mobilizing tremendous change. The method of reflecting is itself very flexible and conducive to a variety of settings. In a private practice office, the lone practitioner may make reflections to him- or herself as a family listens in. In a clinic or hospital setting, reflections can be made by a team working from behind a one-way mirror, or, where there is no mirror, a reflecting team may sit in the same room as the clients.

Regardless of the team's format, its purpose is to allow shifts between listening and talking, movement that generates new ideas and perspectives for both clients and therapists. Lussardi and Miller (1991) offer this description of the switching from talking to listening made by the clients and the team:

> It is the movement from one explanation to many, which allows information, new meanings, the possibility for new behavior to occur. . . . Listening to a version of their story, as understood by a team of therapists from behind a one-way mirror, can make the story seem bigger than life. The effect may be similar to the phenomenon of watching a movie on a big screen, in which characters and their problems seem more dramatic. [p. 235]

## The Practice of Reflecting

The practice of being a reflector requires adherence to one of the main principles of second-order cybernetics: that is, that family therapists are not separated from the family by their expert status but instead are part of the system they are observing. So, for example, reflectors may comment on their own emotional reactions to case material and may use associations to their own relationships and families.

Over the years, guidelines (Andersen 1991, Griffith and Griffith 1994) have been offered for being an effective reflector. Andersen (1991), for example, suggests that "the rules we have are all about what we shall *not do*" (p. 61). Specifically, he informs us that we should not comment on information we learned about the clients outside of the current context, and we should not make negative comments. As far as what reflectors should do, Andersen advises here, too. Reflections should be made tentatively, without the authority of an expert's opinion, so that clients feel free to reject whatever points of view they do not find helpful. Team members are encouraged to talk among themselves, in order to maintain the separation between listening and talking positions. If the team looks directly at the clients, they may feel pressured to respond rather than listen. Reflectors are coached to present both sides of a dilemma, moving from an "either-or" position to a "both-and" one. If a reflector agrees with a previous comment, he or she is still required to come up with an original reflection so as to suggest that there are multiple points of view and not just one solution. Finally, Andersen urges reflectors to be mindful to pitch their remarks at the optimal level of familiarity. In other words, reflections should not be too similar to the clients' own words that they make no impact. Nor should they be so unusual that the clients reject the comments as bizarre or outlandish. The possible contents of reflections include the following partial list: making a self-disclosure, listening for a metaphor and then expanding on it, posing questions to the therapist about their feelings or ideas, asking the family about a topic that was not discussed during the interview, offering an alternative description of a family's problem, suggesting an experiment for the family to conduct at home, or making a normative comment about family development.

Over the course of several years of using a reflecting team, my colleagues and I have been impressed with the impact of a team's reflections. At times, however, we observed that the impact was greater than a family could absorb in one sitting. Eyes glazed over, or family members told us outright that they felt overwhelmed by the sheer number of comments made to them. Emboldened by research indicating the impact of letters on clients (Hylund and Thomas 1994), we decided to experiment with sending a letter to every family following a reflecting team encounter. The letter includes both a summary of the reflections and the family's comments made in response to the reflections. A letter that summarizes only the reflectors' comments may elevate the team to the status of experts, a status at odds with the nonhierarchical spirit in which the reflections were originally offered.

The feedback to us from families regarding these letters has been uniformly positive. Many clients have told us that the letter was even more helpful than the live reflections. Perhaps the written form promotes true reflection, allowing clients to take in whatever they wish, without any expectation of having to respond. The letter-writing has also been a useful teaching tool, allowing teams to observe, retrospectively, their own reflecting process. For example, the letters document which type of reflections team members are most comfortable offering and which ones they tend to avoid and therefore need to work on.

## Variations on the Reflecting Team Format to Accommodate Adolescents and Their Families

Although using the reflecting team is not a specialized technique for adolescents and families, there are several adaptations that make it well suited to work with this population. How the family can be subdivided and reflected to as a whole and separately and the use of peers as reflectors make the reflecting team an important mode of interacting with adolescents and their parents.

## Dividing Up the Reflections

If, in the course of an interview, it becomes evident that there are certain issues that create tension in the room, the interviewer may suggest breaking into smaller subgroups (typically, parents in one group and adolescents in another) and excusing those who do not want to talk about a particular issue. Then, the reflectors can comment to each of the subgroups as well as to the family as a whole. In this way, the reflections make a "both-and" statement to the family: you are a family *and* you have separate concerns as a couple and as adolescents.

Mr. and Mrs. Leopold and their 18-year-old daughter, Samantha, came to me for a reflecting team consultation. Samantha, the youngest of three, was planning on leaving for college in five months' time. The Leopolds had been in family therapy to work on the bitter fights that the mother and Samantha had been having over the use of the car and the mother's wish that "her daughter not leave home like this." The Leopolds' therapist requested a consultation regarding who should be attending the meetings. Should the mother and daughter come without the father to work on their fights? Should the mother come alone because she seemed depressed? Should Samantha come by herself to explore her feelings about leaving home? Or was there a hidden marital problem that would best be addressed in couples treatment?

Within the first five minutes, the family gave me clues about who they thought needed therapy. As I introduced myself and reviewed the reflecting team format, Mrs. Leopold was quietly weeping. When I asked her about her tears, she told me that it was about "something, not for mixed company." When pressed, she explained that mixed company meant her husband and daughter. Next, Samantha said to me, "I don't care if they stay together or separate, as long as they're happy." Piecing together the unspoken and the spoken, I surmised that the Leopold couple was struggling to stay together for the sake of their daughter, at least until she left for college. I understood Samantha's giving permission to them about separating as her wanting to be out of their marital decision-making and free to leave for college. To help untangle Samantha's leave-taking from the marriage, I suggested that we divide our reflecting time so that part of the interview would be with just the couple and part with all three of them. Correspondingly, reflections were initially made just to the couple, and then Samantha joined her parents and the therapist to listen in on the second set of reflections.

Subsequently, in an adaptation of the reflecting team format, I wrote two letters to the Leopolds, summarizing the reflections: one to the couple and the other to the family.

The reflections and the letters were able to tease apart the overlapping strands—the marital, parent–child, and family issues. By addressing the different subsystems sequentially, the consultation clarified the initial question about who should be in treatment. With Samantha's blessing and to her great relief, the Leopolds began weekly couples therapy to determine whether they had any reason to stay together now that the children were successfully launched.

### Use of Peers as Reflectors

As adolescents' lives become more and more entwined with systems outside the family—from the media to peers to schools to legal and social services—it sometimes makes sense to include these other systems in the treatment of adolescents. Matthew Selekman (1995), a Chicago-based family therapist, has developed a way of using the peer system as reflectors for adolescents in therapy. His method stands out as unusual in my review of peers as adjuncts to family therapy, despite convincing developmental research stressing the often positive role played by peers in the lives of adolescents (Haber 1987, Meire et al. 1984). Selekman advocates several ways that adolescent peers can be used as reflectors. First, when there is an impasse around trust between parents and their adolescents, merely introducing peers can help. For example, parents can interview peers about the activities they do with their son or daughter. Second, peers can be enlisted to act as a support group, particularly when an adolescent is resistant to joining a more established group, such as Alcoholics Anonymous or Narcotics Anonymous. Peers may agree to establish a hot line or share ideas with a friend's parents about what their own parents did to help them become drug-free. Peers may also be asked to act as consultants to ongoing family therapy, perhaps reporting on positive changes they have observed the adolescent client making in school.

The process of inviting peers to family therapy requires several steps, as outlined by Selekman. He recommends exploring the idea of bringing in peers with the adolescent client and the parents. Next, the adolescent is delegated to explain to his or her peers the problem and the rationale for involving peers. If the peers agree to participate, their parents must be contracted by the adolescent's parents to explain the rationale of having these adolescents involved. Selekman also has his clients sign consent forms allowing him to release confidential information to peers and the peers' parents, if necessary. Not surprisingly, peer involvement is contraindicated when there is strong gang affiliation or heavy substance abuse.

### Choosing among the Techniques

There is no formula for deciding which of these techniques to use or in what combination. The approaches can be used singly or all at once, as part of a reflecting team intervention. Life-cycle messages and developmental reframes are helpful when families are so filled with ill will and blame that they have no energy left over to devote to problem solving. Rituals are often most useful when a family is stuck in a paradoxical bind, such as wanting their child to grow up and not grow up at the same time. The fast-forwarding techniques seem most applicable with families who are struggling with the transition to leaving home. Challenging the cultural discourse is helpful when families have preconceived notions about adolescence and when their notions are constraining them from having open, free-wheeling conversations. The story-oriented genogram is the most complicated and, perhaps, the most powerful of all the techniques described. Because it requires so much time on the part of the therapist, it may be the approach of last resort.

These ways of interacting should not supplant the respectful, empathic listening that is the hallmark of any good therapist, regardless of his or her theoretical orientation. Sometimes, too, the sheer act of bringing a whole family together is in itself the most powerful intervention of all. And then there is one last intervention to use, one that also honors a developmental approach. It is the one I think of when all else has failed, a strategy that parents have been using through the ages to deal with their adolescent children. It is a strategy my own parents used with me. It went like this. Behind closed doors, but loud enough to be heard, my mother would say to my father, "You won't believe the trouble Anne got into today." My father would listen, and in his unflappable way, say, "Well, I think it's just a stage she's going through. With time, she'll pass out of it." And my mother would respond, "We should only live so long." Despite my mother's pessimism, there is always the hope, when all else fails, that time will intervene and rescue us, adolescents and their families, ushering us all into another developmental stage.

# PART III

## DEVELOPMENTAL VARIATIONS

# 6

# The Perpetual Adolescent:
# Families Stuck in Adolescence,
# or "We're a Family That Won't
# Grow Up"

One common clinical presentation is an adolescent who appears unable or unwilling to grow up. The picture may be of a young person who has made no attempt to leave home after high school graduation, or one who has dropped out of college and returned home without any plans for the future. It may also be a family whose children are not chronologically the age of adolescents but whose stage of development is that of a family unable to move on to the next stage of launching these young adult children.

This chapter will explore the family drama that accompanies this stage of development in which adolescents—or young adults—are preparing to separate and instead get stuck. While there are certainly many adolescents whose development is tragically impeded by the onset of psychosis, attention here is not directed at severe mental illness. Rather, the focus is on those youths whose difficulties in growing up are related to dynamics within the family.

A clinical case of a family with six children grappling with this stage will launch the chapter. Subsequently, research and theory about the family factors that impede or facilitate such a passage will be discussed. The case presented includes both adolescent and young adult children. They are an excellent example of a family paralyzed by the task of negotiating the departure of the children. A symptomatic family member, a parental loss coinciding with leave-taking, and a tangled web of three-generational beliefs about growing up—all these issues characterize the case and are some of the factors present in other developmentally stuck families.

## THE BRUNOS: A FAMILY THAT DOESN'T WANT TO BREAK UP

Mrs. Bruno, a 57-year-old mother of six children ranging in age from 15 to 25, was referred to me by her internist, a year after her husband's death. She complained to her physician that she felt overwhelmed by difficulties with her children, who were not helping with any of the burdens of running a large house but instead were trying to run her life the way her husband had done when he was alive. She was experiencing occasional anxiety attacks with chest pains and palpitations. The internist referred her for individual psychotherapy and a medication evaluation, in addition to the family therapy consultation with me. She followed through only on this last recommendation. (Much later, she told me that she had been hospitalized many years earlier for postpartum depression, after her fourth child was born in the same number of years, and had not felt helped by medication or individual therapy.)

At the initial appointment, Mrs. Bruno arrived accompanied by five of her six children. She was a small-boned Irish woman with a raspy smoker's voice and porcelain, unlined skin. She spoke rapidly, with a frankness that was disarming. In the first few minutes she told me her chief complaint: "We're a family that doesn't want to grow up," referring to the fact that of her six children, only her eldest daughter, Rose, had moved away. Rose, age 24, had driven from Maine to Boston for the appointment. She had the unique status in the family of having left physically; that leave-taking had taken place four years before when, pregnant, she eloped with a man whom her father disliked and whom she divorced soon after her daughter was born. Next oldest was Ted, age 23, who was born prematurely with a congenital heart defect. He announced that he and his mother had always had a combative relationship, including her abuse of him when he was young. Peter, age 22, had been engaged to be married for two years and continued to live at home. Kevin, age 18, had been diagnosed with learning disabilities and was completing a vocational program. Helen, age 15, made it very clear that she had been dragged to the appointment and wished that she were with her friends. Missing from the meeting was Robert, Jr., age 25, whom the rest of the family discussed with a mixture of concern and fear. Ted told me that Robert had been abusing cocaine and selling drugs since their father's death. When I asked why Robert had not come to the initial meeting, Mrs. Bruno told me that he had not been told about it. She believed that it would be dangerous to confront him with their knowledge of his substance abuse, and she had instructed her children to pretend that nothing was awry. To me, she said, "I would be afraid he would punch a hole in your wall if he were to come here."

Curious about what else besides Robert's drug abuse had occurred since the father's death, I asked if there had been any other changes. Most striking were all the ways in which the family continued to be organized the same way it had been before the father's death. When the father was alive, the children never listened to the mother but would wait for the father to tell them what to do. Since his death a year earlier, they were still turning a deaf ear to her requests for help, but without the father there, the house was falling apart. In addition, just as the father had been abusive to the mother, Robert had now become abusive toward his siblings by threatening violence if they asked him of his whereabouts. Just as no one was allowed to comment on the father's drinking and out-of-control behavior, so the family now had an unspoken pact not to interfere with Robert's drug abuse. I got the distinct impression that the family was stuck in time.

This first session ended with my observation that there was a controversy in the family about whether the family needed a replacement father, in the guise of one of the sons, or whether all members could share in filling the hole left by the father and together make a new family. As we made plans to meet in two weeks, Mrs. Bruno said wryly, "We're a household of all heads with no hands."

In the second session, attended by Mrs. Bruno, Rose, Ted, Kevin, and Helen, the conversation focused on the late Robert, Sr. The family reviewed the course of his long illness, his chemotherapy treatments, and the long-standing competition among the siblings over whom the father loved most. It became apparent that this was the first family conversation about the father that the Brunos had had in years. Quite spontaneously, what followed this talk about the father were contrasting stories about leaving home that Mrs. Bruno offered about herself and her husband. She had gotten a job at age 16 and had been on her own by age 21, while her husband, who came from a large first-generation Italian family, had not left home until years after becoming a husband and father. Mrs. Bruno recounted that her husband had forbidden Robert, Jr., from attending college in a nearby state because that would have meant leaving home. Ted added that he had been the only one to attend college, tearfully explaining that he had felt kicked out of the house and had been so depressed over his leave-taking that he had never studied. The session ended with the family making predictions about who would be next to leave home. They were in agreement that it would be Kevin, now 17, who, as the eldest of the second group of children, had been far more influenced by the mother than the father.

In the third session, Mrs. Bruno, at her own suggestion, came alone. She wanted to discuss many difficult subjects without her children present. She spoke regretfully of the physical abuse she had visited on her children, particularly on her son Ted, who had had multiple heart operations as a child. She told me that the seeds of abuse had been sown by her own mother, who was abusive toward her, and by her father, who had threatened to murder her mother. She talked, too, of the burden of caring for her elderly and infirm mother, who had moved into the Bruno home a month before coming to family therapy. With resignation she stated, "In this day and age, everyone pushes everyone out the door. No one wants to be bothered with an elderly parent. But she's a little bird, and what do you do? You assume the responsibility." She then talked about the years of sacrifice she had made to her husband, who had been ill for almost a decade, a husband who had been physically abusive toward her in her younger years. She talked about his family, whom she bitterly resented for the multitude of ways they had meddled in her marriage. However, she conceded that she and her husband agreed on at least one thing—the importance of taking care of one's own parents as they became aged. With these comments, she added another generational layer to the conversation about leaving home—that while she believed that her children should learn independence in adolescence, they should not turn their backs on their parents in time of need. (As it turned out, many years later when she fell ill, her children heeded this legacy.)

In subsequent sessions, attention focused on Robert and what to do about his substance abuse. The family (except for Robert) and I met to discuss the different ways that they could confront Robert about his substance abuse, including involving members of the extended family. His potential for violence was talked about as a real and frightening possibility, and a safety plan was drawn up to deal with this possibility. The safety plan included a shared willingness to call the police and to vacate the house as soon as any member of the family felt intimidated by Robert. I emphasized the need to take a small action initially and to learn from it, rather than to take on Robert's substance abuse, his potential for violence, and his stealing from family members to pay for drugs, all at once. However, it soon became clear that the family was unable to follow through on any of the plans they committed themselves to in our family meetings. It seemed that this approach—directive, mobilizing of the family to deal with a crisis—was insufficient because it did not take into account the function that Robert's substance abuse served for this family: that of keeping the father in the family past the time of his death.

Because of the dilemma I faced in doing therapy with a family that would not allow a critical family member to attend meetings and because of the failure of more straightforward strategies to confront Robert, I decided to take a very different tack: I proposed doing a story-oriented genogram with a lengthy message back to the family, which I could then share with Robert by sending it to him. Over the course of two sessions I conducted a story-oriented genogram with different constellations of the Brunos, including Robert at one session. In particular, I tracked the themes, over the past generations, of leaving home and staying in contact with the family once leave-taking had occurred.

During these two sessions, I found out that when the father was alive, the major difference in opinion between the mother and father had been about leaving home. The mother fiercely believed in the importance of getting out into the world by age 20 or 21, while the father and his family had considered leaving home to be a major betrayal. In fact, the father was the only one of five children who had managed to get married, and then only at age 37. He and his new wife had lived with his parents for another three years until his wife insisted that they rent their own apartment.

The genogram letter, read during the tenth session to Mrs. Bruno, Ted, Kevin, and Helen, with copies sent to every family member separately, contained the following excerpts:

I want to say that I have been very impressed with your family, with your willingness to talk about many different topics even when this was painful and involved disagreement. You have been willing to persevere with these sessions, even when some members have felt bad after them, and you have all managed to find a way to come to some meetings, offering a great deal of information to think about. It seems that these efforts reflect your dedication to each other and your caring for one another.

In all formal verbal and written communications to a family, I begin with something positive about the family as a whole. This immediately conveys the systemic message that the family, rather than any single family member, will be my focus. Also, I believe that family members will be more open to another's point of view in a context of respect—I expect that the Bruno family will be less defensive and more interested in what follows after an introduction that conveys an appreciation of them.

When you first came to see me and as the months have rolled on, the main dilemma you presented me with is, "Can we pull together as a family or should we break up and go our separate ways?"

This is a summary statement of the family's polarized views about growing up. It is also a very common construction of the possibilities available for growing up, one that leads many families to feel stuck. There appear to be only two routes available to the children, with each represented by either the mother or the father: a Bruno becomes an adult by breaking away from the family and having little to do with them (the mother's stated view) or, a Bruno stays physically close to the family of origin, forgoing commitments to one's own home and family (the father's view). But neither of these trajectories to adulthood is possible for most of the Bruno children. Staying close pulls the family into an organization that existed when the father was alive but that is no longer viable now that he has died. Since his death, the three eldest males have moved into a competition with each other, vying over who will replace the father. Robert, as the eldest, seems to have appropriated the father's role as a substance abuser and physical threat. The path that the mother seems to be advocating is not straightforward either. While saying she wants the children to leave, she seems to need them at home to take care of her own mother and her house and to distract her from her grief over her husband's death. Moreover, a move out of the house could be seen by the others as being disloyal to the father, who had asked Robert on his deathbed to take care of the mother. Thus, the two paths that are offered as models are not available in practice. It is this contradiction that is contributing to how stuck the family is.

> Usually, Mrs. Bruno, you have represented the view that your children should grow up and move away, pointing to your own experience that you grew up by getting out of your family's house. Ted, on the other hand, you seem to be pulling for family cohesion, even though you, along with Rose, have learned the lesson best from your mother about how to grow up. Ted, you tell your mother that the way for family cohesion is for her to be more of a guiding spirit, especially to Robert, whom the family sees as a lost soul.
>
> However, in my thinking about your family, I do not think that the problem is whether to pull together or split apart. Rather, I think the main dilemma is how to keep the memory of Robert, Sr., father and husband, alive in the family.

Once I have located the recurring polarized beliefs that contribute to the family's being stuck, I try to reframe them.

Instead of the dilemma being about growing up, where the battle lines have been drawn for years, I suggest that it concerns the most fitting way to observe the memory of Robert, Sr. This perspective, because it is new and has not been talked about much, is far more fluid and permeable to conversation, new ideas, and stories.

> It seems that the main way you remember him right now is by keeping alive a debate about leaving home, a debate that raged when he was alive. This is a very familiar debate to all of you. When your father was alive, he took the position that the family should stay together at any cost. His life experience was that he lived at home until he was 37 years old and even when he married he maintained very close ties with his mother and siblings. He vigorously discouraged his kids from leaving home. In particular, he didn't want Robert to go away to college and he was unhappy when Rose moved away. When he was alive, he and your mother had many disagreements about when was the right time for you to leave home. Mrs. Bruno, you have believed that your children should be on their own by 21 or 22, while your husband thought that they should never leave home. With your husband and father gone, you have each come up with a way of keeping this lively disagreement going and so of remembering your father in a daily way.

I have taken stories that are very familiar to the Bruno family and created a new montage with them. I am suggesting that the different stories about growing up represent a debate that existed when the father was alive and that persists even after his death as a memorial to him. I then address a paragraph to each family member, highlighting the personal cost to him or her of participating in this kind of memorial.

> Mrs. Bruno, you keep the debate alive by insisting that you want the kids to move out even though it is clear to me that your feelings on this subject are far more complex. In particular, you seem

to have a yearning to be more connected to your children, but perhaps that can only happen when they have won your respect by becoming more self-sufficient.

Rose, I am not sure of your role in the debate. It seems as though you have taken your mother's advice about leaving home, which is that through assuming responsibility for your own family, you grow up.

Robert, you have made the greatest sacrifice of all to keep your father in the family. It is not surprising that as the oldest son in a family that has placed high expectations on oldest sons, you would take your role so seriously, so seriously it is a matter of life and death. Moreover, Robert, before your father died, he asked you to make sure that your mother didn't lose the house and indeed you have made it near impossible for her to give it up as long as she feels that you need her. Although talented in so many ways (for example, in sports, in caring for the elderly), you have gotten your family to focus not on your talents but on your self-destructive actions, for in your self-destruction you provide a way to keep the family together and so honor your father. I am sorry that you have not yet been able to come up with another way to carry out your father's wishes, another way that wouldn't cost you so much.

I have been deliberate here in my use of language. The family has not yet spoken directly to Robert about his substance abuse and drug selling. Therefore, I do not have permission to write about this behavior and use instead language of "self-destruction" that I introduced during the genogram meetings.

Ted, you continue to ask your mother to be "more of a mother," to return the family to a time when the kids were young and needed the guidance and protection of your parents. In doing so, you sacrifice your relationship with your mother because these requests make her upset with you.

Peter, you are in a very interesting position in this debate. With a serious girlfriend, you may be wanting to start your own family soon, but you are still busy battling with your brothers over who will take over as head of the family. I wonder whether you will sacrifice your relationship with your fiancée in order to keep the memory of your father alive or whether you will figure out some other way to honor him so you can get on with your own life.

Kevin, you have one foot in the family, and one out, treated like a child by your older brothers but often respected as a man by your mother. I think that this is a very tough position to be in—to be on both sides at the same time, loyal to your father's vision of the family staying together and to your mother's hopes for you to grow up.

Helen, you seem to be the freest of everyone to do as you please and have even envisioned yourself being able to leave home when you are ready to. I am intrigued and puzzled about how you have managed to stay so free of the debate that rages all around you.

I don't know how you may change this debate and remember your father in other ways besides having struggles about leaving home, struggles that lead so many of you to make so many sacrifices. Mrs. Bruno feels exhausted and even physically ill from the stress of these unresolved issues and Robert has almost given up on his future. Rose often can't feel as proud as she should for growing up and moving away.

What follows is a list of ideas about growing up that are not as polarized as their current beliefs. Some of the ideas suggest that pulling in and breaking apart are related to each other rather than polar opposites. Other suggestions aim to loosen up the "debate" by offering alternative mourning strategies.

I don't know if it would help to talk about Robert, Sr., father and husband, and about how much he is still missed by all of you.

I don't know if it would help for more members of your family to keep up more contact with your father's side of the family, even though that would be difficult for Mrs. Bruno.

I don't know if it would help to pull together as a family to help Robert overcome his self-destructive behavior. By pulling together, you would eventually be helping everyone to grow and get on with their own lives.

I don't know if it is possible to plan more things to do as a family that are fun, for clearly this is a family that is fun-loving and that has given up a lot of laughs in order to keep disagreeing about staying together or splitting apart.

I think that there is a greater chance of your feeling connected emotionally to one another and of your really getting to know each other once you resolve the debate about the family physically staying together. There are already indications of this. I have noticed a change between Ted and his mother, in that they are able to listen to each other and respect each other as long as they are not disagreeing about the future of the family. Also, Helen and her mother have gotten closer since your father's death. I think that people in the family can get closer to one another when they are not in a heated argument about leaving or staying. I think that as long as you push to stay physically closer to one another, this will involve so many individual sacrifices that you will be too depleted to feel emotionally connected to one another.

If things in the family should start to change and if someone starts to miss Robert, Sr., and feel that he has been forgotten, you can always renew the arguments about leaving home. Ted and Rose can come home and criticize mother's raising of Kevin and Helen. In this way they will be saying that the family needs to be all together again. Or Robert, Jr., can act as though he's still doing self-destructive things, because then he knows the family won't be able to split apart. Or any of the kids can ignore the mother's requests for help—in this way, you will all be reminded of how things were when your father was alive.

The last paragraph is a Milan-style "restraint from change" prescription. By prescribing the very behaviors the family had been doing, but with a new spin—that they are in the service of honoring the father—the therapist ensures that even if the family reverts to these previous behaviors, they will have a new meaning.

I am hopeful about this family's ability to pull together and to be able to move on to the next stage.

This last line is again an attempt to interrupt the repetitive polarity in the family and suggest that pulling together and moving on go hand in hand, rather than exist in opposition to one another. I am saying to the Bruno children: you can have your cake and eat it, too—you can stay connected *and* make your own lives. You do not have to choose between loyalty to your mother or father; you can be loyal to both.

## The Bruno Family's Feedback to the Letter

The feedback to this letter was swift and varied. Mrs. Bruno called me four days after hearing the letter to tell me that Kevin was moving out into his own apartment. He had explained that he could no longer tolerate "being bossed around" by his three older brothers. Ted called a week later to ask me for a referral for himself to individual therapy. He explained that he was tired of putting all his energy into the family and felt that it was time to get some help for himself. He added that he and his brothers had broken the silence regarding Robert's substance abuse. They had been talking with Robert about their concern and anger toward him. In turn, Robert asked Ted to get a referral from me for a substance abuse evaluation. According to Ted, Robert had felt too shy to call me directly.

A year later, I received a call from Ted who had, indeed, been in individual therapy since the end of family therapy. He told me that, through his individual therapy, he had uncovered a wellspring of rage toward his mother for her physical abuse of him as a child. At this point he wanted either to try to work through his feelings toward his mother in family therapy or to choose never to see her again. When his mother readily agreed to family sessions, Ted decided to take the route of therapy, too. During a six-month therapy, he confronted his mother with all the abusive incidents he could remember and discussed the continued impact of her past abuse on his adult life. Over time, she was able to listen empathically to him and offer heartfelt apologies. By way of explaining, though not excusing, her behavior toward Ted, she described her psychiatric hospitalization after his birth and her struggle with depression throughout his childhood. At the end of therapy they conducted a ritual together in which Ted talked about those abuses that he could forgive and those that he could not.

Years later, I received another call from Ted. He told me that his mother had had cardiac surgery and needed help from her children, who had now, except for Robert, all left home. He suggested a family meeting to coordinate the caretaking of his mother so that it could be done equitably. Everyone now had their own lives apart from their mother— Rose continued to live in Maine with her child; Ted had had several job promotions and now had a circle of friends; Peter had married and had two daughters; Kevin was engaged to be married; Helen had gone off to college; and Robert, though still at home, had long since stopped abusing drugs. Ted explained that despite their busy lives they wanted to ensure that their mother had the company and help she needed. I heard this as a fundamental change in the family's beliefs about growing up. Where independence and connection had been construed as incompatible forces, now they were viewed as two goals to pursue simultaneously.

This case contains many of the earmarks of other families grappling with making the passage from adolescence to adulthood. There was a symptomatic member, Robert, who was abusing and selling cocaine. He was the initial focus of concern, although just below the surface it became apparent that every member of the family was struggling with a similar dilemma: How does one grow up in this family while maintaining connection?

The death of a parent at a critical point in the family's development had complicated this passage. Often, when a parent's death coincides with movement away from the family, that movement is interrupted, to accommodate the pulling in toward the family that accompanies grief. In addition, the Brunos had constructed a common, constraining polarity for themselves regarding the transition to adulthood—that is, either the family would need to break up to allow individual members to pursue independent lives or the family members would be stuck in time, connected but without their own homes and families. Before therapy, there was no model for staying connected while making their own separate lives.

Questions regarding the previous generations' experiences with growing up revealed a tangled set of conflicting stories. The genogram was a powerful tool for eliciting these stories and for helping the family develop a new narrative. In addition, the genogram was useful in engaging Robert in therapy when his family was ambivalent about his attending family sessions.

The Bruno family's debate about growing up—as either requiring separation from the family or unwavering connection to the family—is echoed in a debate in the theoretical literature on the meaning of intimacy, identity, and separation. The traditional psychodynamic view (Blos 1962, Erikson 1968, Freud 1958) is that separation from the family and the creation of an adult identity must precede the capacity for intimacy. The revisionist view (Apter 1990, Chodorow 1978, Gilligan 1992, Offer and Schonert-Reichl 1992) is that identity and the capacity for intimacy happen in conjunction with an adolescent's ongoing connection to family.

The traditional view holds that the acquisition of a full adult identity will be tumultuous and difficult. In this model, fights between parents and children are seen as an essential tool for expressing the adolescent's wish to renounce childhood. Adolescents are expected first to separate from their families in order to be able later to form intimate attachments outside of the family.

## Revisions of Erikson's Model
## of Identity Development

Despite Blos's and Erikson's emphasis on separation from parents as being the critical antecedent to identity formation, many researchers (Campbell et al. 1984, Gilligan 1992, Steinberg 1990, Waterman 1982) have found connectedness to parents to be the key factor in predicting identity achievement. One of the most articulate, persuasive critiques of Erikson's view of identity development is offered by Terri Apter (1990) in her book *Altered Loves: Mothers and Daughters during Adolescence*. Apter refers to Erikson's view of growing up as the "school of mourning." Instead, she offers a less polarized view of growing up that allows for creating a distinct self as well as maintaining connection with parents. Rather than seeing fights as a tool of separation, she views them as a vehicle for adolescents to engage parents in recognizing who they are becoming.

During the process of interviewing sixty-five mother-and-daughter pairs in the United States and Britain, Apter discovered that her questions, which highlighted separation, were inadequate to elicit the full range of experiences that her subjects wanted to discuss. So, she began asking different questions, including: "How are you retaining your attachment to your mother?" and "How are you trying to persuade her to see you differently?" She found that instead of hearing about the daughters' need to be independent from their mothers, the young women spoke about "what their mothers saw or did not see" (p. 15). Apter interprets these comments as the daughters' attempts to get their mothers to see them as they really are, not as bids for independence. She writes:

> What I found throughout these interviews was that adolescent daughters continued to care deeply about their parents, and in particular retained a strong attachment to their mother, which they very much wanted to preserve. . . . Daugh-

ters worked deliberately upon their mothers to get recognition and acknowledgment of the newly forming adult self. They offered a hundred reminders each day that the habitual ways of viewing them were not quite right. Mothers responded to their daughters' efforts, but themselves offered reminders . . . of what the daughter should be doing, thinking, feeling, or becoming. Communication itself was a type of argument about self-definition and self-justification. The arguments were sometimes more and sometimes less hostile. They were often filled with love and delight. They were often filled with anger and frustration. *But the aim of the argument was never to separate; it was always characterized by the underlying demand, "See me as I am, and love me for what I am."* [p. 22, emphasis added]

Drawing on research conducted by Nancy Chodorow (1978) and Carol Gilligan (1982), Apter emphasizes the relational context in which all of female development (and some male development) takes place. She argues that girls develop at each stage in reference, rather than in opposition, to their parents.

## Expanding the Time Frame

In addition to offering a critique of Erikson and the generational conflict model of adolescence, Apter also challenges the customary time frame offered for accomplishing the tasks of adolescence. She writes, "If we view adolescence as a time when the child separates from her parents in order to establish an adult identity, then we pack too much into this phase. Few girls in their late adolescence had a sense of an adult identity. At best, they felt prepared to form it" (p. 145). When asked about the meaning of their daughters' leaving home, the mothers in Apter's study explained that they did not view their daughters as leaving home when they left for college. Rather, the mothers felt that leaving home occurred when their daughters bought their own houses, set up house in another city, or moved their belongings out of the family home. I think these observations could as easily apply to adolescent boys, although they were not the focus of her study.

## Separation as a Mental Health Story

Several researchers (Offer and Schonert-Reichl 1992, Quadrel et al. 1993, Silverstein and Rashbaum 1994) offer a critique of the cultural discourse on adolescence by debunking ideas held sacrosanct by the mental health profession. Silverstein and Rashbaum, in the *Courage to Raise Good Men* (1994), for example, challenge a cluster of cultural ideas regarding the "need" for boys to separate from their mothers. They challenge the belief that boys must separate from their mothers in order to achieve a satisfactory male sexual identity. If mothers encourage physical and emotional closeness, they run the risk of raising emasculated men; the definition of a healthy male identity, in this view, is synonymous with separation. In *Leaving Home: The Therapy of Disturbed Young People* (1980), Jay Haley focuses on men who become sick at the time of leave-taking, and he recommends that families learn to let go of their sons. Silverstein and Rashbaum argue that young men may became sick at the time of leave-taking because they are not ready to leave home. They quote Barbara Ehrenreich (1983), who writes in *The Hearts of Men*, " 'Grown-up' . . . should have some meaning for a boy other than 'gone away' " (p. 181).

## Separation as a Cultural Story

The concepts that the adolescent must separate from the family before achieving intimacy, that adolescents can best form an identity by disconnecting from their parents, and that one is only grown up when one has gone away are elaborated in many cultural stories. The biblical story of the Prodigal Son resonates with these themes of loss and identity. It is a story that has been used by Helm Stierlin (1974), a psychoanalytically oriented family therapist, to typify family members' issues as they grapple with an adolescent's leaving home.

In this story, two sons are each given a portion of their father's wealth. The younger son takes his money, travels the world, and squanders his fortune while the older son stays home, abiding by his father's wishes. After a time, the younger son returns, ready to beg forgiveness from his father and willing to live like one of his father's servants. To the younger brother's surprise, and to his older brother's chagrin, their father welcomes the prodigal son back with a feast and much celebration. To the outraged older son, the father explains what this celebrating is all about: "My son, thou are always at my side, and everything that I have is already thine, but for this merrymaking and rejoicing there was good reason; thy brother here was dead, and has come to life again; was lost and is found" (Luke 15:31–32). Is the son who gives up his family better than the son who never really separates? This seems to be the central premise of Erikson's view of identity development during the transition to adulthood: a boy must physically separate from his family before developing a fully realized identity.

## Impediments and Aids to Making the Transition to Adulthood

Despite a persistent cultural and psychodynamic mandate to encourage adolescent separation from parents, the research on identity development emphasizes the salutary effects of parent–child connection. Over and over, researchers offer the same advice to families and the therapists who are helping them: stay connected to your adolescents and tolerate their ideas and opinions, no matter how different they are from your own.

In a review of much of the research in this area that draws on Marcia's (1966) operationalizing of Erikson's identity development, Waterman (1982) concluded that differences in parenting styles will predict the different pathways into identity formation. In seeming contradiction to Erikson's emphasis on separation from parents as heralding successful identity development, Waterman concludes that when attachment to parents was paired with parental tolerance for their children's autonomous viewpoints, adolescents were most likely to attain the most desirable state of identity achievement.

Campbell et al. (1984), in a study of identity development using college-aged men and women, concurred with previous findings that connection *and* independence are needed for optimal development. He added another layer of complexity to the equation, a layer that includes distinctions between mothers and fathers. The researchers found that a moderate level of connection to the mother and a moderate degree of independence from the father was the combination of family factors most closely associated with establishing a moratorium, or identity-achieved status, during late adolescence.

There are, however, many ways that connectedness can be overdone and become a problem. One way is when the transition to adulthood coincides with another event, such as divorce or the death of a parent, which often has the effect of pulling the family members in close to each other. When a parent or a grandparent dies as a child is getting ready to leave home, that child may feel that he or she is needed at home to replace the loss or to distract the grieving parent. At the very least, in the acute aftermath of grief, families will often pull together for comfort, which makes any move toward independence seem out of step or downright disloyal.

Similarly, when parents divorce during late adolescence, the child may feel an obligation to stay home with the custodial parent, who may be depressed or overwhelmed by the responsibilities of being a single parent. Rather than feeling free to invest energy with peers and in activities outside the family, the adolescent may be pulled back to the family as a caretaker. Wallerstein and Kelly (1980) advise that the best prognosis for adolescents whose parents divorce during the leaving-home stage is to practice "strategic withdrawal." This term refers to the strategy of concentrating on those activities and relationships outside the family that remain intact, despite the parents' divorce, such as involvement on a soccer team, a church group, or an orchestra.

Keshet and Mirkin (1985) write about another way in which the adolescent's moving-out process can be impeded by divorce. They argue that the normal separation process is characterized by the adolescent using anger to intensify the relationship with each parent in an alternating manner, so that at any one time, he or she is angry with only one parent. But after divorce, this method of experimenting with separation becomes too dangerous. The adolescent may fear losing the noncustodial parent altogether if anger is expressed. The authors assert that the moving-out process is most impeded for the second-eldest child when parents divorce at the time when the oldest sibling is leaving for college. When this occurs, the next-oldest adolescent experiences the double loss of the sibling and the parent. With the oldest child leaving home, the second-oldest loses the buffer to the intensity of the divorce and instead experiences it full force.

Fullinwider-Bush and Jacobvitz (1993) approach the perils of overconnectedness during late adolescence from another vantage point. They examined the consequences of parent–daughter "boundary dissolution" for young women's identity development. Boundary dissolution refers to intrusive interactions between parent and child in which there is little respect for each other's opinions or there is a reversal in the hierarchy so that the child is asked to provide support and comfort to the parent. The researchers found, in concurrence with many previous findings, that young women whose parents fostered both closeness and independence engaged in higher rates of exploration, particularly in the area of dating. Conversely, when bonds between the daughter and either parent were overly close, there were detrimental repercussions for the daughter in her interpersonal relationships.

They also found distinct disturbances in identity development for each parent–child bond. When mother–daughter relationships were characterized by boundary dissolution, those daughters were more likely to prematurely adopt an identity based on the mother's or the family's beliefs without an exploration period. Perhaps these daughters forgo their own development in order to maintain a role as caretaker. When there was father–daughter boundary dissolution, the daughters responded with less exploration in the career domain. The researchers conclude that women's career pursuits are more influenced by the father than by the mother.

## Family Therapy Implications

The art of therapy for the family with adolescents who are having difficulty growing up is, then, a paradoxical one. Often, the therapy requires bringing the adolescent closer into the family in order to be able to move out. There are several fruitful areas of inquiry for the therapist confronted with a family who is stuck in transition: first, it is important to assess the extent to which the family subscribes to polarizing beliefs about growing up. Do families like the Brunos believe that staying connected as a family is mutually exclusive from growing up and moving out on one's own? If so, the therapist will want to introduce into the conversation the notion that both ideas can be true simultaneously. As was true of the Brunos, the family's beliefs about growing up are likely part of the inherited wisdom from previous generations.

The therapist may want to ask what stories from the parents' and grandparents' lives are told within the family about making the transition to adulthood. In the stories told, were relationships sacrificed or enhanced by this passage? In the current generation, have there been any successful leave-takings by cousins?

Taking into account the research on identity development (Campbell et al. 1984, Waterman 1982), the therapist may want to assess the family's tolerance for ideas and opinions that depart from parental values. How have individuals been treated in this family when they challenge an important family value or live on the edge of what is allowed (for example, an artist in a family of doctors, an aunt who chooses not to have children, an uncle who is gay)? How do the parents show respect and interest for beliefs that differ from their own?

In light of the ways that other parts of the family system can have an impact on the family's willingness to let an adolescent leave home, the therapist will also want to ask: "Are there other forces at work that are placing extra demands for closeness and dependency on the family, for example, a recently diagnosed illness, a death, divorce, remarriage?" In the case of the Brunos, the recent death of the father caused the three eldest brothers to stay home, vying for the position of surrogate father, and to respond to their mother's implicit request for their company and help.

## IMPACT OF ADOLESCENTS' SEPARATION ON THE COUPLE

Because there is no marital couple in the Bruno family, this case is missing a key element in the drama of an adolescent preparing for leave-taking. Very often, the couple's relationship will be profoundly affected by the sea changes that accompany a child's transition to adulthood. As the parents lose their focus on heavy caretaking responsibilities, their own relationship will be spotlighted. The therapist may want to ask the parents (in a couples meeting) about the impact on their marriage of having an adolescent. How are the parents responding to the emotional charge surging through the family system that usually accompanies having an adolescent in the house? What effects have the parents noticed in their sexual relationship, their reflections on the future, and their satisfaction with their careers? How do the parents imagine their relationship will change further when their adolescents leave home? How do they feel they have done as parents? Do they have any dreams about their relationships with their children in the future, once their adolescents have left home?

As adolescents bring in new ideas, new music, and new peers to the family, the whole system becomes charged with the possibilities for change. The adolescent's focus on the future is often contagious: the parents are in turn propelled to ask profound questions about their future and how it will be different from the preceding years. How the couple responds to the influx of new stimuli and to the waning of their parenting responsibilities is the focus of the next chapter.

# 7

# The Absent Adolescent: Treating the Couple When the Adolescent Is Not Present

Writing a book about adolescence without highlighting the parental couple would be like reviewing an improvisatory play and leaving out the audience. For just as the audience influences the performance on any given night and leaves the theater somewhat altered, so the couple shapes the child's passage through adolescence and, in turn, is profoundly affected by their shared journey. Two waystations on this journey are particularly affecting for the couple—the adolescent's transition to puberty and the anticipation of the adolescent's leave-taking from the home.

The reciprocal relationship between adolescents and their parents has been captured by many writers and therapists. Fishman (1988), in his classic book on family therapy with adolescents, also includes a separate chapter on the parental dyad. His version of the reciprocity between adolescents and their parents is a homeostatic one: a troubled marriage is often stabilized by adolescent trouble so that once the adolescent is doing better, the marriage needs to be the next therapeutic project. Fishman uses the metaphor of peeling away layers of an onion, suggesting that marital therapy is one treatment in a sequence, one that often follows on the heels of the adolescent's improvement.

Several researchers have studied the reciprocal relationship of adolescents and their parents' marriage. They have probed the effect of marital tension on adolescent adjustment (Emery 1982, Emery and O'Leary 1982) and looked at the impact of the two dramatic denouements—the adolescent's entrance into puberty and the adolescent's leave-taking from home—on the marriage. During the past twenty years a sizable body of research has accumulated that probes the effect of puberty (Farrell and Rosenberg 1981, Glenn 1975, Silverberg and Steinberg 1987, 1990, Steinberg and Silverberg 1987, Swenson et al. 1981) and the empty nest (Brim 1968, Deutscher 1964, Harkins 1978, Lowenthal and Chirboga 1972, McCullough and Rutenberg 1989, Neugarten 1968, Wallerstein and Blakeslee 1995) on the midlife marriage. If young couples with young children are the most likely to divorce, then middle-aged couples with adolescents are the next most susceptible to breaking up. This body of research grapples with the question: What is it about these marriages that invites heightened conflict and risk of divorce?

This chapter begins with the Palmers, a midlife couple with two adolescent children on the cusp of leaving for college. The story of the Palmer couple will introduce a discussion of the developmental literature on midlife marital issues, noting how these issues sometimes conflict and sometimes dovetail with adolescent issues. Subsequently, several typical midlife presentations for couples therapy will be offered, followed by guidelines for doing therapy with this population. Just as there is a dominant cultural story about adolescence and the necessity of separating from parents, so there are cultural stories about midlife. These stories—particularly the inevitability of the "midlife crisis" and the "empty nest syndrome"—will be explored and compared to data from clinical research. The research findings suggest that the child's transition to adolescence and the anticipation of a child's leave-taking are the two most challenging times for midlife couples.

## CASE VIGNETTE: THE PALMERS—PARENTS WITH CHILDREN ON THE CUSP OF LEAVING HOME

Sam Palmer called me to make the initial appointment for couples therapy, hours after his wife, Sally, had given him this ultimatum: either go to therapy or she would file for divorce. On the phone, Sam told me confidentially that he and his wife needed merely "a tune-up." However, within the first few minutes of their initial visit Sally made it clear that if she were to stay married, the marriage needed a complete overhaul. This difference in perception of the magnitude of marital difficulty is quite common among middle-aged couples. One spouse takes the position that only adjustments and accommodations are required in the relationship, as they go from being a family with children at home to being a couple. The other partner, meanwhile, takes the position that a dramatic, discontinuous change is required, where the old order will have to be substantially altered to make room for a marriage with new rules. The therapy often begins with this disagreement about the degree and extent of change required.

Sally, a 45-year-old, fit, sportily dressed, attractive woman had been on a low simmer for several years; overwhelmed by feelings of resentment she could no longer contain, she insisted on having her litany of complaints heard. Sally's frustration had boiled over as she contemplated life with her husband alone once her two children, ages 17 and 18, left for college. Their older child, Ellen, a high school senior, had just completed her college applications. Their son Michael, a high school junior, would soon be leaving home as well. Without the children there as buffers and companions, Sally dreaded the future. She was most upset about Sam's anger at her, which seemed to flare up unpredictably and then last for days.

Sam, a 42-year-old, sporting sneakers and a briefcase, was alternately morose and irrepressibly exuberant. He was unabashed in describing his passion and love for his wife, whom he described as the most beautiful woman he had ever met. He acknowledged that he was easily hurt by her coolness toward him and that this hurt moved quickly to anger. He wished that he could ignore his feelings of hurt and focus on all the things he loved about Sally.

In the first ten minutes of the first interview, Sam sighed and stated softly, "I should really talk about my family if you are to make sense of my marriage." His biological father had died in a car accident when Sam was 3. His mother remarried within in a year, to a man who became increasingly abusive to Sam as he reached adolescence. Sam left home at age 17, eager to get as far away as he could from his abusive stepfather. Throughout his adolescence he lived with friends' families and worked two or three jobs after school to earn money for college. A school counselor took an interest in him and helped him win a college scholarship. His maternal grandmother, who lived to be almost 100, was another source of comfort to him. Sam took care of her for the last twenty years, until one year earlier, when the old woman had died.

Sam told me that he had never seen a therapist before. He believed that through hard work and a resolutely optimistic temperament he had been able to overcome the impact of his childhood. He did note, however, that his usual strategies for keeping negative feelings at bay were not working. Instead, he was plagued daily by the same kind of feelings of rejection from his wife that he had experienced from his mother and stepfather growing up.

I hypothesized that the combination of his beloved grandmother's death, his children's reaching the age at which he had left home and never again returned, and his attainment of financial security, which allowed a slowing down of his work ethic, all contributed to the emergence of unresolved feelings about his traumatic childhood. This is a common presentation at middle-age: a problem that has been shelved for many years now demands to be addressed.

When asked how they would like the marriage to be different, Sam and Sally offered answers that reflected an emerging assertiveness on her part and a longing for more intimacy on his. Sally said that she wanted to be able to speak up more, to offer her opinions, to take more control of their social life—all without fear of hurting Sam's feelings or of angering him. She described Sam's anger as a time bomb. When angered, Sam became verbally abusive to her and had tried to keep her housebound by taking her keys and checkbook. She added that as she faces her children leaving for college, she would like to get a job but fears that her husband will vehemently disapprove. In summary, she said, "I don't want to have a life that is just about pleasing my husband."

Sam had worked tremendously hard at his own business for the first twenty years of marriage and now in his early forties had attained enough wealth to retire. Worried that his wife stayed with him only because of his ability to provide for her, he longed for more affection from her and for signs that she "really wants me."

During the course of my evaluation, I asked them to do an imaging exercise, one loosely based on an exercise that Peggy Papp (1983) describes in her book *The Process of Change*. I asked the couple to close their eyes and for each to picture him- or herself transformed into another life form, such as an animal, a tree, or a part of the landscape. Then I asked each to transform the other spouse into a life form that embodied the other's essential qualities. Finally, I asked them to put the two images together and have each one move in response to the other. In this way, the partners give a powerful, evocative description of their relationship that surprises and informs each of them.

Sam's image of himself was a flowing rapid that was full of energy. He pictured his wife as a sleek mare running through the sunset, being chased by the rapid. Sally imagined herself as the ocean, "peaceful and wild." She pictured Sam as he had pictured her—as a stallion. This stallion was "dominating and independent." He ran through the water "with no feeling for the water." These images were striking for their similarity in theme and image choice. Both Sam and Sally felt that their needs and wants were not taken into account by the other. Each felt that the other had greater freedom and power and was using it against the other to control and dominate.

With all couples I see, I conduct a four-session consultation: a joint session, two individual sessions, and a fourth session in which I offer tentative observations, impressions, and recommendations. In the fourth session, this is what I offered the Palmers:

> It seems that you are working at cross purposes with one another. When Sally says, "I don't care what you think," she is practicing having her own voice and opinions. She is working out her version of the transition to the children moving away. But these are fighting words for Sam, who takes them literally and then wants reassurance that Sally really loves him. Sam, you are asking for more signs of love and caring at the same time that you, Sally, want to try out more freedom to explore the world outside the confines of the family. Each of you is at a challenging time for you individually, and as a couple. Sally is facing the loss of her job as a full-time mother. She wonders what her days will be like without the daily tasks of caring for the children and knows that a dramatic change is needed to accommodate this shift in role.
>
> Sam, perhaps with the death of your grandmother, turning 40, and seeing your own children reach the age when you fled your family, you are more vulnerable to experiencing the pains of the past, pains you thought were long since tucked away. But your past is like a trick knee that acts up under certain circumstances. You notice this vulnerability when you are more reactive to slights from your wife. You, Sam, entertain the possibility that your angry reactions to your wife may be colored by a history of abuse

and neglect that is rearing its head again. Perhaps this would be a time to reexamine the demons of your past as you make plans for the second half of your life. I don't know if that would best be done individually or with Sally present.

In the first half of your marriage, you found the closeness and intimacy with each other that was sorely lacking in the families you grew up in. Married in your teens, you helped each other grow up. But now as you look ahead to the next chapter without children, you have many questions and uncertainties. Sam wants this marriage to be filled with more moments of closeness—for example, he wants Sally to lie down with him on the couch, to hug him in the middle of the night, to seek out his company, to desire him sexually. Sally, on the other hand, wants to know if this marriage can make room for her to speak up more, to tell her true feelings, even when they include annoyance and disappointment, the desire to get a job, and the wish to live without fear of his temper. I think that these changes can happen but will require a new period of courtship with one another—a time of revealing parts of yourselves that have not had the time to come out because of the daily pressures of caring for children and providing for the family. This courtship may include revisiting your childhoods and talking about dreams and disappointments, small and large.

This is a time of reevaluation for each of you and for the two of you as a couple. I think that therapy may be helpful in order to have a series of conversations about the past and the future that have been difficult to initiate on your own. I picture the therapy like improvisational theater, where new roles and ideas can be played with before committing to an ongoing performance. We could talk about how you feel about your jobs as parents. We could talk about your fantasies about your marriage once your children are away at college. These fantasies could include conversations about vacations, time spent separately and together pursuing leisure, changes in your house, the type and frequency of sexual intimacy, the kind of relationships you want with your adult children, the balance of work and relationship, the time set aside for spending with friends, and anything else that is on your minds but has not yet been spoken about.

I saw Sam and Sally for several months in couples therapy. Early on, the Palmers reported a recent fight that they agreed was typical of fights they had been having for years. Apparently Sam had come home late after days of being out of town on a business trip. He was enraged to find that upon his return, his wife had gone to sleep instead of waiting up for him. He turned on all the lights and started barraging her with questions about why she was asleep. Sally, groggy and upset, said nothing. Sam then started to throw magazines at her and did not stop until Sally was sobbing. After I registered my outrage at Sam's abusive behavior, Sam expressed his surprise. He told his wife that by observing my response to him, he was able to acknowledge for the first time how hurtful and angry he had been to Sally. He was willing to explore the similarities between how his stepfather had treated him and how, when angry, he treated his wife. This vulnerability—that when rejected, he lashed out—we acknowledged as his "trick knee."

A few weeks after these insights, another incident occurred that deeply hurt Sam's feelings. He had made travel plans for them to vacation at a favorite island but had been unable to get reservations at their customary hotel. When Sally heard that they would be going to a new hotel, she declared that she did not want to go at all. Ordinarily, they agreed, Sam's response would have been to call her names and take away her house keys. Instead, he cried, telling her how hurt he was that she hadn't felt that being with him, no matter which hotel, was the most important thing. Sally answered, "I can respond to your hurt and I want to. It feels so different when your hurt doesn't come out as anger." Sally told Sam that this was the first time that he had ever showed his hurt to her, a response that made her feel warm, responsive, and giving. Together, they worked out an agreement with each other: they would regard any lashing out from Sam as a sign that he felt hurt and would take time apart so that Sam could get beneath his anger. Sam would then describe his feelings to her rather than telling her what he wanted her to do. It had been the telling that made Sally feel controlled and made Sam feel humiliated for having to ask.

As the therapy progressed, Sam realized that while he had the desire to, he often lacked the emotional vocabulary to describe his feelings. Consequently, he agreed to keep a journal that was a daily record of his emotional life, including physical sensations, dreams, precipitants to feeling hurt or angry, and events that prompted positive feelings, such as elation and pleasant anticipation. Sally, for her part, decided to keep her own journal with a different focus: she kept track of ideas and dreams she had about her future, once her time was freed up from being a full-time homemaker. She also recorded any thoughts that she might have censored in the past out of fear of Sam's reactions. Many weeks were spent moving between Sam and Sally's self-explorations and their sharing of journal entries with each other. In this way, therapy reinvigorated their relationship. After twenty years of marriage, they were getting to know parts of each other that were new to both of them.

## Developmental Issues: The Couple at Midlife

Throughout this chapter, it is assumed that the couple at midlife has adolescent children. Of course, it is also possible to be a midlife couple without children, with infants, with grandchildren, or with some combination of these, but these marriages are qualitatively different than those inhabited by adolescents. There has been relatively little written, clinically, about couples at midlife. To compensate for and augment the paucity of such literature, the more extensive life-cycle literature that documents the intrapersonal changes for men and women at midlife has been drawn upon. Many of these expected individual changes translate into dyadic dilemmas for couples at midlife. The dyadic consequences of individual shifts in sexuality and gender role are next discussed.

## Middle Age from the Perspective of Life-Cycle Developmentalists: Intrapersonal Changes

Over the last thirty years, there has been a proliferation of studies on the individual development of middle-aged men and women (Levinson 1978, Lowenthal and Chirboga 1972, Masters and Johnson 1966, Neugarten 1968, Neugarten and Gutmann 1968, Sheehy 1974, 1995, Vaillant 1977). Much of this writing focuses on the significance of loss at midlife as individuals grapple with their own illnesses, the death of parents, the waning of youth, and the dawning realization that the time left to live is finite. Counterbalancing this emphasis on loss has been an interest in middle age as a time of burgeoning possibilities. For men who have been striving in their careers for twenty years, midlife offers the chance to relax and enjoy these achievements, with a new focus on family and friends. For women who have put family first, midlife offers a time of increased freedom from family responsibility and a chance to pursue school or career. For women who have been in the workforce all along, midlife can be a time to pursue achievements with more energy and focus than was available during the years of juggling family and work responsibilities.

## The Dyadic Effects of Intrapersonal Shifts at Middle-Age

The literature on midlife is rife with other comparisons made between male and female experiences of this stage of life. In general, the observed shifts are for women to become more in touch with their masculine side and men with their feminine one. As Bernice Neugarten (1968) observes, "Important differences exist between men and women as they age. Men seem to become more receptive to affiliative and nurturant promptings; women, more responsive toward and less guilty about aggressive and egocentric impulses" (p. 286). Gail Sheehy (1974) names this process of men and women taking on feminine and masculine qualities respectively, the "Switch-40s." Sheehy observes that women become more autonomous and achievement-oriented as their family responsibilities decrease and as they no longer rely on procreative powers to define their creativity. Men, she writes, tend to become more nurturant with their children and wives. She argues that biological processes parallel these psychological ones: in men, testosterone decreases, while estrogen decreases in women.

Sexually, things get more complex during midlife. In general, hormonal and vascular changes make for sexual changes in men and women at midlife. Both genders, for example, may require more direct stimulation to the genitals as they age.

Levinson (1978) believes that the difference between male and female sexual responsivity is at no time greater than at middle age. If women have been expected to reach their sexual peak at 38, many men reach theirs in their late teens. By middle age, a man's first physiological response and refractory period take longer than it did in his twenties. Orgasms may be less forceful. In general, Levinson suggests that men become increasingly affected by their bodily changes, while many women continue to be multiply orgasmic, with sexual desire and responsiveness peaking at midlife and declining only very gradually afterward. There is a subgroup of women, however, who report a dramatic dip in sexual interest and responsiveness after menopause. Both the gender role and the sexual changes require the couple to continue getting to know each other. Bodies and roles are in flux. To paraphrase Jung, what was true in the morning may not be true in the noon of life.

## Couples Work: When the Adolescents
## Are Not Invited to Therapy

While the midlife couple is not destined for inevitable crisis, many couples do present for the first time during midlife. When is a recommendation for couples, rather than family, therapy warranted? Many middle-aged couples are as hesitant as their privacy-conscious adolescents to bare their souls in a cross-generational context. These couples present at a crossroads that marks an uncertain future. Many ask, as the Palmers did: Can we and do we want to follow the path we have been on for the first half of our marriage? Or can we, and should we, go in some other direction, like divorce, an affair, a new job, or fashioning a whole new set of rules and expectations for this marriage? What follows are the most common reasons for requests for couples therapy at midlife.

### *Presenting at a Crossroads*
### *Regarding Their Adolescent Children*

Some couples trace their difficulties to their adolescent children but still prefer to meet without them. These couples present when their children are just approaching puberty or on the threshold of leave-taking, prompted to anticipate the road ahead by their teen's rapid development. The adolescents are implicated in their parents' confusion but are not central to solving it. They may legitimately have had their marriage stressed by an adolescent's severe difficulties, such as the diagnosis of schizophrenia or cancer, or by negotiating multiple treators and schools to accommodate a child with learning disabilities. Other couples barely mention their adolescents, but their impact on the marriage can be inferred. As adolescents challenge their parents' choices and dream freely about the future, the process can be infectious, prompting the couple also to question, take stock, and consider the time that lies ahead.

## Sexuality

Normal aging in men and women may leave couples vulnerable to misunderstandings and hurt. Imagine this scenario: a husband, in response to vascular changes and lower testosterone, finds himself taking several minutes, rather than a few seconds, to achieve an erection. His wife may interpret his change as a sign that he no longer finds her attractive or even that he is interested in another woman. In order to reassure herself about her attractiveness to him, she may demand that he respond to her the way he used to. These requests may make him impotent, which will only aggravate her feelings of being unloved. Or, his sexual changes may merely make the lovemaking feel unfamiliar to her and make them both feel uneasy about sex that was once so effortless.

## Career Issues

If the couple had a traditional division of labor between home and family, there was parity achieved by the woman taking care of the home front while the husband worked as provider. But this equitable situation becomes unbalanced when the children leave home. Husbands may envy their wives' freedom. Wives may feel guilty about their newfound freedom. Another way that work changes create havoc in a midlife marriage occurs when one member loses a job. Not only is it difficult to land another job when you are in your fifties, but it can also shake the foundation of the marriage. All of these changes challenge the basic givens of the marriage and require a flexibility and a willingness to renegotiate the earlier contract. Such a reexamination can throw many questions up in the air, questions that had been happily resolved for years; for example, what shall we do with our free time? Shall we spend it together, with our own friends or developing a new pursuit? How much money do we really need and for what?

## Changes in the Self

Many couples at midlife declare to their partners, in one way or another, "I am no longer the man or woman you married twenty years ago." After a productive therapy or the transforming experience of parenting or a serious illness, or after the death of one's parents, profound questions about identity get raised. A core issue for marriages at midlife is about the choice between growth or stagnation. Ross Goldstein, in his book *Fortysomething* (1990), writes: "Extramarital issues aside, the third party in a mid-life marriage is usually the evolving self, which often feels confined. How do you explore your need for personal growth without upsetting the dynamic of the marriage? How do you breathe new life into a relationship that seems to have stopped growing?" (p. 182). He advises that couples need a new obsession with each other, they need to study what the other is becoming. Often, this process began during the children's adolescence, but the couple was too preoccupied with the demands of parenting to notice each other's changes.

## Guidelines for Doing Couples Therapy with Middle-Aged Couples

*Assessing how much change is needed to make this marriage workable.* Many middle-aged couples, like the Palmers, will begin therapy with a hotly contested difference of opinion about the magnitude of change required. At their most polarized, one member may take the stance that only a few adjustments are needed, while the other member may feel that a complete overhaul of the original wedding vows is warranted or else divorce proceedings will commence. This difference mirrors the normative pulls of middle-age development faced by the individual: Are drastic change and starting over warranted, at the crossroads or midpoint of one's life, or is this a time to add and subtract elements to a life that is basically left intact? The couples therapist working with middle-aged couples needs to inquire about the extent and depth of felt dissatisfaction with the marriage and other aspects of each individual's life, including his or her work life, friendships, leisure pursuits, sexual and physical well-being, and relationships with children, parents, and other relatives. Where there is a gaping discrepancy in the extent of marital transformation needed, it must be addressed at the start of therapy in a forthright manner.

*Dealing with losses of many kinds comes with the territory of middle-age, regardless of parental status.* The losses of youthful dreams, of youthful bodies, and of the constancy of one's parents are linked to the process of aging. However, being parents of adolescents highlights some losses and introduces others that childless middle-aged couples do not face. For parents of adolescents, many losses take on an added poignancy: not only is one's body aging but there is a daily reminder of what is being left behind, in the form of one's own exuberant adolescent. The fact of these ready-made comparisons with youth makes many parents feel sad and even resentful of their children. Then there is the loss of one's children that middle-aged couples must confront, first as being dependent, then, as they move away, the loss of their presence on a daily basis. For Sally Palmer, it was the impending loss of her children that brought her and Sam into treatment. As she contemplated her son and daughter moving away, she felt lost as she tried to imagine a purpose to her life and a reason to stay married.

The therapist may wonder with the couple: Is this the first time in the couple's relationship they have faced loss? Are there previous losses, such as a miscarriage, death of a parent or sibling, or job loss, that were confronted earlier in the marriage? What was helpful to them in these previous situations?

Then, on a different tack altogether, some couples will divide up their feelings around loss so that one is the bearer of sadness, while the other voices feelings of excitement and anticipation for the future. One middle-aged couple with two adolescent sons planned to move to a new house that was far grander than their previous house. The wife tearfully sorted through all of their possessions, wanting to keep some of the old and reliving many of the sad times they had shared in the house. The husband, on the other hand, wanted to throw out all of their old furniture and paintings. For him, these were reminders of their own painful illnesses and of his mother, who had recently died in their house. Instead, he saw this move as a chance to start afresh and leave the losses and grief behind. For such a couple, it is helpful to point out and question the emotional division of labor that they are employing around loss: Do you notice that one of you is in charge of mourning the past, while the other has taken on the job of looking ahead to a brighter future? What would happen if you shared these tasks between you? Would that make the work easier or harder?

*Making room for the inner changes that accompany the development of a more complex and mature self can be the focus of therapy for middle-aged couples.* In her book *Dreams of Love and Fateful Encounters* (1990), Ethel Person writes about the salubrious effects on a marriage of sharing one's unconscious. She maintains that marriage partners who share their inner lives with each other have a limitless supply of excitement and novelty to sustain a lifelong passionate relationship. At middle-age, mutual access to each other's interior worlds can revitalize a relationship that is flagging under the strains of loss, reevaluation, and the pressures of parenting adolescents.

Can marriage partners expand their conversations with each other to make room for the inner changes that accompany the external changes of aging and loss? In Virginia Woolf's *Mrs. Dalloway* (1925), a novel about a day in the life of a middle-aged wife planning a dinner party, a former suitor offers these reflections on reaching middle age: "The compensation for growing old, Peter Walsh thought, . . . was simply this: that the passions remain as strong as ever, but one has gained—at last!—the power which adds the supreme flavour to existence, the power of taking hold of experience, of turning it round, slowly, in the light" (p. 119).

Whether marriage partners are willing to turn their experiences round in the light with each other becomes a central developmental question and a ripe area for couples work. Partners can be invited directly to share their dreams with each other. Or they can be asked to speak to each other as though writing in a journal, where the listener offers no judgments or opinions in response to the journal writer's offerings. Or they can be asked what topics they are aware of leaving out of conversations with the other partner and then to contemplate what would be lost or gained by bringing these topics into the conversation. In the novel *The Pull of the Moon* (Berg 1996), the heroine uses many of these strategies in a journey that leads her first to leave her husband for a meandering road trip and finally to return to him, hopeful about their future together. In her travel journal she finds that she writes in the way she wished she could speak to her husband. The central discovery of her journey is how much of her interior life she has kept from him and how important her inner life is to her. Eventually, she realizes that she wants to return to her husband and understand the "underside of his rock" as she has come to appreciate her own hidden parts.

For the Palmers, their journals focused each of them on a part of their inner world that had been overlooked. For Sam, it was a place to focus on nuances of emotion that had been overshadowed by the prevailing feeling of anger. For Sally, it was allowing herself to dream about a life unencumbered by mothering responsibilities. The Palmers went one step further than the heroine in *The Pull of the Moon*. They chose to share the underside of the rock with each other.

*Midlife is a time of reevaluation of the first half of life, a reevaluation that includes the marriage.* The couple may raise several questions about themselves and each other, as if the "givens" of the marriage are now up for grabs; for example, how much time will we spend together, alone or with others? How did we do as parents? What will engage our energies now that our children are preparing to leave or are actually gone? This reevaluation is spotlighted by the simultaneous public scrutiny that takes place as adolescents get graded and ranked through the process of applying to college. It is accentuated by the idealistic and sometimes harsh appraisals made by one's own adolescents as they question their parents' choices.

The couples therapist can loosen the pressures of internal and public scrutiny by asking questions that fast-forward the couple's relationship: In ten years, how would you like to be spending a weekend? What do you hope your sexual relationship is like then? Once your children have graduated from college or have gotten their first real job, how do you think you will look back on this time? The couples therapist may also introduce the idea of therapy as improvisational theater, where new roles and ideas can be played with before committing to an ongoing performance.

*Problems that required too much energy to confront before (when providing for the financial and emotional needs of the family took precedence) now come to the forefront.* Many middle-aged couples present with a problem in one partner that neither member of the couple wants to put up with any longer—such as obsessive compulsive disorder, depression, drinking, lack of sexual desire, a violent temper, or the lingering effects of childhood trauma. One of the goals of the evaluation is to figure out whether individual therapy is warranted to work on these long-standing issues. Even if warranted, however, the couple may prefer to work on such an issue together.

The Palmers offer an example of a couple in which the husband's long-standing individual issues demanded immediate attention by his wife. If Sam had been willing, I could have made a referral for individual treatment to explore his childhood abuse, which seemed to be at the root of his volatile temper. However, for Sam, the main impetus for change came from his wife. It was really for the sake of his marriage and his family that he was willing to tackle his "trick knee." For his own sake, he would have been happy to limp along without any therapeutic help. But for the sake of his marriage, he was willing to examine the roots of his volatile temper and make a commitment to talking about his hurt feelings before they metamorphosed into anger. For Sally, the turning point in the therapy came when Sam stopped himself from lashing out at her and instead sobbed about his feeling rejected by her. Sally told him that at that moment of courage and vulnerability, she had fallen in love with him again.

The Palmers illustrate the possibility for getting a second chance at midlife. This is a view that is subversively at odds with the popular view that midlife is merely a time of crisis and loss. Berg (1996) echoes the notion of midlife as a time of growth, as a time when aging offers perspectives that were not available in youth: "But why not get old, when what it means is more time with all that is here? When you learn to turn from the mirror, when you look up from your hands, you have a chance to see a garden truly because you are not in your own way" (p. 190). Therapy with midlife couples is an opportunity to attend to that garden; to help couples figure out whether it is the time to resow or to pull out bulbs that have stopped flowering, to rotate crops or to learn to enjoy the colors and species that have sprung up while they were too busy to notice. Before a therapist can embrace this view of midlife as a time of possibility and growth, it is important to examine some of the constraining cultural stories about midlife (shared by therapists and patients) and compare them to the more recent clinical research.

## Comparing the Cultural and the Scientific Discourse on Midlife Marriage

Midlife marriages, like adolescence itself, have been shaped by cultural and historical factors. For example, late middle life, which typically coincides with children leaving home, has grown dramatically in length since the beginning of the twentieth century. This stage, marked by the first child leaving home until the death of a spouse, has increased from a median of two years to almost twenty years, making the post-childrearing years now the longest stretch in a marriage. This dramatic change occurred because of smaller family size, women being younger when they have their last child, and a longer life expectancy (McCullough and Rutenberg 1989).

Another historical change in midlife marriages is the cultural expectation of a midlife crisis. British psychoanalyst Elliott Jacques (1965) first coined the term *midlife crisis* after studying the creative development of several outstanding artists, musicians, and writers. He concluded that all of the artistic geniuses had work crises in their late thirties. The crises took different paths: for some, like Gauguin, who at age 37 left his staid banking job and wife, the creative urge asserted itself for the first time. For others, like Mozart, the artistic flame burned out or died altogether. Of the 310 gifted painters, writers, and musicians Jacques studied, there was a dramatic death rate between ages 35 and 39, a rate that was far higher than the one reported for the general population during a comparable historical period. For those who survived this dangerous period, middle age was a time of reinventing creative gifts to allow the process to be slowed down and infused with new themes of loss and death, as had happened with Shakespeare, who moved from comedies in his twenties to tragedies in his late thirties.

This linguistic construct has so powerfully shaped what we expect of ourselves and each other at midlife that when a crisis fails to crystallize, many individuals feel that they have missed out on something critical. As one husband put it in describing his marital boredom, "I'm forty-five and I've been looking forward to something shaking us up, but instead it's just the same old thing day after day. Are we getting too old for a midlife crisis?" The psychological necessity of experiencing a midlife crisis is made manifest in Daniel Levinson's book *The Seasons of a Man's Life* (1978). Levinson argues that men who fail to go through a tumultuous time, or who go through the midlife transition only blandly, will pay a high cost later on. They will lack the vitality necessary for growth in subsequent adult stages of development.

Recent research (Cromie 1997) involving interviews of 15,000 midlifers over a period of eight years, however, reveals that midlife crisis is more a social construction than fact. The study, headed by Oliver Brim, found no evidence that crises occur more frequently in midlife than at any other age. Rather, most people in the study reported that these were the best years of their lives.

In the family life-cycle literature, midlife crisis is most often paired in time with adolescents leaving home, or the emptying of the nest. However, despite the popular notion that the empty nest, like the midlife crisis, is a time of great loss, research fails to confirm this view. Brim (Lowenthal and Chirboga 1972), summarizing several studies of marital happiness, concludes that the

postparental period is one of greater satisfaction in marriage than before. For most this is not a crisis period but rather a "golden period" in which there is an increase in shared activities with the spouse, a decrease in mutual concerns about money . . . there is possibly a "discovery" of the personality of the marital partner as it has evolved during the 25- to 30-year-period of childrearing. [p. 8]

In a study of more than 300 women, Harkins (1978) concluded that, on objective criteria, there was no difference in psychological well-being between the empty nest and non-empty nest women. On subjective criteria, the empty nest women reported significantly more positive well-being. Only one variable was found to account for a difference among women in reaction to their child's leave-taking: mothers whose children did not leave home on schedule, relative to their peers, experienced less psychological well-being.

If the research suggests quite solidly that the postparenting years are more halcyon than hellish, why is there a dread of the empty nest and a fear of midlife as a time of crisis? Kathy Weingarten (1988) argues that we use language and are used by it. Rather than merely reflecting a common experience, the language of "midlife crisis" has shaped how we view this passage. She suggests that we might view this transition differently if we used less dramatic language to describe it—for instance, a "midlife simmer." Interestingly, Wallerstein, in *The Good Marriage* (Wallerstein and Blakeslee 1995), observes that among happily married couples there were no serious midlife crises. For these couples, the impending change of children's leaving home was anticipated and welcomed. They viewed the empty nest as providing more time for each other and new pursuits, and they committed themselves to renewing the marriage.

The linkage of midlife crisis and empty nest obscures the more common simmering points for midlife marriages. These points come earlier, when the first signs of puberty occur and when the couple starts to anticipate their children's leave-taking.

## Two Common Simmering Points
## for Midlife Marriages

### *When a Child Enters Puberty*

Clinical anecdotes abound that tell of the impact of parent–
child relationships at early adolescence on parents' well-being. One mother of a 12-year-old son is stunned by the
changes brought over the course of a single summer. Six
inches taller and mustachioed, the boy she thought had lar-
yngitis turned out to have had a permanent voice change.
Tearfully, she tells of the way he recoils now from her touch,
as if there is an electrical charge attached to her hand. Once
eager to share confidences, he now grunts out monosyllabic
answers; his mother, devastated by the loss of easy conversation, feels sure that the boy she has loved and nurtured is
gone for good. A father of a 13-year-old girl tells of intensely
missing his daughter, who now spends most of her time with
friends, but he says he will not consider "holding her back" by
asking her to spend time with him. Another father confides
that he feels incompetent parenting his young adolescent son,
who is constantly questioning and arguing. Parents of young
adolescents frequently report on these themes of shock at the
physical changes brought on by puberty; loss of an earlier,
idealized relationship; and incompetence in the face of conflict.

There is some corroborating research to back up these clinical impressions. Small and colleagues (1983) suggest that
parents report greater stress when their children are early
adolescents than when they are preadolescent or middle adolescent children. In a three-year study of 200 families whose
oldest child was on the verge of puberty, Silverberg and
Steinberg (1990) reported that almost half of the parents
suffered a dramatic decline in well-being that was strongly
linked to the adolescent's changing self. Parents' distress was
correlated with feeling rejected by their adolescent's increased

autonomy and feeling stressed by increased parent–child conflict. As their children begin to question rules and detach themselves, parents may also engage in a period of reassessment and feel less sure of themselves as parents and spouses. In addition, the surge in disputes about rules at the cusp of puberty may make parents feel less competent, consequently making them perceive themselves and each other in a less favorable light.

Same-sex parent–child relationships are particularly vulnerable at the onset of puberty. In an earlier study, Silverberg and Steinberg (1987) looked at 129 families with firstborn children who were between the ages of 10 and 15; they found that a husband's marital satisfaction was predicted by his relationship with his son, whereas a wife's marital satisfaction was predicted by her relationship with her daughter. Mothers and fathers were more susceptible to midlife concerns when their same-sex children were more emotionally autonomous. That is, fathers were more likely to launch themselves on a journey of self-reevaluation if they had sons who no longer idealized them and had begun to form a differentiated sense of self. Similarly, mothers also reported heightened feelings of introspection when their daughters were emotionally separate. Mothers' midlife concerns were even more pronounced when their daughters were socially active and more physically mature.

In another study (Steinberg and Silverberg 1987), the researchers looked directly at the impact of parent–child distance on the marriage. They concluded that same-sex parent–child distance actually *leads* to marital dissatisfaction, rather than merely reflecting it. They also report that women's midlife concerns, though not men's, are predictive of marital satisfaction. They interpret this gender difference as suggesting that a woman's heightened sense of midlife issues may lead her, more than her husband, to challenge the power relations in the marriage and to demand a renegotiation of the marital contract. This focus on midlife concerns may itself be a factor in producing lower marital satisfaction. Or, it may happen that one partner (or both) has been growing a separate interior life and has been too busy to share it when the demands of caring for small children pressed on the couple's time and energy. As the first child enters puberty, and as the pressures mount to reevaluate, there is greater need for the adults to reveal their own psyches, checking out whether these changing selves still have a place in the marriage.

Papini and Roggman (1993), in a study of parents' experience of their attachment to early adolescents, found that parents who saw themselves as having a strong attachment to their adolescents also experienced less anxiety and depression. Intriguingly, they also reported less marital closeness. Must marital happiness be sacrificed to make way for a secure attachment with adolescents? In *The Pull of the Moon* Elizabeth Berg provides a partial answer.

In the novel, Nan, a 50-year-old mother and wife, takes off by herself on a literal and metaphoric journey of self-discovery. The dawning of how lost she feels in her marriage began when she realized that her daughter would be leaving home in four years. By the time she decides to return to her husband, she has found out things about herself that were unable to be spoken of in her marriage. In alternating journal entries and letters home to her husband, Martin, she records her revelations, highlighting all the experiences, fears, and fantasies that had been unspoken inside her marriage.

Near the beginning of her trip, Nan writes to Martin about the way she has kept so much of her inner life out of the marriage.

> I have felt for so long like I am drowning. And we are so fixed in our ways I couldn't begin to tell you all that has happened inside me. It was like this: I would be standing over you, pouring your coffee . . . and I would be loving you, Martin, but I would feel as though I were a ship pulling away from the

shore. . . . I would put the coffeepot back on the warmer and
sit opposite you and talk about what was in the newspaper,
and inside me would be a howling so fierce I couldn't believe
the sounds weren't coming out of my ears, from beneath my
fingernails. I couldn't believe we weren't both astonished—
made breathless—at this sudden excess in me, this unman-
ageable mess. There were a couple of times I tried to start
telling you about it. But I couldn't do it. There were no words.
As even now, there are not. Not really. [p. 6]

There is a great deal of wisdom in this passage. She is describing the crisis that can occur when marital partners fail
to keep each other abreast of the internal changes they are
making in response to their own aging process and in response to the development of their adolescent children. When
a couple has a child entering puberty, so much gets stirred
up that not pausing to reflect, and then not talking, can lead
to marital trouble.

### The Effects on the Couple of Anticipating a Child's Leave-Taking

There are hints in the life-cycle literature that the period immediately preceding the launching stage is more difficult for
couples than the period of the empty nest. Glenn (1975), in
his review of national surveys, found that there was greater
marital satisfaction in the postparental stage than in the
period just before the children were launched. In another
study, when Deutscher (1964) interviewed thirty-one parents
with children who had all left home, the majority indicated
that the postparental period was better than earlier stages.
These parents, aged 40 to 65, stressed the freedom that came
from having their children out of the house: freedom from
daily household responsibilities, freedom from having to be
role models, and freedom to travel. They also mentioned the
positive impact of feeling that they had accomplished the job

of parenting and did not have to wrestle with the uncertainty of the prelaunching years when they had not yet known how the children would turn out.

As the intense parenting years draw to a close, it is inevitable that couples evaluate each other and themselves. At the cusp of launching their children, they ask, "Have we done enough? Have we been good enough parents?" This can be a time of deep regrets for actions not taken, of anxiety about the future. When such self-evaluation becomes too uncomfortable, it may turn into blame of one's partner. This period preceding a child's leave-taking is a time of taking stock as a parent, in the face of uncertainty regarding how the child will do independently. It is often a time of heightened conflict with a child, who, in preparing to leave home, may be initiating more fights as a way to ease the transition. As if this weren't enough, the prelaunching stage is often a time of public scrutiny: as the child prepares college applications, takes SATs, goes for interviews, and is accepted and rejected by colleges, the parents must grapple with the judgments that others are making about their child. Self-evaluation, increased fighting, and uncertainty about one's child's future and outsiders' judgments can contribute to marital turbulence. The Palmer couple represents an example of a marriage that boiled from the heat of anticipating their eldest daughter's departure for college. For the Palmers, once their daughter left home, they were granted some closure about their uncertainty and were able to enjoy increased freedom and less daily conflict. In addition, they were able to share the pride of having completed a project and done it well.

Lil Meachum, in the film *The Great Santini,* voices the parental satisfaction of sending an adolescent off into the world. On her son's eighteenth birthday she writes him a letter about what it means to her that he has become a man: "Whatever you do and wherever you go, you go with my blessings. I knew nothing about love, and about the boundaries of love until I raised you. This has been your gift to me." His impending leave-taking makes her aware of the powerful love she has for him and how much he has given her. Parents in therapy, as they stand on the threshold of saying goodbye to their children who are heading off to college, sometimes make the same kind of statements. At its best, it is a time of taking stock and reflecting on the ways that parenting has made them grow up themselves. Couples therapy with the absent adolescent, or the adolescent about to absent himself from home, can help couples notice with pride the changes that have been wrought in them through their parenting and to talk about what they will do with this legacy in their time ahead.

# PART IV

## STORIES THAT PROFESSIONALS LIVE BY

# 8

# Understanding the Stories of Clinicians Who Treat Adolescents and Their Families

For more than a decade I have been teaching and supervising family therapy. Repeatedly, I am amazed by the passionate opinions held by beginning clinicians toward work with adolescents. These reactions fall into two major categories. The first is the view of the clinician who declares a great eagerness to work with adolescents and asserts a confidence that he or she has a flair for such work. The other reaction is one of great trepidation, accompanied by a conviction that work with adolescents will certainly not be part of any future career plans. Both groups of clinicians, usually fresh out of medical or graduate school, have only recently transversed their own adolescence. Since these reactions are not based on much, if any, previous work with adolescents, they must derive from the clinicians' own experiences as adolescents.

My intrigue at these visceral reactions toward adolescent work propelled me to question my trainees about their own stories of adolescence. Later, I became interested in how these early stories become transformed as clinicians entered midlife. Do therapists feel the same way toward their work with adolescents now as they did as young adults? How do they regard the parents of these youngsters now, as compared to when they were so much closer in age to the adolescents? Do they find that working with adolescents and their families infuses their therapeutic work with different characteristics than working with other populations? What do they find most difficult and most enjoyable about working with adolescents? A group of clinicians who defined themselves as therapists of adolescents and their families were posed these questions.

In this chapter the findings from this qualitative and exploratory study of clinicians are presented. These therapists' stories are examined at different points in their development and highlight the recurring stumbling blocks as well as the sustaining excitement that these clinicians navigate in their work with adolescents. Then, the therapists' responses are used as a springboard for discussing training and supervision. This discussion includes a review of countertransference, with an emphasis on Helm Stierlin's analysis of three common countertransference reactions to working with adolescents and their families. Subsequently, I discuss Bowenian and systemic approaches to integrating therapists' impasses in doing family therapy with an exploration of family-of-origin material.

## How Are Family Therapists Made?

The literature about therapists' own families is surprisingly scant. Bruce Lackie (1983) explains the paucity of material about caretakers' families this way: as therapists, we may be protecting our own families from exposure, a stance that is in keeping with our caretaking role.

In Krull's biography of Freud (discussed in Lowenstein 1980) Krull echoes this tendency for therapists to silence themselves about their own families. She argues that Freud gave up on his seduction theory out of loyalty to his father, who died a year before his delineation of the theory, leaving him with a dream message, "It is suggested to close the eyes." Krull writes that Freud interpreted this message to mean that he should not delve further into seduction theory, in which he might have discovered that his father was guilty of a seduction, like marital infidelity. Krull argues that the consequences of Freud's loyalty were great: he turned instead to elaborating the oedipal complex, which allowed him to identify his hostility at his father without uncovering the real reason behind it (Lowenstein 1980). While most family therapists are not writing and rewriting theories to protect their families of origin, the tendency as a therapist to repeat a role that one knows from childhood is borne out in studies of therapists' families of origin (Lackie 1983, Titelman 1987).

In a study of 1,577 clinical social workers (Lackie 1983), more than two-thirds described themselves as being mediators, good children, or of assuming a role of precocious autonomy in the families they grew up in. Consequently, Lackie argues, these parentified children decide, at an unconscious level, to become therapists in order to provide for others the parents they never had. Or as Lackie puts it,

> Professional caretaking, at least in the beginning then, may be an attempt to make symbolically one's own parents, or our parental introjects, more capable of parenting. It is an attempt to distort history. It can be a trade-off, a compromise, an attempt at individuation from the specialized role of parents to the parents. It can be an attempt to put to rest an impossible legacy through more limited, more manageable caretaking. [p. 317]

These insights into what motivates certain people to become therapists are intriguing. More questions arose. How would a therapist who had been a parentified, good child in his or her own family handle the acting out and rebelliousness of adolescent patients? Perhaps, I hypothesized, those therapists who do a substantial amount of their clinical work with adolescents had a somewhat different family role. Lackie's research raised more questions than it answered.

Were there gender differences? If it is "in the beginning" that therapists are motivated professionally by a wish to redo their childhoods, what happens to them, say, "in the middle"?

## The Study of Clinicians Who Are Drawn to Work with Adolescents and Their Families

To explore some of these questions, I interviewed sixteen therapists, all of whom spend at least a third (though a majority spend between half and two-thirds) of their professional lives doing therapy with adolescents and their families, or teaching and supervising this work. The therapists are all white, practicing in the greater Boston area, and range in age from 34 to 72, with the median age of 45. Of the sixteen, three are social workers, six are psychiatrists, and seven are psychologists. The sample was evenly divided by gender. All of the female clinicians wrote their answers to the questions, while the male therapists answered the same questions verbally as I wrote down their answers. This gender difference is one of many and is indicative of the nonscientific, qualitative approach I have taken. (As an aside, the gender difference in response style came about because I initially sent out the questions to about twenty clinicians. Only the women in my sample returned their questionnaires. When I recontacted the men and asked them if they would prefer a live interview to the questionnaire, every one responded affirmatively. Since this is not a study about research compliance, I am not going to interpret this gender difference, only report it.)

This study is exploratory and the findings, such as they are, are offered tentatively and without any presumption of scientific rigor. The questioning began by asking clinicians to tell three or four stories that captured their own experience of adolescence. The assumption was that these few selected stories would be charged with meaning in much the same way that earliest memories give a snapshot of major themes and conflicts. Subsequently, I asked them whether there were any stories or memories of adolescence that particularly struck them as significant now in middle age that might not have seemed so important when they were in their twenties.

There were then a few questions about professional development. In light of my supervisory experiences with clinicians in their twenties who had strong opinions about adolescent work, I was curious about the pathway into this work. I assumed that the choice would happen early on for those clinicians who ended up working with this population. I was also interested in changes that occurred as these clinicians aged and wondered whether their initial loyalty to the adolescents would give way to a more complex shared loyalty with the parents as well. In addition to a longitudinal look, I wanted to use a cross-sectional lens and asked clinicians how their work with adolescents compared with their other clinical work. Finally, I wanted to know what was particularly challenging about working with adolescents and families. (See Appendix 1 for the actual wording of the questionnaire.)

## The Therapists' Stories: Gender Differences and Commonalities

The male and female stories differed in some rather classic, predictable ways. A majority of the women therapists told stories about learning, as adolescents, the healing and transformative power of being listened to or of listening to others. Several women, for example, told of finding a therapist or teacher during adolescence who made them feel that they had something of importance to say. One woman, Ashley,[1] a 38-year-old psychologist, remembers calling a hot-line "to talk

---

1. All of the names of the therapists have been changed to protect their confidentiality.

with someone about my feelings and wishes to run away. The fact that they listened and I could talk about my feelings kept me from having to run away." Another psychologist, Molly, remembered running away to a teacher's house where she was sure to be listened to. Female clinicians also reported many stories about listening attentively, as a child, to someone else. Ashley writes, "as a parentified child, I felt it was my duty to listen to and solve [my parents'] problems."

The second most frequent female memory was of fights with their mothers, usually from the perspective of remembering their power as adolescents to inflict hurt on their mothers. Hannah, a 40-year-old psychologist and mother of two young sons who moved from Manhattan to rural New England to raise her family, recalls her adolescent power in this terse but evocative memory: "Telling my mother to go to hell and seeing her cry for the first time in my life at age 14." There was a startling absence of memories about fathers, except in the context of their illnesses or death.

The stories told by the male therapists in the study clustered around two predominant themes. The first was of remembering an injustice done to them, and their response to this injustice as a critical turning point in their identity formation. For example, a psychologist, Justin, now a chief administrator at a large Boston teaching hospital and father of two adolescent boys, was tearful thirty years later as he told of being reprimanded by a teacher and told to sit in a corner for something he did not do. He told the teacher he would not let himself be punished for a crime he didn't commit, then walked out of the classroom and told the principal. When the principal didn't correct the injustice, Justin walked out of the school and went home, where he stayed for several days. At the time, Justin was new to the school, and this incident served to define who he was in his peers' eyes, as well as in his own. As he sat with his legs stretched out on top of the desk, Justin told me that it still made him sad to tell the story about being "arbitrarily wrongly accused and whammed for standing up." But he discovered an important truth about himself, which is central to his current identity as an outspoken clinician: "When I think something is unfair, I can't stop myself from doing something about it."

And from another psychologist, Greg, age 41, the father of four small children and a clinician known as much for his ability to convulse a departmental meeting into gales of laughter as he is for his superb clinical skills, came this resonating story. "In my junior year I didn't make the football team and I thought it was an injustice." About a year later, after proving his athletic ability, the coach made up a special award for Greg that acknowledged the coach's earlier injustice. Greg said, "To win the award was the turning point of my life. The award was from the coach who never said he was wrong." In both of these stories, the experience was critical of having weathered and then transformed an injustice visited on them by an adult.

The second distinctly male adolescent story was one of adventure and travel with peers that helped define the young man as separate from the family left behind. There were several variations on this theme. One version, recounted by several men, was of an exhilarating trip taken with peers, "finding places to stay, pretending that we were older than we were—we could be more independent than we could be at home." John, now a prominent psychiatrist, recalled going to a foreign country for medical school, at age 19, and the thrill of being unreachable even by phone from a family that had been overly involved in his life up until then. Still another psychiatrist, Harry, now in his seventies, described his adolescence as being framed by going off to boarding school at one end, and, at the other, being stationed abroad during World War II. For each of these men, the memories of leaving home and spending time with peers was pivotal in their figuring out who they were going to be as adults. Only two women included comparable stories of adventure outside the family as defining their adolescence.

These stories were not the only tales told. There were two themes that ran through most of the clinicians' recollections of adolescence, regardless of gender: of being helpers and outsiders in their world of family and peers. That therapists would have learned to be caretakers in their own families was the most predictable story, based on the literature about therapists' family of origins (Lackie 1983, Titelman 1987). Many of the stories were about a parent becoming ill, through psychosis, alcoholism, or cancer, when the clinician was an adolescent.

Bob, a tall, congenial psychiatrist and administrator in his late thirties, told about the summer after his eleventh grade when he returned from camp and his parents came home after being away on vacation.

> When my father came back, he was grossly crazy, psychotic. My mom took to bed. I stayed up with him for a couple of days. I felt overwhelmed and blown away for a couple of days. . . . I had been a great basketball prospect, but I missed a bunch of practices because I was so distracted. Was I still a popular kid who did well in school, or a person marked by a manic parent? It was so difficult to integrate that smart popular kid that was tainted by this crazy parent.

This poignant story, which is clearly told from the perspective of a man looking back at the adolescent he was, suggests a confluence of themes that seems to characterize many of the therapists' stories. Not only is this a memory about being a caretaker, but it is also about the feeling of being on the outside, of being different from other kids because of the caretaking role he assumed.

A male social worker, Stan, also linked his memory of being a helper during adolescence with feeling like an outsider with his peers. An only child growing up in a single-parent family on the West Coast, Stan assumed early responsibility for taking care of himself. He recalled that at surfing parties, when everyone else was drinking alcohol, he was "the one who got everyone home and made people coffee." Commenting on his social role as a helper to his peers, he reflected, "I was outside a set of experiences; I felt outside adolescent culture because I wasn't high or drunk." In addition, he knew that he could never wreck the family car because it was the one that he and his mother depended on.

Many of the female therapists also told stories about bearing this dual mark of caretaking while feeling on the margins. One psychiatrist, Karen, a highly regarded teacher and clinician at a Boston teaching hospital, recalled feeling academically successful as an adolescent "but socially in the shadows of more attractive and sexual peers." While conscious of being on the outside looking in on her more popular peers, Karen became a confidante to male and female friends. This status as listener allowed her "to understand their experiences, using them as shields against having to act myself in the scary arena of sexuality." From the vantage point of midlife, Karen saw her role in adolescence, that of confidante for issues she felt too immature to grapple with herself, as preparing her for the person she grew into. She reflects, "I appreciate how my insecurities led me to become psychologically minded, which is a piece of myself I now value highly."

This particular mixture of being a helper and feeling on the outside of one's peer group or family seems to be the most common thread in the stories told by therapists who are drawn to work with adolescents. There were many different brews of this mixture. Sometimes the status of outsider conferred on the adolescent a sense of being more mature and therefore capable of helping his or her peers. In others, the ability to listen to others masked a feeling of being different from or less mature than peers. In still others, the experience of being different from peers, when based on confronting a parent's illness or death, developed into a heightened, precocious sensitivity to others. In any case, these stories raised the question of whether previous reports about therapists' childhood roles as parentified children, or mediators, were incomplete as they applied to therapists who work with adolescents. While it seems that many of the therapists in this study fit the portrait of having been helpers in their families, many also described a powerful sense of having been different from their peer group. Perhaps this sense of differentness, albeit inextricably linked with their identification as a caretaker, is what predisposed this group of clinicians to be drawn to the particular vicissitudes of adolescence.

## Professional Development

With this predisposition as a starting point, the question remained of how these clinicians decided to work with adolescents. Did they know, as some of my beginning trainees seem to, that they would be well suited to working with adolescents? If they did have an idea at the beginning of training that they wanted to work with this population, how did their views of themselves as clinicians change as they became closer in age to the parents of adolescents?

As predicted, almost all of the clinicians in my study started working with adolescents very early in their careers. In fact, almost all of the women and a few of the men reported that they began working with children while they themselves were adolescents—for example, tutoring children and working in day-care centers and camps. All but one of the five male psychiatrists started out as pediatricians and then segued into child psychiatry. In other words, it seems that these clinicians got an early start, often as adolescents themselves or during the opening chapters of their careers.

I initially thought that this early pull toward working with children signaled a precocious self-knowledge that one was well suited to this work. What the study found was somewhat murkier. Many therapists said that they had stumbled into their work, that it had chosen them rather than the other way around. These clinicians referred to their decision to work with adolescents as the "luck of the draw" or "slipping into it" because it offered administrative responsibilities. One psychiatrist, Allen, a 50-year-old father of three adolescent boys, stated simply, "It's always been a little mysterious how I ended up in working with adolescents. I don't think I appreciated what it was going to be like." A few therapists observed that they had gone into this work when they noticed that many of their peers were made uncomfortable by adolescents. It seems that for these clinicians, their relative ease with adolescents was something to capitalize on as their own burgeoning identities were unfolding.

A handful of therapists reflected that they were drawn to work with adolescents because their own adolescence had been so memorable. In particular, two clinicians felt that being profoundly helped during adolescence, by a therapist and by a teacher, propelled them toward wanting to perform the same service for others.

And still another group of therapists reported being far more deliberate in choosing this work. They cited a compelling constellation of qualities that even at the very start of their careers they associated with adolescents. Adolescents' intensity, directness, and aliveness were noted by these clinicians as uniquely appealing. In addition, the stage of development itself, a "time of tons of possibility," was identified as exciting because of its fluidity, plasticity, and the opportunity for change afforded for the individual and the family. As one psychiatrist put it, "This is this last chance to do an anticipatory and preventative piece of work; that's what I enjoy."

Among therapists who were drawn to adolescent work and among those who stumbled into it, many mentioned that the therapeutic relationship with adolescents was particularly interesting to them. Clinicians reported being stimulated by establishing just the right amount of distance and being challenged by adolescents' unwillingness to let them hide behind a professional mantle. Consequently, many therapists reported feeling more "real," "self-disclosing," and "straightforward" and reported using more humor with adolescents than they did with other clients. Stan, reflecting on his experience as director of a facility for emotionally disturbed adolescents, said, "They taught me how to be straightforward with myself about what I'm doing and carry that over with all my clients. When I'm asked by kids, 'Why do you do this work?,' I answer it, and that is not the way I was taught."

## The Shift at Midlife

Many clinicians observed that the kind of therapist they learned to be with adolescents early on in their careers has generalized over time and has come to define the kind of therapist they are now with all of their clients. Justin described how his early work with adolescents came, by midlife, to inform his typical therapeutic style:

> I have gotten more relaxed. I have more fun. I don't care about clinical theory. I know that my irreverence is grounded in a lot of experience. When I was younger, I used to feel that I had to be more parental. Now, I think I have learned to treat other populations the way I do adolescents. I think that everyone has to go back to limbic reality, which is so present with adolescents. I have generalized to other populations what I learned with adolescents.

Justin is describing a process that was echoed by others as well. Initially drawn to clinical work with adolescents because it allowed them to be more emotionally present, to show humor, to be flexible about self-disclosure, they reported that by middle age, this way of being a therapist came to define all of their clinical work.

There were other changes that therapists observed as a function of their becoming older and more experienced. Several clinicians poignantly stated that their work with adolescents had made them aware of what they themselves had missed out on as teenagers. Stan, who as an only child had assumed precocious responsibility for himself and his more risk-taking peers, wished that he had learned as a teenager to draw more attention to himself, since that is a skill that is required again at midlife. Another therapist, Sarah, wished that she had been less compliant in the face of her parents' multiple divorces and moves, a stance she believes in retrospect would have made her less depressed. Still others experience vicariously with their adolescent patients aspects of childhood that they missed out on, like fighting with parents and having teenage romances. Some therapists described a process of becoming more understanding of their adolescent selves, as they reexperienced through their patients some of their own earlier struggles. Harold, a psychiatrist in his fifties who described a lonely childhood as a highly intellectual only child, stated, "As I've grown older, I've become more charitable about my younger self. I did pretty well with what I had. This helps me help kids be more charitable with themselves."

By far the most frequently mentioned change was in therapists' work with parents of adolescents. This change was attributed both to reaching midlife and to becoming parents themselves. Bob, a psychiatrist who recently became a parent, told me,

It used to be, "You [the adolescent patient] and me against those bastards." As soon as my wife was pregnant, it was "You poor parents with those impossible kids." I had had almost no perspective on parents. Whatever parents told me before I was a parent, I thought they were putting a spin on it. I didn't appreciate that most parents are doing the best they can.

Another psychiatrist, Allen, the father of three adolescents, described a shift in perspective this way:

> In having my own adolescent, I have a feeling of "we" with parents. I feel less like a perfectly sane parent who knows what he's doing. I often use the words "we as parents." I won't talk about my experiences with my own sons, but I will make references to "us as parents." . . . Having three sons keeps me appropriately humble. I'm dealing with issues in real life and then in the office.

This shift in perspective brought on by parenthood made some therapists report that they felt more comfortable jumping into the middle of generational conflict because they finally felt that they could understand both perspectives and not be unfairly swayed by one. A unique perspective on the therapist's role in generational conflict was offered by one psychiatrist, Harry, age 72, who said that for the last decade he has used the fact of his age more actively. "It's easier now working with adolescents," he explained, "because I'm considerably different from their fathers. It's an advantage that I'm different from their parents because I can stay out of the generational tug of war. I'm safer."

Other therapists described a change at midlife in their eagerness to draw parents out about the pain that they are in. One female psychologist, Molly, noted this change in her clinical work, a change that she attributed to reaching midlife, becoming a parent, and remembering her mother's silence about her breast cancer when Molly was an adolescent.

> Now I'm keenly aware of the topics that parents keep silent about, perhaps to protect their children, perhaps because they believe that parents, and particularly mothers, should not have pain of their own. Where I was mainly interested in what

kids had to suffer silently, now I pay attention to the editing that parents do about their difficulties and sorrows. I question parents about why they only talk about certain experiences and not others—about their work, for example, but not about their alcoholism.

This change toward increased sympathy with parents also prompts many therapists into being less dismissive of parents and instead trying to include them in the treatment whenever possible. I was surprised at the lengths that therapists go to involve parents, devising far more flexible strategies for engaging them than they do with their other clients. Many therapists described a treatment that began with an assessment of the child and the family together and separately, and then an ongoing treatment plan that included continued involvement of everyone. I think that these flexible treatment plans, although described by each therapist as a unique solution to working with this population, arise from a wish to honor their divided loyalties in families with adolescents, as well as to uphold the crucial contribution and attachment of parents to their children.

## What Is Most Difficult?

If there was a great deal of overlap and resonance among therapists regarding their developmental changes, there was little agreement in response to the last question, "What is most difficult about working with adolescents and their families?" There were almost as many different responses as there were clinicians in the study. The only answer that was offered by several therapists was that they now find it difficult to respond clinically to teenagers acting out their pain impulsively and self-destructively without becoming parental. Otherwise, therapists answered this question in idiosyncratic ways.

Sue, a social worker and director of an adolescent inpatient evaluation center, stated that she was most stymied by the intensity of an adolescent's rage and depression, an intensity that carried with it "an indictment of you. You are an adult and therefore responsible." This is the same woman who in writing about her own adolescence described several incidents of feeling overly responsible for another's pain. She remembered her father's last Thanksgiving dinner before his death from cancer a few months later. Sue recalled that she heard her mother tell the family to go ahead and eat without their father present. Later, after the meal had commenced, Sue's mother brought her husband in his wheelchair into the dining room, where he was surprised to find that the family had started eating without him. Sue felt devastated that she had not known to wait for her father and recalled running "out of the house in a frantic self-hating fit. After running, out of breath, for some time, I lay my face in the dirt and broken glass of the bend in the road to hurt myself. My father's last Thanksgiving ruined." It seems hardly surprising that a therapist who felt such intense self-loathing and responsibility in the face of her father's dying would be unraveled years later by her adolescent patients' intense outpourings of rage and depression.

Lucy, a thoughtful, soft-spoken 40-year-old psychologist specializing in women's development, makes an overt connection between what is difficult for her today in working with adolescents and what was most challenging in her own adolescence. As an adolescent Lucy was shy and introspective, gravitating to a group of less popular kids at church. Decades later, she observes that she still feels anxiety when faced with a popular, outgoing teenager and worries about whether she will be able to make a connection. She notes,

> The anxiety feels like a throwback to my own teenage years where fitting in with all the different groups, especially the "popular kids," was a big deal. I am sure that this has dimin-

ished over time, as I have experienced the difference between how awkwardly I related to such kids as a kid myself and the relative ease with which I form relationships with them as an adult.

I think that the idiosyncratic nature of these responses about what is difficult for the clinician suggests that they tap the therapist's unique history. More than the answers to any of the other questions asked, the responses offered were too individualistic and varied to present a pattern or trend. Rather, what is difficult for a particular clinician seems to have more to do with emotional make-up, and his or her role in the family of origin than with overarching developmental trends or properties endemic to working with adolescents. The intersection of a therapist's particular history as an adolescent and his or her impasses as a family therapist is a challenging area for supervision.

## Application to Supervision

In supervision, when a trainee seems to encounter a recurrent stumbling block that is not related to his or her skill level or knowledge of theory, I am curious about the young therapist's own experiences as an adolescent but cautious about overstepping the bounds of supervision. The weaving back and forth between impasses in the current clinical work and the therapist's own family of origin has been written about by many family therapists who run the theoretical gamut (Chasin and Roth 1991, Framo 1976, Guerin and Fogarty 1972, Roberts 1994, Stierlin 1977, Titelman 1987).

Frank Pittman, family therapist and author of *Turning Points* (1987), has written, "I'm not sure that people are truly adult until they have been through adolescence from both ends . . . . Those years of children coming of age can be a more vivid experience than a comparable period of psychoanalysis, and often bring them far closer to their own parents" (p. 176). I think that for therapists working with adolescents and their parents, this work can be an incomparably vivid experience as well. The drama of this stage of the life cycle usually pulls therapists toward an identification with one grouping or the other. Perhaps professional maturation comes when as therapists we have learned to side with both adolescents and their parents and when we can see both sides of their dilemmas simultaneously.

Helm Stierlin, a family therapist and psychoanalyst, writes about these impasses as countertransference reactions and describes three that are particularly common among therapists who work with adolescents and their families (Stierlin 1977). He argues that family therapy with adolescents is particularly vulnerable to countertransference because of the heightened conflicts of loyalty inherent in working with this population. Two of these reactions are more typical among younger therapists, while the third is more characteristic of middle-aged therapists such as the ones in my study.

In the first type, the therapist—often a younger therapist not long out of adolescence—sides with the sick, victimized adolescent. Typically, says Stierlin, this siding is enticing to a therapist who believes that the patient's parents are using projective identification to locate all of their own disturbance in their child. Stierlin cautions that this therapist should resist the urge to side with the adolescent against the parent and instead should acknowledge the power that the adolescent wields over the parent. Stierlin maintains that this countertransference reaction is most likely to arise if the therapist has not truly separated from his or her own parents and is hoping that the patient's parents will feel badly for the things that the therapist's own parents did to him.

The second countertransference reaction, like the first, is more common among younger therapists. In this one, the therapist sides with the rebellious adolescent who overtly seems to be waging a battle for independence against his parents and with the support of the therapist. Stierlin warns that this therapist may miss a critical piece of projective identification: that the adolescent, rather than rebelling, may be conforming to the parents' disowned rebellious impulses. Stierlin concludes that this therapist, often still stuck in late adolescence himself with unresolved issues concerning individuation and separation, may try to enlist his rebellious patients to continue the therapist's own rebellious struggles.

With the third countertransference response, therapists feel bad for the beleaguered parent who is being pushed around by the incorrigible teenager. Stierlin states that these therapists, who often have their own adolescent children, may encourage the parents to reject their own teenagers. Stierlin cautions that these therapists may be taking their adolescent patients to task for what was once done to them by their own parents. Regardless of the type of countertransference reaction, Stierlin advises the therapist to pay attention to it and to develop understanding by exploring any difficulties that the therapist had during adolescence in separating from his or her family.

This exhortation to examine one's family of origin is echoed by several Bowenian family therapists (Bowen 1978, Guerin and Fogarty 1972, Titelman 1987). In a now legendary presentation at a family therapy conference in 1970, Murray Bowen discarded his planned theoretical paper and, at the last minute, delivered instead a highly personal account of a therapeutic journey he made to his family of origin. Using his own constructs of triangles and self-differentiation, Bowen identified those triangles in which he played a primary role and then took actions that allowed him to become both more differentiated and more intimately connected with family members. By his example, Bowen demonstrated how inextricably linked are family theory and practice, and he urged therapists to work on their relationships with their own families in order to become better family therapists.

Guerin, a devotee of Bowen, argues that supervisors of family therapy should model the importance of these journeys by doing their own family-of-origin work in front of trainees. Fogarty underscores the urgency of doing personal exploration as a part of supervision. He writes, "Any supervision that limits itself to the trainee and the family he is seeing is practically worthless. It becomes only an intellectual exercise. Supervision as such should cease" (Guerin and Fogarty 1972, p. 20).

The process of teaching Bowenian concepts as they apply to a therapist's own family exploration is most succinctly described by Guerin (Guerin and Fogarty 1972). He advises supervisees to make a three-generational family genogram and focus on defining those primary triangles that are working well and those that are problematic. Subsequently, the trainee, using letter writing, phone calls, and visits home, attempts to extricate him- or herself from some of these triangles by, for example, refusing to gossip with one member about a third. The desired goal of working on one's own family is the ability to carry on one-on-one relationships with each family member.

Narrative family therapists, too, have offered creative ways of connecting a trainee's family stories with their clinical work. Janine Roberts (1994), in *Tales and Transformations*, describes the powerful process unleashed in the trainee as he or she studies family therapy. "For most people this study evokes reflection and thinking about their own experiences on a number of levels" (p. 148). For one young therapist, the study of narrative therapy meant learning a new vocabulary that helped make sense of his own family history in some new ways. "For other trainees it might mean becoming aware of stories that have been painfully silenced for a long time, such as that of an alcoholic mother, sexual abuse by a brother, a violent father" (p. 148). She advocates working with trainees' own stories as a way of using the intense engagement that comes from linking one's own experiences with theory. As a further advantage, eliciting trainees' stories keeps them out of the role of expert, since they are involved in a parallel process to their client families. (For examples of several inventive exercises for working with trainees' stories, see *Tales and Transformations: Stories in Families and Family Therapy*, pp. 147–182.)

Roth and Chasin (1991), therapists at the Family Institute of Cambridge, have designed a consultation technique that moves clinicians from current impasses in their clinical work to corresponding difficulties in their families of origin. Working with a small group of trainees, Chasin and Roth (1991), focus on one clinician's dilemma in a single consultation. Using other group members to constitute the clinical "family," the therapist re-enacts the therapy just to the point of impasse. The consultant then amplifies this moment by drawing attention to unique spatial configurations, idiosyncratic language, and unusual body language used. The purpose of this intensification is "to trigger a significant 'flash-back' to a problematic time . . . in the therapist's family of origin" (p. 3). Subsequently, the therapist is asked, "When in your childhood have you been in such a predicament or felt or reacted this way?" (p. 2); then he or she is invited to enact the family-of-origin scene that has been triggered by these connecting questions. Again, other group members are enrolled as the therapist's own family members.

The consultant does not leave the therapist in this difficult role-play. Instead, the therapist is asked to repair his or her own painful past recollection with inquiries such as "What needs to happen here?" or "What would have had to have been different in your parents' childhood for them to respond differently in this scene you just enacted?" In short, the therapist is asked to throw caution to the winds and rewrite history, going back as many generations as is needed. The consultee typically plays each of the family roles, acting as the transformer and the transformed.

After this intervention, which requires the therapist to re-write his or her own life, direct, and star in it, the clinical case at hand is revisited. The free-wheeling approach that the therapist took to revamping his or her own family history should infuse the clinical material. The therapist is encour-aged to address the initial impasse through another role play of the clinical case, by "saying anything that comes into your head." The therapist may be asked to switch places with the clients to feel fully the impact of the new therapeutic posi-tion or direction. Roth and Chasin conclude that while thera-pists rarely repeat verbatim what they have enacted in the consultation group, they do come away with a more flexible, open approach to their case.

For those consultants and consultees who are less comfort-able with a psychodramatic approach, Roth (Chasin and Roth 1989) suggests a verbal adaptation of the model that she terms *genographic*. The therapist first describes the clinical impasse and then discusses the impasse so the consultant gets a feel for the distinctive language and affect that surrounds the difficult spot. Then the therapist is asked to look at his or her own genogram for parallel impasses in past relation-ships or events. The consultant has a conversation with the therapist "about the past in a language that deliberately evokes feelings, using charged images and metaphors" (p. 3). The therapist is then asked to tell a story that would repair the difficult pattern identified in the genogram. On the heels of this storytelling, the therapist is redirected to the original clinical dilemma. The hope is that the freshness and sponta-neity of his or her own rewritten story will be released and will revitalize the clinical impasse.

These psychodramatic and genographic consultation ap-proaches are both derived from narrative theory and a belief in the power of altering stories to effect change. As with the Bowenian approach discussed earlier, the therapist's treat-ment impasses are construed as being directly linked to his or her own troublesome patterns in the family of origin. But rather than return to one's family of origin and try out new positions in troublesome triangles, Roth and Chasin advocate changing the patterns by rewriting history. Furthermore, they seem to suggest that the freedom found in healing one's own story through rewrites will carry over to a more creative, spontaneous approach in one's clinical work.

My main criticism of the Bowenian and the narrative approaches to connecting clinical impasses with family-of-origin material is that they are too time-intensive and demand a willingness for self-disclosure that a training setting may simply not permit. In a busy private practice or pressured hospital setting, both of these supervisory approaches seem luxurious, even extravagant. I have made my own adaptations so that some of the ideas contained in these approaches fit the time constraints I am under as a supervisor in a time-pressured medical setting. For example, I am mindful of Stierlin's three countertransference reactions and will ask clinicians who they feel more pull to, the adolescent or the parents. I may then ask what they think the risks are to the family of maintaining such a position and what they think it will take for them to develop a dual loyalty to adolescents and parents. I often ask my trainees to tell me some stories about their own adolescence and then ask them to reflect on the connections between these stories and their current beliefs about adolescence and middle-aged parents. Finally, when a trainee hits an impasse that does not seem solely related to skill level or knowledge base, I will ask, "What do you think the child in the family needs? What do you think the parents need? And what did you need when you were in a similarly difficult spot as an adolescent?"

I recognize that these interventions are so pared down that they may seem like the very poor relations of the richly complex techniques proffered by Roth, Chasin, Bowen, and others. Mainly, I am trying to introduce the idea to my trainees that their adolescence may be continuing to exert some influence on their clinical work. Sometimes, when a supervisee is stuck in a repetitive impasse that is impervious to direct advice from me, I help supervisees sift through several layers of obfuscating debris. One layer to sort through consists of their tightly held beliefs about adolescence, garnered from their own experiences as adolescents and from resonating cultural messages. Another layer addresses their current stage of development, particularly if they are in the process of separating from their parents through an impending marriage or ongoing analysis, or if they are parents of adolescents. It can be helpful, too, to share with trainees the cultural and scientific stories that are told about adolescence. Making each of these distinctions helps bring a more fully textured, flexible, and creative approach to the clinical work.

# 9

# Cultural and Scientific Stories about Adolescence

Everyone has a comment or a story about adolescence. It is an extremely powerful idea in our culture that reverberates through the psyches of all ages—from young children looking up in awe at older siblings and teen stars, to middle-aged parents remembering and reinventing their own adolescence, to elders longing for the vitality and sense of immortality associated with their youth. Coming of age, as a theme, is more frequently represented in film and in novels than perhaps any other idea. The allure of the coming-of-age story is universal, regardless of the age of the reader or viewer. There is a little adolescent in all of us, if by adolescent we mean in the process of becoming someone.

Adolescence is concurrently a set of biological changes, a significant element of our culture, a historical construction, and the subject of recent, prolific scientific study. The emphasis here is on comparing the cultural discourse on adolescence with scientific findings. The content of the cultural discourse has been gleaned from three sources: first, from social historians who study adolescence as a historical construction; second, from novels with adolescent protagonists, which have been widely assigned to teenagers in school or have proven their appeal to adolescents over several decades; and third, from popular movies that also portray the adolescent as the hero, beginning with movies of the 1940s and continuing to those of the present. This cultural material was approached with several questions:

"Have our ideas about adolescence, as they appear in the popular culture, changed over the last fifty years?"

"Are there any notions about adolescence that seem *not* to be influenced by historical and economic changes, but rather continue to be put forth in novels and movies, from one era to the next?"

"When adolescence is studied by scientists in mental health and by public health researchers, how is their picture of adolescence similar to and different from popular views?"

This exploration of the cultural discourse on adolescence reveals that as a culture, we hold many compelling stories about adolescence, some of which illuminate more about the fantasies and longings of the adolescents' parents than about the adolescents themselves. Ideas and stories about adolescence powerfully inform the experiences of family members presenting for therapy and the therapists who listen.

## ADOLESCENCE AS A HISTORICAL CONSTRUCTION

Stanley Hall, an American psychologist who championed the child-study movement at the turn of the century, published a tome in 1905, *Adolescence: Its Psychology and Its Relations to Physiology, Anthropology, Sociology, Sex, Crime, Religion, and Education*. With the publication of this book, Hall is widely credited with inventing adolescence (Demos and Demos 1969), if inventing means formally labeling and describing adolescence as a universal stage of development. His book, so vast as to almost defy summary, emphasized adolescence as a stage that all humans pass through, characterized by powerful "antithetical impulses" and as a time of great turmoil. In fact, as the Demoses (1969) point out, there were books and magazine articles written in the 1820s about "youth" that anticipate Hall's writing and suggest that his work was not groundbreaking but rather built on popular ideas of his time (Beecher 1844).

Hall's descriptions so closely resemble later psychoanalytic notions (Blos 1967, Erikson 1958) and current popular ideas of adolescence as a period of inevitable *Sturm und Drang* that one might be tempted to credit Hall with discovering a truly universal, ahistorical phenomenon. However, social historians have formulated a different way of looking at adolescence; rather than viewing adolescence as a universal, psychological stage, they see it as an invention of a particular historical time. They point to the transformation from an agricultural to an industrial society as the impetus for creating adolescence as a stage of development. This transformation, which began at the beginning of the nineteenth century, had broad implications for family life. In farm families, children and parents tended to share the same tasks, leisure pursuits, friends, and goals. As young farm workers, children functioned like miniature adults and were expected to contribute from a young age to the economic viability of their family. Their lack of a separate identity as children was underscored by their isolation from peers. As families began to move into cities, children no longer shared the same work roles as their parents and came into close contact with peers. The industrial economy could not absorb as many workers as the rural economy, and so the idea of adolescence as a time of moratorium from work came to be widely accepted.

## THE CULTURAL DISCOURSE ON ADOLESCENCE

The cultural discourse on adolescence is shaped by social institutions, such as the mental health field, juvenile courts, and schools, as well as by the language used by families and in the media, novels, and films. Michael Ventura, in the *Utne Reader*, offers fascinating reflections on the language surrounding adolescence:

> Adolescence is a cruel word. Its cruelty hides behind its vaguely diagnostic air. To say someone is "adolescent" or "going through adolescence" or, worse, "being adolescent" is to dismiss their feelings, minimize their trouble, and (if you're their parent) protect yourself from their uncompromising rage. The words teenager and teen are worse. They reek of cuteness. But we all know that being a "teen" doesn't feel cute. [p. 63]

When the language that is available for a particular subject is awkward or inadequate (consider the arcane language around the topic of infidelity, for example), it usually reflects discomfort on the part of the language makers, in this case parents, teachers, and therapists. When adolescents speak of themselves, their descriptors are far richer and evocative: hippie, yippie, beatnik, greaser, punk, geek, rapper, home-boy, and freak are some of the names generated by adolescents over the last four decades (Ventura 1994).

Ventura offers an explanation for why adults have invented such awkward language for their youth, an explanation that addresses the pull of adolescence as a projective for adults:

> Our secrets, our compromises, our needs, our lacks, our failures, and our fear that we're going to fail again—all this stirs and starts to growl somewhere deep inside when the young look hard into our grown-up eyes. It's as though, in some dark way, they are privy to our secrets, even to what we don't know about ourselves, and when they so much as glance toward

those parts of us, oh, our old panics resurrect those demons
we thought we'd dealt with, grown out of, transcended, es-
caped—it only takes this goddam kid, and the beasts awake.
As a parent you may measure your fears by the extent of your
distance from that kid. [p. 64]

Films and novels offer a way to look further at adolescence
as a middle-age projective, since so many coming-of-age films
and novels are told from the perspective of a parent and are
rarely written or directed by an adolescent.

## NOVELS ABOUT ADOLESCENCE

For the past four years, I have read almost nothing but coming-of-age novels during my leisure time. Even so, I have only
skimmed the surface of this literary genre. My selections were
guided by a wish to revisit the books I had enjoyed as an
adolescent and by suggestions from high school English teachers, librarians, and colleagues, as well as my adolescent patients and friends. In general, the books seem to cluster into
four different subgroups. Rather than discuss all the books
listed in each subgenre, I have chosen to highlight one as an
illustrative example of each type. As it turns out, most of
these exemplars are books I read with binocular vision: I read
them first as an adolescent and then, twenty-five years later,
as an adult.

By far the largest subgroup is the novel that features an
adolescent protagonist who is very much on the margin, by
dint of being a mental patient or a social pariah. Usually,
though not always, the female heroine of these novels finds
her voice through an inward search, while the male counter-
part finds his by outward risk-taking. Most boldly stated, the
female protagonists tend to be crazy while the males are social outlaws. Some examples of this genre with female protagonists who are psychologically eccentric are: *Go Ask Alice,*

by Anonymous; *I Never Promised You a Rose Garden*, by Joanne Greenberg; *Girl, Interrupted*, by Susanna Kaysan; and *Not the End of the World*, by Rebecca Stowe. Examples of novels with male protagonists who rebel through action include: *Mystery Ride*, by Robert Boswell; *The Outsiders*, by S. E. Hinton; and *Adventures of Huckleberry Finn*, by Mark Twain. Two other novels feature male heroes whose rebellion is introspective and psychologically complex: *Portrait of the Artist as a Young Man*, by James Joyce; and *The Catcher in the Rye*, by J. D. Salinger.

*The Catcher in the Rye* is a classic example of this subgenre of novel with the adolescent hero as a rebellious and unflinchingly honest observer of his world. Perhaps because *The Catcher in the Rye* is about a boy who acts out through drinking and getting expelled from school, and who is *also* psychologically unstable in the tradition of female heroines, the book has appealed to both boys and girls since its publication in 1954. Over the years, the novel has elicited a range of response from adult authorities, who have periodically banned it and made it required reading in high school English classes. Told in the first person, from an institution that is probably a psychiatric hospital, it is the irreverent account of Holden Caulfield's journey home following his fourth expulsion from a prep school.

Rereading it as an adult, I was struck by the book as a critique of what is expected of male adolescents in upper-middle-class America. Olga Silverstein (Silverstein and Rashbaum 1994), a clinical social worker, writes that "Holden is a dismal failure at conventional masculinity" (p. 114), if masculinity is defined by the values of Pency Prep, from which he has just been expelled. At this all-male boarding school, the conventional values, which Holden summarily rejects, are getting good grades, making money, scoring with girls, and winning at sports. Instead of following his father's plan for him to attend an Ivy League college and make a lot of money, he envisions a future as "a catcher in the rye," a distinctly noncorporate job: his dream is to become someone who stands on the edge of a cliff where children are playing, ready to catch anyone who starts to run over the edge. He rejects, too, the prep school ideal of having sex with as many women as possible. Instead, he only wants to talk with a prostitute and confesses that he is admiring of girls and believes them when they say "no" to intercourse. His closest relationships are to his younger sister Phoebe, his dead brother, and his mother. Such close ties to the family are hardly the stuff of an independent male hero.

The dual task of resisting the social order and figuring out where one fits in is a theme that has captured the imagination of writers over the ages. Patricia Spacks (1981) argues in *The Adolescent Idea* that there is a predominance of literature about adolescence because this dual theme lends itself to novelistic treatment. How else to explain why so many books are written about a time of life when so little is accomplished in the external world? Coincidentally, it is also a dual task that parents expect and fear from their adolescents. This subgenre reminds adults to question the existing social order—the rules about gender, class, and the meaning of happiness. At the same time, such novels sanction adolescents to perform a role that adults expect of them and of novelists—to stand outside of the adult world, holding a mirror up for us to see ourselves and ask if this is the best we can do.

Another substantial subgenre is the adolescent apprenticeship novel, which features an adolescent moving from comfortable surroundings to difficult circumstances and who, in the process, becomes an adult. Examples of this group include *The Diary of Anne Frank*; *Lucy*, by Jamaica Kincaid; and *Candide*, by Voltaire. *The Diary of Anne Frank* is one of the most remarkable books about adolescence ever written. First published in Amsterdam in 1947 and in the United States in 1952, it has since been translated into at least thirty languages and has sold many millions of copies. It is the only published work of a 15-year-old girl, written during her two years of hiding from the Nazis during War World War II.

John Berryman's (1976) interpretation of the significance of Anne Frank is astute: the "subject of Anne Frank's diary (is) even more fundamental and mysterious than St. Augustine's and . . . is the conversion of a child into a person" (p. 93). With only her own resources of a keen intellect, acute observational powers, and a fertile imagination, she manages to separate herself from her family, awaken sexually and spiritually, and fall in love. She manages all the tasks of adolescence outlined by Blos and Erikson, and without the moratorium to do so. As an adult reader, I was most struck by Anne's imaginative powers, that I closely associate with adolescence. Consider her love for Peter, a 17-year-old young man who is incarcerated with her. Although he is lacking in many ways as a boyfriend (for example, he seems dishonest and insecure to her), Anne manages to transform him into someone worthy of her respect and affections. At the same time, she differentiates herself from her mother and gives up the fantasy of having her father as a soul mate. Out of her own resources she develops a life credo that is worlds apart from the advice her mother has imparted: when unhappy, her mother advised Anne to think of all the misery in the world and be thankful that she is not sharing in it. Instead, Anne learns to take advice of her own making: "Go outside, to the field, enjoy nature and the sunshine, go out and try to recapture happiness in yourself and in God. Think of all the beauty that's still left in and around you and be happy!" (p. 171).

One of the compelling themes contained in *The Diary of Anne Frank*, which is also captured in other apprenticeship novels, is that adolescents are more creative, intense, and resilient than adults and are able to face apparently impossible challenges with courage and humor. This cultural story suggests that adolescents are worthy of adults' admiration.

Another subgenre is the school novel, which can again be subdivided into the pro-school and the anti-school novels (Taliaferro 1981). Examples of the school novel are: *A Clockwork Orange*, by Anthony Burgess; *Lord of the Flies*, by William Golding; *Good-bye Mr. Chips*, by James Hilton; *The World of Henry Orient*, by Nora Johnson; *Up the Down Staircase*, by Bel Kaufman; *A Separate Peace*, by John Knowles; and *The Prime of Miss Jean Brodie*, by Muriel Spark. The school is usually a stand-in for the family, with the teachers functioning as substitute authority figures for parents. The school novel grapples with a timeless conflict: "the struggle of order and anarchy" (Taliaferro 1981, p. 89). In the pro-school novel, "school is the seat of order and civilization, the clean, well-lighted place where conventions are learned and values accepted." By contrast, "anti-school novels assume that school is the place where we learn the conventions of oppression and hypocrisy" (p. 89). In each type of school novel, the adolescent has a particular role—either of learning how to take his or her place in society, or of questioning the rules.

*Lord of the Flies*, by William Golding, is a classic anti-school novel. It is a British story about an airplane carrying a party of schoolboys that crashes on a desert island. The boys attempt to set up a democratic society by electing a chief and making up rules to ensure that each boy can speak up. No sooner has a fair system been instituted, however, than it blows up, the children are at war with one another, and two children are killed. While this book appears to be about adolescent boys, it really carries a message about the fallacy of depending on any institution to control individual aggression. The children are rescued at the end of the book by a navy officer who is involved in an unrelated manhunt. Golding asks about this officer, "And who will rescue the adult and his cruiser?" There is no higher authority here. The children, who initially were presented as the symbol of nature and innocence, behave as badly as their adult counterparts. Similarly, adults cannot be seen as the symbols of order and reason. This anti-school novel turns child and adult, chaos and order, nature and reason on their heads as polarized categories. Golding is presenting a distinctly unromantic view of children—they do not lead adults to a less constricted, truer path but back to our worst, most destructive selves.

Another subgenre are books that are told as a reminiscence by a middle-aged narrator of a particular moment during adolescence, usually a transformative summer. The summer remembered typically features a pivotal relationship and a loss of innocence. Powerful insights about the past are perceived only in retrospect. The narrator's adolescence is reinvented, or at least reinterpreted, to make sense of the past and the present. Memory takes on a transcendent and palpable quality. As events and relationships of adolescence are revisited in middle age, they become transformed. As events are relived, the middle-aged narrator can make poignant predictions of how things will turn out in the future. Examples of this genre are: *The Finishing School*, by Gail Godwin; *Rich in Love*, by Josephine Humphries; and *Who Will Run the Frog Hospital?* by Lorrie Moore.

In *Who Will Run the Frog Hospital?* the middle-aged narrator, Bernie Carr, tells the story of a summer when she was 15 and worked in an amusement park with her friend Sils. She remembers her devotion to Sils, who was far more interested in and attractive to boys than Bernie was. When Sils becomes pregnant, Bernie steals money for Sils's abortion.

Bernie's loss of her youth is experienced many years after the fact. When she returns to her childhood town for a high school reunion, she feels inexplicably sad at hearing of Sils's happiness surrounding her engagement. She finds that the sadness is a longing for the time when their futures were open with possibility. She muses that she longs "for a feeling again, a particular one: the one of approaching a room but of not yet having entered it" (p. 134). The feeling is of "that anteroom of girlhood, with its laughter as yet only affianced to the world, anticipation playing in the heart like an orchestra trying and warming, the notes unwed and fabulous and crazed—I wanted it back!—those beginning sounds, so much more interesting than the piece itself" (p. 134). Only after the orchestra has played on into adulthood does she yearn for the opening bars that hold out unlimited possibility. Memory allows an appreciation for the freedom that she had as an adolescent but did not then understand.

Memory also allows an appreciation for the wisdom that she possessed as an adolescent. Bernie remembers that when she was a child, she tried to split her voice to send part of it toward the horizon and part up toward the sky. She remembers, too, one moment in high school when the girls sent a song into the heavens together. "All of us could hear it, a valedictory chorus to our childhood. We never sounded that beautiful again" (p. 148). In middle age she wonders how far those united, bell-like voices had soared. As an adult she learns, too, about Asian monks who could split their voices into a "choir of brokenness, lamentations" (p. 8). With hindsight she realizes that that was the sound she had been trying to make as a child. Her memories that allow her to appreciate her younger self come at a cost—she realizes how much she has lost, before she had the capacity to grab hold.

We have here two stories juxtaposed against each other. The first is the narrative of an adolescent friendship that estranges Bernie from her parents. The second is the story of a middle-aged narrator who is trying to make sense of what she has lost and given up and how much wisdom she possessed as a child but did not then realize she had. If adolescence is a time when we reinvent ourselves, the middle-aged narrator reminiscing about her adolescence reinvents that time to make retrospective sense. The sense made is bittersweet: it is appreciative of the adolescent self and deeply mournful for what is lost through growing up—in particular, the feeling that life stretches out ahead with limitless possibilities. Although the adult observer can now appreciate what the adolescent had, it is too late to use that wisdom because the middle-aged life has a horizon, no longer a wide open landscape.

Adolescence, according to these novelists, is a time when teens are expected to hold up a mirror to the adults in their world and challenge them to act more ethically and creatively. Adolescence is a time to be revered for its resilience and creativity. Conversely, adolescence is also a stage to be feared because of the wild, uncontrollable, destructive impulses that are unleashed. These wild adolescents ask adults, "Do the frightening impulses you see in us belong to you, too, or can you keep them at bay by regarding us as alien to you?" And finally, adolescence is portrayed as a container for the wisdom and freedom that could not be appreciated at the time of being an adolescent but only retrospectively, in middle age, when memory evokes a tremendous feeling of loss.

## FILMS

A broad historical view of films about adolescence allows one to see which attitudes toward adolescence have changed and which have persisted over the past fifty years. One feature, constant across different time periods, is the lack of a direct correlation between the concerns of teenagers at a particular time and the films made about them. The fact that movie directors, producers, and writers make movies that often reflect little of the actual adolescent experience is especially puzzling, given the high numbers of adolescents who have flocked to movie theaters over the last fifty years. Since the end of World War II, teenagers have made up a substantial portion of the movie-going population (Izod 1988). Despite the large numbers of adolescents attending films, however, there is no strong relationship between the content of films and the social and economic concerns of adolescence at any given time in history. For example, between 1937 and 1946, as teens confronted the Depression and then the war, MGM produced seventeen Andy Hardy films, featuring a middle-class American fantasy. In the 1940s, too, more girls than ever before attended college, and yet the cult of the bobby-soxer, rather than the intelligent coed, is portrayed in the movies. In the 1960s, as adolescents were outspoken and articulate about Vietnam, civil rights, and the women's movement, few movies of that decade reflected the sophistication of their viewers. A handful of movies were made about serious adolescent concerns regarding the Vietnam War, such as *Strawberry Statement* (1970), and all of them were box office failures. While adolescents have surely had an impact on Hollywood through their financial vote, Hollywood has also shaped how adolescents see themselves and are seen by their parents.

In every decade, films portray adolescents as free of parental authority or at war with parental authority. An adversarial parent–child relationship or one characterized by neglect is a constant backdrop for teen movies, regardless of the historical period. Across decades, films oscillate in their depiction of adolescence; they alternately offer a picture of adolescents engaged in conflict with the older generation or wrapped up in defining a subculture with its own rules and mores, cut off from parental influence.

In the films of the 1940s, adolescence seems to first emerge as being a distinct phase of life, although one cannot yet discuss teen movies as a distinct subgenre. According to David Considine (1985), a film historian, the word *adolescence* is first uttered on screen in a 1949 movie, *Father Was a Fullback*, when a frustrated father (played by Fred MacMurray) tries to arrange a date for his mortified daughter. When the mother tries to interpret their daughter's upset feelings to her husband, she says, "It's just adolescence, dear, she'll live through it." Considine argues that during war, with men off at war and women off in factories, adolescence was the one area of society left intact. Hollywood seems to have ignored the hardships faced by teenagers during this era and instead presents a frothy cinematic world beset only by solvable peer dilemmas.

In the 1940s, the most popular teenager movies were the Hardy films, featuring a wholesome Mickey Rooney making the transition from boyhood to manhood in the halcyon stability of suburban life, under the watchful eye of mother and father. Other films of this period include *Tomboy* (1940), *A Date with Judy* (1949), *Janie* (1944), and *Kiss and Tell* (1945). In each of these, the families are defined by their adolescent, whose problems are surmountable and humorous. Adolescence will never appear so easy again.

By the 1950s, cinematic families are fractured, although most adolescents are still appealing to their parents for answers and help. Their problems are no longer about what to wear to the prom or whom to date, as they were in the '40s. Adolescents have big problems now, especially delinquency. The first genuine teenage films emerged in the '50s, with James Dean as their poster boy. He is the image of the surly, sexy adolescent at odds with grown-up society. Once James Dean appeared, the idealized cinematic teen would never again be a team player who emulates his parents. The teen was forever transformed as other.

The '50s and the James Dean image are inextricably linked with Dean's image as an adolescent, repeatedly disappointed by his weak father and turning instead to his delinquent peers. With the war over, many American men were at loose ends in terms of their identification with manly goals. The father in *Rebel without a Cause* (1955) is a classic example of this floundering male. In this movie, the James Dean character, Jim Stark, asks his father, "What can you do when you have to be a man?" His father answers, "When you look back on this in ten years, you'll laugh. It happens to all boys." This dismissive answer propels Stark to find his own solution, one that ultimately results in the death of another boy. During the film, Jim Stark moves through several phases—from wanting his father's advice, to giving up on him and relying on his peer group, to a tentative rapprochement with father at the end, when the father comforts his son after a boy is shot, promising, "I'll try to be as strong as you want me to." The message here is that parents can learn to care about their adolescents but only if faced with the dire consequences of these adolescents being on their own.

In the '60s, the films seen most frequently by adolescents, like *Bonnie and Clyde* (1967) and *Easy Rider* (1969), were not directly about them but represented an attack on the conventional values of getting ahead through hard work and responsibility. Parents receded from these films and many films were about fantasy (Academy Awards for best film included *The Sound of Music* [1965] and *My Fair Lady* [1964]), a trend that Considine interprets as a retreat from the serious questions asked about the family by the films of the '50s. But there are also popular films like *West Side Story* (1961) and *The Graduate* (1967) that deal with the generation gap, the profound misunderstanding and mistrust that was accentuated during the '60s between parent and child generations.

Popular films of the '70s included a proliferation of satanic narratives, such as *The Exorcist* (1973), *Carrie* (1977), and *The Fury* (1978), featuring powerfully demonic children capable of wreaking havoc on their families. At the same time, there were several nostalgia films, indicating Hollywood's retreat from the conflicts of the '60s. These nostalgia films include *The Way We Were* (1973), *Summer of '42* (1972), and *American Graffiti* (1973). *American Graffiti* is an anthropological study of an ordered teen society that is absent of adults. The film takes place during the 24-hour period before two boys are due to leave home for the first time to attend college. Adolescent culture is depicted as a comfortable, predictable world in which everyone knows his or her place. The question of whether or not to leave home is recast here—instead of a dilemma of leaving one's family, it is about leaving the comfort of the well-defined contours of a peer group. Parents are absent from this film but peer society is one governed by its own set of morals and principles.

In the '80s the family returned as a presence in many successful films about adolescence, like *Ordinary People* (1980), *The Great Santini* (1979), and *Smooth Talk* (1985). In each of these films, however, the parents' marriage is severely impaired, and, as parents, they are distracted and ineffectual. The adolescents grow up through painful experiences (the death of a brother in *Ordinary People*; a father's alcoholism and abusive behavior in *The Great Santini*; a girl's rape in *Smooth Talk*) that their parents are too self-centered and immature to guide them through.

In the '90s, there are several powerful films about teenagers that depict a separate subculture, removed from parental influences, but the subculture now is no longer guided by its own order and set of morals, as it was in movies like *American Graffiti* or *West Side Story*. Instead, the peer subculture is cut off from parents and is itself completely anarchic and grim. *Pump Up the Volume* (1990), *Welcome to the Dollhouse* (1995), and *Kids* (1995) are examples of this new variation.

*Kids* represents a new vision of adolescent as outsider that is frankly shocking. The teenagers in *Kids* are not rebelling against an older generation or searching for new meaning. As one reviewer put it, "instead of being portrayed as alienated, they are simply aliens" (Pareles 1995, p. 23). The teenagers in this movie behave like animals who live in their own jungle. The movie uses a documentary style to record the 24-hour period in the life of a group of urban teenagers. The central figure is Telly, whose only raison d'être is to con unsuspecting virgins to have sex with him. Meanwhile, one of his victims discovers that Telly has infected her with the HIV virus and she frantically tries to find him. The viewers never know whether Telly is aware of the deadly aspect of his sexual conquests. In a film that is resolutely about teens, there is only one cameo made by a parent. Telly's mother sits nursing an infant while Telly steals money from her, sweet-talking her just as he sweet-talks his virgin prey. The movie is horrifying. It seems to be saying that adolescents are so alien that adults need not even bother to help them or connect with them.

One movie that stands out as an exception to the general cinematic pattern of adolescent alienation or parental neglect is *Breaking Away* (1979), a film about four friends in a midwestern town who have just graduated from high school. The film focuses on one of these boys, Dave, a passionate bicyclist, who appropriates Italian culture because the best bikers are Italian. Initially, his father, a granite cutter, is disgusted with his son's rejection of the family's working-class values. Near the start of the story, the father laments his son's rejection of work: "He's worthless, that one—a lazy freeloader. I tell you, I die of shame every time I see him." By the end of the film, however, the father's attitudes toward his son have been transformed and, in the process, so has the father's own marriage. Not only does the father cheer his son on at a bike race, but through the catalyst of his son's passions and rebellions, the father becomes more sexual and romantic with his wife. At the close of the film, the father is expecting a baby and riding a bike. Dave is able to mature and grow up, too, not through the usual narrative twist of leaving home or coming to terms with a parent's death or other tragedy, but within the confines of his family. The son's adolescence has a salutary effect on his father and on his parents' marriage. They are mutually transformed and are able to reconnect with one another. This is adolescence at its best.

## THE SCIENTIFIC DISCOURSE

Some ideas are so powerful and persuasive that they have defied modification even by mounting scientific evidence. Offer and colleagues (1992) argue that until the 1970s the mental health profession's understanding of adolescence was informed solely by findings from clinical populations. Only more recently have normal populations of adolescents and their families been studied empirically, releasing findings that systematically stand the myths on their heads.

The first myth about adolescence that was dispelled by such research is that the normal passage into adulthood is tumultuous. This notion, rooted in Hall's (1905) writings, and echoed by Blos (1962), Erikson (1968), and Freud (1958), has as its corollary that when adolescents manage to bypass their tumultuous teens, they run the risk of growing up to become disturbed adults. "Tumultuous" is generally a shorthand reference to bitter conflict between parents and their children. Citing several studies of nonclinical populations (Csikszentmihalyi and Larson 1984, Douvan and Adelson 1966, Offer and Offer 1975), Offer concludes that turmoil is not a pervasive characteristic among adolescents. Instead, he points to recent evidence suggesting that most adolescents have very positive feelings toward their parents (Douvan and Adelson 1966, Offer et al. 1981, 1984) and that most adolescents take on beliefs and values similar to those of their parents (Steinberg 1990, Youniss and Smollar 1985).

"Tumult" may also be a euphemism for psychiatric problems. Interpreted this way, however, adolescence does not appear to be any more tumultuous a time than adulthood. Studies of the prevalence of psychiatric problems in adults (Burnam et al. 1987, Klerman and Weissman 1984) and adolescents (Rutter et al. 1976, Whitaker et al. 1990) both hover around the same number—about 20 percent of the population.

The myth of adolescence as a time of great turmoil is closely related to the second myth: adolescence as a time of increased emotionality, marked by having more intense mood swings than do either children or adults. This heightened emotionality is commonly attributed to the surge of hormones that occurs during adolescence. In one study by Larson and Lampman-Petratis (1989), the hypothesis of increased adolescent emotionality was confronted directly. Using the experience sampling method, which allows subjects to give dozens of self-reports at random times when paged electronically, the moods of adolescents and preadolescents were studied. The researchers found that the moods of the preadolescents and the adolescents were not significantly different from each other. In other words, adolescents were not found to be any more emotionally labile than their younger counterparts.

In another study (Csikszentmihalyi and Larson 1984) of seventy-five suburban high school students, also using the experience sampling method, a new interpretation of adolescent emotionality emerged from the findings. The researchers found that adolescents whose moods changed most often reported being as happy and as much in control as their more even-keeled peers. They also appeared well adjusted on other measures. The authors conclude that mood variability cannot be regarded as a sign of a weak ego or pathological mood disturbance, like cyclothymia. Rather, they interpreted the heightened emotionality among some subjects as an expectable response to adolescents' rapid and frequent shifting among multiple contexts—such as studying, having fun, being with their families, planning for the future—that is at the core of most adolescents' daily life. Seen this way, variability in mood has nothing to do with hormonal changes and everything to do with adolescents' response to negotiating the conflicting experiences of "tak(ing) adult responsibilities seriously and at the same time reap(ing) the celebrated pleasures of youth" (p. 125).

A third popular myth is that puberty is a negative event during adolescence and that pubertal hormones produce moodiness and emotionality. This myth is not irrefutably dismissed by science. Cultural expectations of puberty continue to hold some sway, so that adolescents who encounter menarche much earlier or later relative to their peers (Simmons and Blyth 1987) experience more negative feelings than do their on-time peers. In another study (Paikoff et al. 1991), the confluence of menarche in the daughter with menopause in her mother was associated with increased mother–daughter conflict and heightened adolescent concerns around eating and gaining weight. In addition, regardless of the mother's hormonal status, the normal weight increase that accompanies menarche is associated with dissatisfaction in girls (Blyth et al. 1985). However, in one set of interviews, few of the girls viewed menarche as entirely negative (Ruble and Brooks-Gunn 1982).

Boys' parallel pubertal experience with spermarche has been studied far less often than menarche. In one study (Gaddis and Brooks-Gunn 1985) two-thirds of the boys' responses were generally positive, with some mention of their feeling frightened by their first ejaculation.

Another popular notion that has been partially challenged by recent scientific evidence is the idea that adolescence is a time of heightened risk-taking. In one study (Csikszentmihalyi and Larson 1984), male and female adolescents were asked to rate which pursuits they found most enjoyable, and risk-taking activities were not at the top of their lists. Playing sports, being with friends, and playing music were listed as the top leisure activities, none of which can be considered risky, while having sex and taking drugs were mentioned only a few times and never in first place.

In another study (Quadrel et al. 1993), the researchers asserted that adolescents "experience the negative consequences of some risk behaviors to a disproportionately high degree"

(p. 102), but they challenged the common explanation given for high rates among teens of sexually transmitted disease, drinking, smoking, and car accidents. They reject the popular "adolescent invulnerability hypothesis," the notion that adolescents ignore or underestimate the likelihood of bad outcomes and see themselves as invulnerable.

The "adolescent invulnerability hypothesis" has gathered steam from many quarters (e.g., Blum and Resnick 1982, Kegeles, Adler, and Irwin 1988, Whitley and Hern 1991), but these discussions leave out a comparison to adult risk-taking. When adults' perception of invulnerability has been studied, the results do not clearly differentiate adults from adolescents. In one study (Weinstein 1987), for example, adults were asked to evaluate their risk for several negative events over which they had some or no control. In general, they rated their risk as lower than that faced by someone else of their same age; they felt somewhat more invulnerable when faced with a controllable event and somewhat more vulnerable if they knew someone well who had been confronted with the negative event.

In Quadrel and colleagues' study (1993), the adolescent invulnerability hypothesis was tested by directly comparing adolescents with adults. Three groups were studied: low-risk teens (recruited from organizations at public schools), their parents, and high-risk teens (recruited from homes for teens with legal and chemical abuse problems). The study found that all three groups saw themselves as facing somewhat less risk than other people they knew. This finding was no more pronounced for adolescents than for adults. While the authors acknowledged that adolescents do seem to experience the negative effects of risky behaviors to a higher degree than other age groups, they challenged the usual interpretation of this data. They argue that rather than the negative effects being due to adolescents taking more risks, maybe these effects are due to adolescents being less skillful and knowledgeable than adults, or because their indiscretions are more visible, or because they have more opportunities to take risks.

Related to the myth that adolescence is a time of increased risk taking is the notion that adolescence is a time of increased risk of suicide. Offer maintains that compared to rates of adult suicide, the incidence of adolescent suicide is far lower. Offer's refutation of this myth is built on a demographics argument (Hollinger and Offer 1992). He states that the dramatic increase in youth suicide rates from 1956 to 1976 coincided with a proportionate increase in the youth population. With the end of the baby boom in the late '70s, there was a concomitant decrease in adolescent suicide, until 1983. Since then, Offer argues, the suicide rate has stabilized and not returned to the high watermark of 1978. Offer suggests an economic explanation for these trends. That is, the self-image of adolescents is better when adolescents make up a smaller proportion of the total population, as was true in the early 1960s and 1980s. Perhaps when adolescents make up a larger segment of the general population, they have more difficulty obtaining jobs and getting into good colleges. In an environment of scarcer resources and more competition for those limited resources, suicide rates go up. We are currently experiencing another great boom in numbers of young people. There are 22 million American youths between the ages of 12 and 17, which represents a greater number than in any single year of the previous baby boom (Stepp and Morin 1995).

This argument, which places the explanation for adolescent suicide on demographics rather than on something inherent in adolescence, is compelling but is challenged by chilling statistics from public health research. For example, according to Christie Robinson, Director of the Division for School Age and Adolescent Health in the Massachusetts Department of Public Health (Gilligan et al. 1991, Robinson 1991), reporting on national data, every 78 seconds an adolescent attempts suicide and every 90 minutes, one adolescent suicide is completed. In addition, she states that adolescents are the only age group in this country in which the mortality rate has increased over the last thirty years because of an increase in deaths from car accidents, drugs, AIDS, and pregnancy. While these causes of death may not be regarded as suicide, they do fall under a larger category of adolescents behaving self-destructively or, at least, not self-protectively.

Additional pessimistic data comes from a ten-year study on adolescence conducted by the Carnegie Council on Adolescent Development (1989). In this report, the authors conclude that almost half of American adolescents are at significant risk of ruining their futures if the soaring rates of teen drug and alcohol use, unprotected sexual activity, delinquency, depression, violence, and eating disorders are taken into account.

The numbers that tell of increases for each of these negative life events are alarming. For example, the number of teenagers who drink alcohol has increased by more than 30 percent since the 1950s, with two-thirds of adolescents saying they have started drinking by the ninth grade (Office of Educational Research and Improvement 1988, Takanishi 1993). The Children's Defense Fund (1990) reports that the rates of sexually transmitted diseases are higher among adolescents than any other age group, with 25 percent of adolescents carrying sexually transmitted infections before graduating from high school. Despite available contraception, the rate of unwanted pregnancies among 10- to 14-year-olds increased 23 percent from 1983 to 1987, and rates for gonorrhea among the same age group quadrupled during that period.

## PUTTING THE CULTURAL AND SCIENTIFIC DISCOURSES TOGETHER

From the myths and scientific evidence, there emerges a dual picture of adolescence. On the one hand, researchers such as

Offer sound a note of optimism about adolescents and their families—arguing that adolescence is not a time of increased risk-taking or a time when children automatically disconnect from their parents. Yet the data from another scientific corner, from public health, suggest that adolescence is more perilous than ever before.

To a large extent, the messages from films and novels mirror the public health data. The dominant story in these narrative forms is that adolescents grow up disconnected in one way or another from their parents, who misunderstand, reject, and neglect them or are simply too clueless and incompetent to be helpful. Left to their own devices, in both novelistic and cinematic renderings, adolescents are sometimes admirably creative and resilient and at other times, frighteningly out of control, engaging in a dizzying array of self-destructive behaviors, from body-piercing to reckless sexual activity to suicide to eating disorders. The view of adolescents as being in conflict with their parents is one that has not changed over fifty years of filmmaking. Instead, with few exceptions, films tell a dominant story of adolescents in heated conflict with their parents or of adolescents who have given up on adults and instead create their own separate peer culture.

This dual picture of adolescence presents a challenge to the family therapist. We cannot ignore the real dangers faced by adolescents at this time in history: the prevalence of violence and drugs, the life-threatening risks of sexual experimentation, and the increase in a range of self-destructive behaviors. But the dominant cultural narrative—that adolescents should discount their families and turn only to each other—must be challenged by therapists. The family therapist must know how to help families hang in with their adolescents when they engage in dangerous behaviors. The family therapist must have some creative, compelling strategies and ideas to compete with the powerful negative cultural views of adolescence. The family therapist must be able to tolerate and encourage the simultaneous desire for autonomy and connection. The family therapist must also know when family therapy is contraindicated so that couples therapy, individual treatment, or hospitalization can be recommended when warranted.

If the perspective offered in this book has questioned the cultural discourse on adolescence, it has also held up another set of narratives, narratives that have been linked throughout this book to evaluation and treatment. Some of the new narratives proposed include the notion that separation and connection can occur in tandem, that parent–child fighting can be a sign of wanting to be known better, and that parents and their adolescents, in facing some similar developmental struggles, can learn from each other about becoming someone.

# Appendix

**Questions for therapists who are to drawn to work
with adolescents and their families**

1. What are your most vivid experiences and memories of
   adolescence? Please tell a few stories that evoke this
   time of life for you.
2. Why were you drawn to work with this population? Was
   it early in your career, after a few years, after many
   years? What do you like now about working with this
   population?
3. Are there stories about your adolescence that you remember now or that seem significant now that did not
   stand out when you were entering the field or when you
   were in your twenties?
4. How has your work changed with this population as you
   have become older and more experienced?
5. Do you find that you are different as a therapist with
   adolescents and/or with their families, as compared to
   how you are with other clients?
6. What is most difficult about working with adolescents
   and their families? Has this changed over time?

# References

Andersen, T. (1995). Reflecting processes; acts of informing and forming: you can borrow my eyes, but you must not take them away from me! In *The Reflecting Team in Action*, ed. S. Friedman, pp. 11–38. New York: Guilford.

———, ed. (1991). *The Reflecting Team: Dialogues and Dialogues about the Dialogues*. New York: Norton.

Anderson, H., and Goolishian, H. (1988). Human systems as linguistic systems: preliminary and evolving ideas about the implications of clinical theory. *Family Process* 27:371–393.

Anderson, H., Goolishian, H., and Winderman, L. (1986). Problem-determined systems: toward transformation in family therapy. *Journal of Strategic and Systemic Therapies* 5:1–14.

Andreas, S. (1989). The true genius of Virginia Satir. *The Family Therapy Networker*, vol. 13, no. 1 (Jan.–Feb.): 50–80.

Anonymous (1971). *A Real Diary: Go Ask Alice*. New York: Prentice Hall.

——— (1972). Toward the differentiation of self in one's own family. In *Family Interaction: A Dialogue between Family Researchers and Family Therapists*, ed. J. L. Framo. New York: Springer.

Apter, T. (1990). *Altered Loves: Mothers and Daughters during Adolescence*. New York: Ballantine.

Bandura, A., and Walters, R. H. (1963). *Social Learning and Personality Development*. New York: Holt, Rinehart & Winston.

Beecher, H. W. (1844). *Lectures to Young Men*. Boston: J. P. Jewett.

Berg, E. (1996). *The Pull of the Moon*. New York: Random House.

Berryman, J. (1976). *The Freedom of the Poet*. New York: Farrar, Straus and Giroux.

Blos, P. (1962). *On Adolescence*. New York: Free Press.

────── (1967). The second individuation of adolescence. *Psychoanalytic Study of the Child* 22:162–186. New York: International Universities Press.

────── (1979). *The Adolescent Passage*. New York: International Universities Press.

Blum, R., and Resnick, M. (1982). Adolescent sexual decision-making: contraception, pregnancy, abortion and motherhood. *Pediatric Annals* 11:797–805.

Blyth, D., Simmons, R. G., and Zakin, D. (1985). Satisfaction with body image for early adolescent females: the impact of pubertal timing within different school environments. *Journal of Youth and Adolescence* 14:207–225.

Boswell, R. (1992). *Mystery Ride*. New York: Harper Perennial.

Boszormenyi-Nagy, I., and Sparks, G. (1973). *Invisible Loyalties*. New York: Harper & Row.

Bowen, M. (1978). *Family Therapy in Clinical Practice*. New York: Jason Aronson.

Brim, O. G. (1968). Adult socialization. In *Socialization and Society*, ed. J. A. Clausen, pp. 182–226. Boston: Little, Brown.

Bruner, J. (1990). *Acts of Meaning*. Cambridge, MA: Harvard University Press.

Burgess, A. (1962). *A Clockwork Orange*. New York: Norton.

Burnam, M. A., Hough R. L., and Escobar, J. I., et. al. (1987). Six-month prevalence of specific psychiatric disorders among Mexican-Americans and non-Hispanic whites in Los Angeles. *Archives of General Psychiatry* 44:687–694.

Campbell, E., Adams, G. R., and Dobson, W. R. (1984). Familial correlates of identity formation in late adolescence: a study of the predictive utility of connectedness and individuality in family relationships. *Journal of Youth and Adolescence* 13:509–525.

Carnegie Council on Adolescent Development (1989). *Turning Points: Preparing American Youth for the 21st Century*. New York: Carnegie Corporation.

Carter, B. C., and McGoldrick, M., eds. (1989). *The Changing Family Life Cycle: A Framework for Family Therapy*, second edition. Needham, MA: Allyn & Bacon.

Carter, E. A. (1978). Transgenerational scripts in nuclear family stress: theory and clinical implications. *Georgetown Family Symposium*, vol. III (1975–76), ed. R. R. Sager. Washington, DC: Georgetown University Press.

Chasin, R., and Roth, S. A. (1989). *Changing the therapist's history: psychodramatic and genographic approach*. Unpublished paper.

———— (1991). *Genodramatic Consultation*: a therapist-centered consulting method. Paper presented at the Family Institute of Cambridge, Cambridge, MA, May.

Children's Defense Fund (1990). *S.O.S. America: A Children's Defense Budget*. Washington, DC: Author.

Chodorow, N. (1978). *The Reproduction of Mothering: Psychoanalysis and the Sociology of Gender*. Berkeley: University of California Press.

Considine, D. M. (1985). *The Cinema of Adolescence*. Jefferson, NC: McFarland.

Coopersmith, E. I. (1981). Development reframing. *Journal of Strategic and Systemic Therapies* 1:1–9.

Cromie, W. J. (1997). Midlife crisis disappears. *Harvard Gazette*, March 20, vol. 93, no. 24, pp. 1, 4.

Csikszentmihalyi, M., and Larson, R. (1984). *Being Adolescent*. New York: Basic Books.

Darling, N., and Steinberg, L. (1993). Parenting style as context: an integrative model. *Psychological Bulletin* 113:487–496.

Davis, J. (1988). Mazel tov: the bar mitzvah as a multigenerational ritual of change and continuity. In *Rituals in Families and Family Therapy*, ed. E. Imber-Black and J. Roberts, pp. 177–208. New York: Norton.

Demos, J., and Demos, V. (1969). Adolescence in historical perspective. *Journal of Marriage and the Family* 31:632–638.

De Shazer, S. (1994). *Words Were Originally Magic*. New York: Norton.

Deutscher, I. (1964). The quality of postparental life. *Journal of Marriage and the Family* 26:52–59.

Dickerson, V., and Zimmerman, J. (1992). Families with adolescents: escaping problem lifestyles. *Family Process* 31:341–352.

Douvan, E., and Adelson, J. (1966). *The Adolescent Experience*. New York: Wiley.

Duncan, B. L., and Moynihan, D. W. (1994). Applying outcome research: intentional utilization of the client's frame of reference. *Psychotherapy* 31(2):294–302.

Ehrenreich, B. (1983). *The Hearts of Men: American Dreams and the Flight from Commitment*. New York: Anchor.

Elkin, M. (1984). *Families Under the Influence: Changing Alcoholic Patterns*. New York: Norton.

Emery, E. (1982). Intraparental conflict and the children of discord and divorce. *Psychological Bulletin* 92:310–330.

Emery, E., and O'Leary, D. (1982). Children's perceptions of marital discord and behavior problems of boys and girls. *Journal of Abnormal Child Psychology* 10:11–24.

Erickson, M. H., and Rossi, E. L. (1981). *Experiencing Hypnosis: Therapeutic Approaches to Altered States*. New York: Irvington.

Erikson, E. (1950). *Childhood and Society*. New York: Norton.

——— (1965). *The Challenge of Youth*. Garden City, New York: Doubleday.

——— (1968). *Identity: Youth and Crisis*. New York: Norton.

Falloon, I. R., and Liberman, R. P. (1983). Behavioral therapy for families with child management problems. In *Helping Families with Special Problems*, ed. M. R. Textor, pp. 121–147. New York: Jason Aronson.

Farrell, M. P., and Rosenberg, S. D. (1981). Parent–child relations in middle-age. In *Understanding the Family Stress and Change in American Life*, ed. C. Getty and W. Humphreys. New York: Appleton-Century-Crofts.

Fishel, A., and Gordon, C. (1994). Treating the family in the emergency department. In *Manual of Psychiatric Emergencies*, third edition, ed. S. Hyman and G. Tesar, pp. 45–52. Boston: Little, Brown.

Fishman, C. (1988). *Treating Troubled Adolescents: A Family Therapy Approach*. New York: Basic Books.

Foucault, M. (1980). *Power/Knowledge: Selected Interviews and Other Writings*. New York: Pantheon.

Framo, J. (1976). Family of origin as therapeutic resource for adults in marital and family therapy. *Family Process* 15:193–210.

Frank, A. (1967). *The Diary of a Young Girl.* New York: Doubleday.

Freud, A. (1958). Adolescence. *Psychoanalytic Study of the Child* 13:253–278. New York: International Universities Press.

Fuligni, A. J., and Eccles, J. S. (1993). Perceived parent–child relationships and early adolescents' orientation toward peers. *Developmental Psychology* 29:622–632.

Fullinwider-Bush, N., and Jacobvitz, D. (1993). The transition to young adulthood: generational boundary dissolution and female identity development. *Family Process* 32:87–103.

Gaddis, A., and Brooks-Gunn, J. (1985). The male experience of pubertal change. *Journal of Youth and Adolescence* 14:61–69.

Galambos, N. L., and Dixon, R. A. (1984). Adolescent abuse and the development of personal sense of control. *Child Abuse & Neglect* 8:285–293.

Gardner, R. (1971). *Therapeutic Communication with Children: The Mutual Storytelling Technique.* New York: Jason Aronson.

Gergen, K. (1985). The social constructivist movement in modern psychology. *American Psychologist* 40:266–275.

Gilligan, C. (1982). *In a Different Voice: Psychological Theories and Women's Development.* Cambridge, MA: Harvard University Press.

——— (1992). Adolescent development reconsidered. In *New Directions for Child Development: Adolescent Social Behavior and Health,* vol. 37, ed. C. E. Irwin, pp. 63–92. San Francisco: Jossey-Bass.

Gilligan, C., Rogers, A., and Tolman, D., eds. (1991). *Women, Girls and Psychotherapy: Reframing Resistance.* New York: Haworth.

Glenn, N. (1975). Psychological well-being in the postparental stage: some evidence from national surveys. *Journal of Marriage and the Family* 37:105–110.

Godwin, G. (1984). *The Finishing School.* New York: Viking Penguin.

Golding, W. (1954). *Lord of the Flies.* New York: Berkeley.

Goldner, V., Penn, P., Sheinberg, M., and Walker, G. (1990). Love and violence: gender paradoxes in volatile attachments. *Family Process* 29(4):343–364.

Goldstein, R. (1990). *Fortysomething.* Los Angeles: Jeremy Tarcher.

Greenberg, J. (1964). *I Never Promised You a Rose Garden.* New York: Holt, Rinehart and Winston.

Griffith, J. C., and Griffith, M. E. (1994). *The Body Speaks: Therapeutic Dialogues for Mind/Body Problems.* New York: Basic Books.

Guerin, P., and Fogarty, T. (1972). The family therapist's own family. *International Journal of Psychiatry* 10:6–50.

Haber, R. (1987). Friends in family therapy: use of a neglected resource. *Family Process* 26(2):269–283.

Haley, J. (1973). *Uncommon Therapy: The Psychiatric Techniques of Milton Erikson, M.D.* New York: Norton.

——— (1980). *Leaving Home.* New York: McGraw Hill.

Haley, J., and Hoffman, L., eds. (1967). *Techniques of Family Therapy.* New York: Basic Books.

Hall, G. S. (1882). The moral and religious training of children. *Princeton Review* Jan: 26–48.

——— (1905). *Adolescence: Its Psychology and its Relations to Physiology, Anthropology, Sociology, Sex, Crime, Religion and Education.* New York: Arno Press, 1969.

Hare-Mustin, R. (1994). Discourses in the mirrored room: a postmodernist analysis of therapy. *Family Process* 33:19–35.

Harkins, E. B. (1978). Effects of empty nest transition on self report of psychological and physical well-being. *Journal of Marriage and the Family* (August): 549–556.

Hauser, S., Powers, S., and Noam, G. (1991). *Adolescents and Their Families: Paths of Ego Development.* New York: Free Press.

Hilton, J. (1934). *Good-bye, Mr. Chips.* Boston: Little, Brown.

Hinton, S. E. (1967). *The Outsiders.* New York: Viking.

Hoffman, L. (1981). *Foundations of Family Therapy.* New York: Basic Books.

Hollinger, P. C., and Offer, D. (1992). *Adolescent Suicide.* New York: Guilford.

Humphreys, J. (1987). *Rich in Love.* New York: Viking Penguin.

Hylund, D., and Thomas, J. (1994). The economics of narrative. *The Family Networker* (Nov/Dec.): 38–39.

Imber-Black, E., and Roberts, J. (1992). *Rituals for Our Times: Celebrating, Healing and Changing Our Lives and Our Relationships.* New York: HarperCollins.

Izod, J. (1988). *Hollywood and the Box Office 1895–1986.* New York: Columbia University Press.

Jacques, E. (1965). Death and the midlife crisis. *International Journal of Psycho-analysis* 46:502–514.

Johnson, N. (1958). *The World of Henry Orient*. Boston: Little, Brown.

Jolly, W. M., From, J., and Rosen, M. G. (1980). The genogram. *Journal of Family Process* 10(2):251–255.

Joyce, J. (1916). *A Portrait of the Artist as a Young Man*. New York: Viking.

Kaufman, B. (1965). *Up the Down Staircase*. Englewood Cliffs, NJ: Prentice Hall.

Kaufman, E., and Kaufmann, P., eds. (1979). *The Family Therapy of Drug and Alcohol Abuse*. New York: Gardner.

Kaysen, S. (1993). *Girl, Interrupted*. New York: Random House.

Keeney, B. (1983). *The Aesthetics of Change*. New York: Guilford.

Kegeles, S. M., Adler, N. E., and Irwin, C. E. (1988). *Adolescents and condoms: associations of beliefs and intentions to use.* Paper presented at the 96th Annual Convention of the American Psychological Association, Atlanta, GA, August.

Keshet, J. K,. and Mirkin, M. P. (1985). Troubled adolescents in divorced and remarried families. In *Handbook of Adolescent and Family Therapy*, ed. M. P. Mirkin and S. L. Koman, pp. 273–293. New York: Gardner.

Kincaid, J. (1991). *Lucy*. New York: Penguin.

Klerman, G. L., and Weissman, M. M. (1984). An epidemiological view of mental illness, mental health and normality. In *Normality and the Life Cycle: A Critical Integration*, ed. D. Offer and M. Sabshin, pp. 315–344. New York: Basic Books.

Knowles, J. (1959). *A Separate Peace*. New York: Doubleday.

Lackie, B. (1983). The families of origins of social workers. *Clinical Social Work Journal* (Winter): 309–322.

Lamborn, S. D., Mounts, N. S., Steinberg, L., and Dornbusch, S. M. (1991). Patterns of competence and adjustment among adolescents from authoritative, authoritarian, indulgent and neglectful families. *Child Development* 62:1049–1065.

Landau-Stanton, J., and Stanton, M. D. (1985). Treating suicidal adolescents and their families. In *Handbook of Adolescent and Family Therapy*, ed. M. P. Mirkin and S. L. Koman, pp. 309–328. New York: Gardner.

Larsen, R., and Lampman-Petraitis, C. (1989). Daily emotional states as reported by children and adolescents. *Child Development* 60:1250–1260.

Lax, W. D., and Lussardi, D. J. (1988). The use of rituals in families with an adolescent. In *Rituals in Families and Family Therapy*, ed. E. Imber-Black and J. Roberts, pp. 158–177. New York: Norton.

Levinson, D. (1978). *The Seasons of a Man's Life*. New York: Ballantine.

Lowenstein, S. F. (1980). Book review of *Freud and Sein Vater* by Marrianne Krull. *Family Process* 9:307–313.

Lowenthal, M. J., and Chirboga, D. (1972). Transition to the empty nest: Crisis, challenge or relief? *Archives of General Psychiatry* 26:8–14.

Lussardi, D. J., and Miller, D. M. (1991). Reflecting team approach to adolescent substance abuse. In *Family Therapy Approaches with Adolescent Substance Abusers*, ed. T. C. Todd and M. D. Selekman, pp. 227–240. Needham, MA: Allyn & Bacon.

Maccoby, E., and Martin, J. (1983). Socialization in the context of the family: parent–child interaction. In *Handbook of Child Psychology: vol. 4: Socialization, Personality, and Social Development*, ed. E. M. Hetherington and P. H. Mussen, pp. 1–101. New York: Wiley.

Madanes, C. (1981). *Strategic Family Therapy*. San Francisco: Jossey-Bass.

Marcia, J. E. (1966). Development and validation of ego-identity states. *Journal of Personality and Social Psychology* 3:551–558.

Masters, W. H., and Johnson, V. E. (1966). *Human Sexual Response*. Boston: Little, Brown.

McCullough, P., and Rutenberg, S. (1989). Launching children and moving on. In *The Changing Family Life Cycle*, second edition, ed. B. Carter and M. McGoldrick, pp. 285–309. Needham Heights, MA: Allyn & Bacon.

McGoldrick, M. (1995). *You Can Go Home Again: Reconnecting with Your Family*. New York: Norton.

McGoldrick, M., and Gerson, R. (1985). *Genograms in Family Assessment*. New York: Norton.

Meichenbaum, D. (1977). *Cognitive Behavior Modification: An Integrative Approach*. New York: Plenum.

Meire, R. F., Burkett, S. R., and Hickman, C. A. (1984). Sanctions, peers, and deviance. *The Sociological Quarterly* 25:67–82.

Miller, D., and Lax, W. D. (1988). Interrupting deadly struggles: a reflecting team model for working with couples. *Journal of Strategic and Systemic Therapies* 7(3):16–22.

Miller, S., Hubble, M., and Duncan, B. (1995). No more bells and whistles. *The Family Networker* (March/April): 53–63.

Minuchin, S. (1974). *Families and Family Therapy.* Cambridge, MA: Harvard University Press.

Minuchin, S., Bernice, R., and Baker, L. (1978). *Psychosomatic Families: Anorexia in Context.* Cambridge, MA: Harvard University Press.

Mirkin, M. P., and Koman, S. (1985). *Handbook of Adolescent and Family Therapy.* New York: Gardner.

Moore, L. (1994). *Who Will Run the Frog Hospital?* New York: Knopf.

Morris, R. J., and Kratochwill, T. R. (1983). *Treating Children's Fears and Phobias: A Behavioral Approach.* New York: Pergamon.

Neugarten, B., ed. (1968). *Middle Age and Aging.* Chicago: University of Chicago Press.

Neugarten, B., and Guttmann, D. (1968). Age-sex roles and personality in middle age: a thematic apperception study. In *Middle Age and Aging,* ed. B. Neugarten, pp. 44–89. Chicago: University of Chicago Press.

Offer, D., and Offer, J. B. (1975). *From Teenage to Young Manhood: A Psychological Study.* New York: Basic Books.

Offer, D., Ostrov, E., and Howard, K. I. (1981). The mental health professional's concept of the normal adolescent. *Archives of General Psychiatry* 38:149–152.

———— (1984). *Patterns of Adolescent Self-Image.* San Francisco: Jossey-Bass.

Offer, D., and Schonert-Reichl, K. (1992). Debunking the myths of adolescence: findings from recent research. *Journal of the American Academy of Child and Adolescent Psychiatry* 31:1003–1014.

Office of Educational Research and Improvement (1988). *Youth Indicators 1988.* Washington, DC: US Government Printing Office.

Paikoff, R. L., Brooks-Gunn, J., and Carlton-Ford, S. (1991). Effects of reproductive status changes on family functioning and well-being of mothers and daughters. *Journal of Early Adolescence* 11:201–220.

Papini, D. R., and Roggman, L. A. (1993). Parental attachment to early adolescents and parents' emotional and marital adjustment: a longitudinal study. *Journal of Early Adolescence* 13:311–328.

Papp, P. (1983). *The Process of Change.* New York: Guilford.

Pareles, J. (1995). They're rebels without a cause and couldn't care less. *The New York Times*, July 16, Section 2, pp. 1, 23.

Patterson, G. (1982). *A Social Learning Approach to Family Intervention: Coercive Family Processes*, vol. 3. Eugene, OR: Castalia.

Patterson, G., and Forgatch, M. (1987). *Parents and Adolescents Living Together: vol. 1, The Basics.* Eugene, OR: Castalia.

——— (1989). *Parents and Adolescents Living Together: vol. 2, Family Problem Solving.* Eugene, OR: Castalia.

Paul, N. (1969). The role of mourning and empathy in conjoint marital therapy. In *Family Therapy and Disturbed Families*, ed. G. Zuk and I. Boszormenyi-Nagy. Palo Alto, CA: Science and Behavior Books.

Paul, N., and Paul, B. (1975). *A Marital Puzzle.* New York: Norton.

Penn, P. (1982). Circular questioning. *Family Process* 21(3):267–280.

——— (1985). Feed-forward: future questions, future maps. *Family Process* 24(3): 299–310.

Person, E. S. (1990). *Dreams of Love and Fateful Encounters.* New York: Norton.

Pittman, F. (1987). *Turning Points: Treating Families in Transition and Crisis.* New York: Norton.

Preto, N. (1989). Transformation of the family system in adolescence. In *The Changing Family Life Cycle: A Framework for Family Therapy*, second ed., ed. B. C. Carter and M. McGoldrick, pp. 255–282. Needham, MA: Allyn & Bacon.

Preto, N., and Trevis, N. (1985). The adolescent phase of the life cycle. In *Handbook of Adolescent and Family Therapy*, ed. M. P. Mirkin and S. Koman, pp. 21–37. New York: Gardner.

Prosen, H., Toews, J., and Martin, R. (1981). The life cycle of the family: parental midlife crisis and adolescent rebellion. In *Adolescent Psychiatry, Vol. IX,* ed. S. Feinstein, J. Looney, A. Schwartzberg, and S. Sorosky, pp. 170–180. Chicago: University of Chicago Press.

Quadrel, M. J., Fischoff, B., and Davis, W. (1993). Adolescent (in)vulnerability. *American Psychologist* 48:102–116.

Quinn, W., Newfield, A., and Protinsky, H. (1985). Rites of passage in families with adolescents. *Family Process* 24:101–111.

Roberts, J. (1994). *Tales and Transformations: Stories in Families and Family Therapy.* New York: Norton.

Robinson, C. R. (1991). Working with adolescent girls: strategies to address health status. In *Women, Girls and Psychotherapy: Reframing Resistance,* ed. C. Gilligan, A. Rogers, and D. Tolman, pp. 241–252. New York: Haworth.

Roth, S. A., and Chasin, R. (1991). *An exercise to stimulate variety and versatility when the therapist feels stuck.* Paper presented at the Family Networker Conference, Washington, DC, March.

Ruble, D. N., and Brooks-Gunn, J. (1982). The experience of menarche. *Child Development* 53:1557–1566.

Rutter, M., Graham, P., Chadwick, D. F. D., and Yule, W. (1976). Adolescent turmoil: fact or fiction. *Journal of Child Psychology and Psychiatry* 17:35–56.

Salinger, J. D. (1945). *The Catcher in the Rye.* Boston: Little, Brown.

Satir, V. (1964). *Conjoint Family Therapy.* Palo Alto, CA: Science and Behavior Books.

Scarf, M. (1987). *Intimate Partners: Patterns in Love and Marriage.* New York: Random House.

Selekman, M. (1995). Rap music with wisdom: peer reflecting teams with tough adolescents. In *Reflecting Team in Action,* ed. S. Friedman, pp. 205–222. New York: Guilford.

Selvini Palazzoli, M. (1974). *Self-Starvation: From the Intrapsychic to the Transpersonal Approach to Anorexia Nervosa.* London: Chaucer.

Selvini Palazzoli, M., Boscolo, L., Ceccin, G., and Prata G. (1978a). *Paradox and Counterparadox.* New York: Jason Aronson.

——— (1978b). A ritualized prescription in family therapy: odd days and even days. *Journal of Marriage and Family Counseling* 4(3):3–9.

—— (1980a). Hypothesizing-circularity-neutrality: three guidelines for the conductor of the session. *Family Process* 19(1):3–12.

—— (1980b). The problem of the referring person. *Journal of Marital and Family Therapy* 6(1):3–9.

Sheehy, G. (1974). *Passages: Predictable Crises of Adult Life.* New York: Dutton.

—— (1995). *New Passages: Mapping Your Life Across Time.* New York: Random House.

Silverberg, S., and Steinberg, L. (1987). Adolescent autonomy, parent–adolescent conflict and parental well-being. *Journal of Youth and Adolescence* 16(3):292–312.

—— (1990). Psychological well-being of parents with early adolescent children. *Developmental Psychology* 26:658–666.

Silverstein, O., and Rashbaum, B. (1994). *The Courage to Raise Good Men.* New York: Viking.

Simmons, R. G., and Blyth, D. A. (1987). *Moving into Adolescence.* Hawthorne, NY: Aldine.

Small, S. A., Cornelius, S., and Eastman, G. (1983). *Parenting adolescent children: A period of adult storm and stress?* Paper presented at the Ninety-First Annual Convention of the American Psychological Association, Anaheim, CA, August.

Smilansky, E. M. (1994). Glossary. In *Crisis at Adolscence,* ed. S. Box, pp. 247–262. Northvale, NJ: Jason Aronson.

Spacks, P. M. (1981). *The Adolescent Idea.* New York: Basic Books.

Spark, M. (1961). *The Prime of Miss Jean Brodie.* New York: Dell.

Stanton, D., and Todd, T. (1982). *Family Therapy of Drug Abuse and Addiction.* New York: Guilford.

Stanton, M. D., Todd, T. C., Heard, D. B., et al. (1978). Heroin addiction as a family phenomenon: a new conceptual model. *American Journal of Drug and Alcohol Abuse* 5:125–150.

Steinberg, L. (1990). Autonomy, conflict, and harmony in the family. In *At the Threshold: The Developing Adolescent,* ed. S. S. Feldman and G. R. Elliott, pp. 255–276. Cambridge, MA: Harvard University Press.

Steinberg, L., and Silverberg, S. (1987). Influences of marital satisfaction during the middle stages of the family life cycle. *Journal of Marriage and the Family* 49:751–760..

Stepp, L. S., and Morin, R. (1995). The teen age. *The Washington Post*, Dec. 10, pp. 1, 22, 23.

Stierlin, H. (1974). *Separating Parents and Adolescents: A Perspective on Running Away, Schizophrenia, and Waywardness.* New York: Quadrangle.

——— (1977). *Psychoanalysis and Family Therapy.* New York: Jason Aronson.

Stowe, R. (1991). *Not the End of the World.* New York: Random House.

Straus, M. (1994). *Violence in the Lives of Adolescents.* New York: Norton.

Swenson, C., Eskew, R., and Kohlhepp, K. (1981). Stage of family life cycle, ego development, and the marriage relationship. *Journal of Marriage and the Family* 43(4):841–853.

Takanishi, R. (1993). The opportunities of adolescence—research, interventions, and policy. *American Psychologist* 48(2):85–87.

Taliaferro, F. (1981). Blackboard art: the novel goes to school. *Harper's* (October): 89–92.

Titelman, P., ed. (1987). *The Therapist's Own Family: Toward the Differentiation of Self.* Northvale, NJ: Jason Aronson.

Tomm, K. (1984a). One perspective on the Milan systemic approach: Part I. Overview of development, theory and practice. *Journal of Marital and Family Therapy* 10(2):113–125.

——— (1984b). One perspective on the Milan systemic approach: Part II. Description of session format, interviewing style and interventions. *Journal of Marital and Family Therapy* 10(3):253–271.

——— (1988). Interventive interviewing: Part III. Intending to ask lineal, circular, strategic or reflexive questions? *Family Process* 27(1):1–15.

Twain, M. (1885). *Adventures of Huckleberry Finn.* New York: Harper, 1951.

Tyler, A. (1995). *Ladder of Years.* New York: Knopf.

Vaillant, G. E. (1977). *Adaptation to Life.* Boston: Little, Brown.

Ventura, M. (1994). The age of endarkenment. *The Utne Reader* (July/August): 63–64.

Voltaire (1759). *Candide.* New York: Modern Library, 1992.

Wachtel, E. F. (1982). The family psyche over three generations: the genogram revisited. *Journal of Marital and Family Therapy* 8(3):335–343.

Walker, G. (1987). AIDS and family therapy. *Family Therapy Today* 2(4):1–7.

—— (1988). An AIDS journal. *Family Networker* (Jan./Feb.): 20–32.

Wallerstein, J., and Blakeslee, S. (1995). *The Good Marriage: How and Why Love Lasts*. Boston: Houghton Mifflin.

Wallerstein, J., and Kelly, J. B. (1980). *Surviving the Breakup: How Children and Parents Cope with Divorce*. New York: Basic Books.

Waterman, A. S. (1982). Identity development from adolescence to adulthood: an extension of theory and a review of research. *Developmental Psychology* 18:341–358.

Weathers, L., and Liberman, R. L. (1975). Contingency contracting with families of delinquent adolescents. *Behavior Therapy* 6:356–66.

—— (1978). Modification of family behavior. In *Child Behavior Therapy*, ed. D. Margolin, pp. 150–180. New York: Gardner.

Weingarten, K. (1988). *On being stirred up: the marriages of midlife couples*. Paper presented at the Treating Couples Conference, Cambridge Hospital, Cambridge, MA, November.

—— (1994). *The Mother's Voice: Strengthening Intimacy in Families*. New York: Harcourt Brace.

Weinstein, N. D. (1987). Unrealistic optimism about susceptibility to health problems: conclusions from a community-wide sample. *Journal of Behavioral Medicine* 19:481–500.

Whitaker, A., Johnson, J., Shaffer, D., et al. (1990). Uncommon troubles in young people. *Archives of General Psychiatry* 47:487–496.

Whitaker, C. (1975). Psychotherapy of the absurd. *Family Process* 14:1–16.

White, M., and Epston, D. (1990). *Narrative Means to Therapeutic Ends*. New York: Norton.

Whiting, R. (1988). Guidelines to designing therapeutic rituals. In *Rituals in Families and Family Therapy*, ed. E. Imber-Black and J. Roberts, pp. 84–109. New York: Norton.

Whitley, B., and Hern, A. (1991). Perceptions of vulnerability to pregnancy and the use of effective contraception. *Personality and Social Psychology Bulletin* 17:104–110.

Woolf, V. (1925). *Mrs. Dalloway*. New York: Harcourt, Brace and World.

Youniss, J., and Smollar, J. (1985). *Adolescents' Relations with Mothers, Fathers and Friends*. Chicago: University of Chicago Press.

Zinner, J., and Shapiro, S. (1972). Projective identification as a mode of perception and behavior in families of adolescents. *International Journal of Psycho-Analysis* 53:523–530.

——— (1974). The family group as a single psychic entity: implications for acting out in adolescence. *International Review of Psycho-Analysis* 1:179–186.

# Index